Informatik-Fachberichte

Herausgegeben von W. Brauer
im Auftrag der Gesellschaft für Informatik (GI)

18

Virtuelle Maschinen

Nachbildung und Vervielfachung
maschinenorientierter Schnittstellen

GI-Arbeitsseminar, München 1979

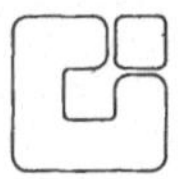

Herausgegeben von H. J. Siegert

Springer-Verlag
Berlin Heidelberg New York 1979

Herausgeber

Prof. Dr. H. J. Siegert
Institut für Informatik
Technische Universität München
Postfach 20 24 20
8000 München 2

AMS Subject Classifications (1970): 68-02
CR Subject Classifications (1974): 4.35, 4.6, 6.29

ISBN-13: 978-3-540-09618-4   e-ISBN-13: 978-3-642-67415-0
DOI: 10.1007/978-3-642-67415-0

CIP-Kurztitelaufnahme der Deutschen Bibliothek
Virtuelle Maschinen: Nachbildung u. Vervielfachung maschinenorientierter Schnittstellen / hrsg. von
H. J. Siegert. - Berlin, Heidelberg, New York : Springer, 1979.
(Informatik-Fachberichte ; 18)

NE: Siegert, Hans-Jürgen [Hrsg.]

Veranstalter

Fachausschuß 3/4 "Rechnerorganisation und Betriebssysteme"
der Gesellschaft für Informatik e.V.

Programmausschuß

A. Endres, Sindelfingen
E. Jessen, Hamburg
F. Kopitsch, München
H.J. Siegert, München
H.R. Wiehle, München
P. Wüsten, München

Tagungsleitung

Prof. Dr. H.J. Siegert
Institut für Informatik
Technische Universität München
Postfach 20 24 20

8000 München 2

Vorwort

Die Zielsetzung des Arbeitsseminars wurde in dem Aufruf zur Vortrags-
anmeldung wie folgt dargestellt:
"Durch eine Virtualisierung der Apparatur, d.h. durch Nachbildung und
Vervielfachung der maschinenorientierten Schnittstellen, können mehrere,
evtl. auch unterschiedliche Betriebssysteme parallel in einer Anlage ablaufen. In den vergangenen Jahren war ein zunehmender Einsatz solcher
virtuellen Maschinen zu beobachten. Gründe hierfür sind u.a.:

- Bei Anwendern wird die Umstellung auf neue Betriebssysteme und/oder
  neue Anlagen teilweise erheblich erleichtert.
- Bei Herstellern kann der Test neuer Betriebssysteme effizienter durchgeführt werden.

Weitere Anwendungen sind absehbar, so daß in vielen Fällen neu zu entwickelnde Rechnerstrukturen von den Anforderungen der virtuellen Maschinen, insbesondere hinsichtlich deren Effizienz, beeinflußt werden.

Die Ziele dieses Arbeitsseminars sind deshalb die Klärung der mit dieser
Betriebsweise zusammenhängenden theoretischen und praktischen Probleme,
der Austausch von Erfahrungen bei konkreten Anwendungen, sowie ein Diskussion der Entwicklungstendenzen ...".

Die eingereichten und ausgewählten Vorträge zeigten, wie erwartet, daß die
aktive Auseinandersetzung mit den Problemen der virtuellen Maschinen der-
zeit im wesentlichen bei den Rechnerherstellern einerseits und den Anwendern andererseits erfolgt. Dementsprechend fehlen Vorträge von Universitäten über Forschungsaktivitäten in diesem Bereich und über die theoreti-
sche Behandlung und Beschreibung virtueller Maschinen. Umso erfreulicher
war das überaus große Interesse, auch der Universitäten, an einer Teilnah-
me an diesem Arbeitsseminar. Dies ist sicherlich unter anderem dadurch zu
erklären, daß virtuelle Maschinen immer mehr zu einem wesentlichen Programm-
produkt werden, an dem Hersteller und Anwender im kommerziellen und tech-
nisch-wissenschaftlichen Bereich gleichermaßen interessiert sind.

Wichtige Anwendungen sind heute unter anderem:

- Test von Betriebssystemen
- Paralleler Betrieb von Betriebssystemen bei Einführung neuer
  Systemversionen
- Einsatz neuer Maschinenkomponenten, insbesondere neuer Geräte, ohne
  Änderung vorhandener Programme
- Paralleler Betrieb von alten und neuen Betriebssystemen (Migration
  innerhalb einer Rechnerfamilie)
- Emulation anderer Maschinen beim Übergang zu einer neuen Rech-
  nerarchitektur (Migration zu neuen Rechnern)
- Bereitstellung benutzerspezifischer virtueller Maschinen, deren
  Konfiguration "weitgehend unabhängig" von der realen Konfiguration
  der Anlage ist
- Bildung unabhängiger und extrem isolierter Subsysteme (Datenschutz,
  Ausfallsicherheit).

Neue Entwicklungen zeigen sich bei virtuellen Maschinen mit Intermaschi-
nenkommunikation. Solche Systeme können funktionell als gekoppelte, dezentrale virtuelle Rechensysteme angesehen werden. Bei der üblichen Realisierung sind reale Betriebsmittel diejenigen einer einzigen realen Anlage. Es lassen sich aber auch dezentrale reale Konfigurationen bilden,
wobei Netze von virtuellen Maschinen auf Netze von realen Maschinen abgebildet werden. Hierdurch eröffnen sich wichtige neue Aspekte.

Insgesamt werden sich die Einsatzgebiete der virtuellen Maschinen, insbesondere aufgrund der derzeitigen technologischen Entwicklung und der damit verbundenen Möglichkeit der Mikroprogrammierung, laufend erweitern.
Dadurch ist ein starker Einfluß auf die Architekturen neuer Rechnergene-
rationen zu erwarten.

Möge das Arbeitsseminar virtuelle Maschinen eine wissenschaftlich anregende Umgebung bieten, um derzeitige Anwendungen und zukünftige Entwicklungen zu diskutieren. Für ihre Beiträge hierzu sei allen Autoren, den
Mitgliedern des Programmausschusses und unserer Tagungssekretärin Frau
E. Seide an dieser Stelle gedankt.

München, den 23.2.1979   H.J. Siegert

Die Tagung wurde gefördert von

IBM Deutschland GmbH

Siemens AG München

Technische Universität München

Inhaltsverzeichnis

A PERSPECTIVE ON VIRTUAL MACHINES

Love H. Seawright

IBM Scientific Center Cambridge

ABSTRACT

A virtual machine is a replica of a real computing
environment and has become of increasing interest to the
computing community. This paper provides an historical
perspective on virtual machine architecture within IBM, a
description of how virtual machines are being used today,
and a discussion of problems associated with virtual
machines and new developments in solving these problems.

INTRODUCTION

In recent years the virtual machine capability has become of
increasing interest to the computing community. More and
more products are being made available that provide virtual
machine capability or enhancements to early implementations
of virtual machines. This paper provides an historical
perspective, a discussion of applications of virtual
machines, and then problems associated with virtual machine
architecture and some advancements that have been made to
address or correct those problems. The perspective
presented here is from the IBM implementation of virtual
machines and not necessarily from other implementations that
have been done.

Typically in a virtual machine system, one computer
called the host machine provides functional simulation or
replicas of one or more other computers, which may or may
not be similar to the host. In addition to a CPU, the
virtual machine is comprised of memory, which is virtual,
input/output (I/O) devices, and associated channels. The
virtual machine will also contain an operating system or
subsystem which will perform the necessary work of the user
or installation. Two categories of virtual machine
architecture have been defined by Goldberg (1):
self-virtualizing, where the virtual machine is identical to
the host, or family-virtualizing, where the virtual machine
is a member of the same computer family as the host. These
terms will be used to categorize the early virtual machine
systems.

<u>HISTORY</u>

In locking back through time several common reasons can be found for the development of the virtual machine architecture and the systems as we know them today. One major reason was to develop a tool for experimenting with both hardware and software system levels. There was a need to understand how these functioned and performed and the impact changes or new architecture might have on these systems. Virtual machines provided a facility for measuring and observing operating systems and applications without having to modify the system being measured. This would minimize distortion of measurements and therefore more accurately reflect the real environment. It also provided a means for analyzing the dynamic interaction between operating systems and their hardware environments. The architecture allowed experiments to be made at the hardware level as well.

A second reason was to provide a testing tool for systems in addition to evaluating systems. This allowed not only traditional software testing to occur but provided another level of system testing to look at timings, trace input/output operations, and to trace interrupt activities. Virtual machines would also allow devices to be simulated that were not currently available on the real hardware and therefore system software could be tested prior to availability of the real device.

Another reason was to provide in-house timesharing facilities for various organizations. This interactive facility would allow research to be done in time-sharing techniques and uses as well as provide certain tools for measuring and testing systems. It would also prove useful to access, manipulate, and analyze the experimental data captured during the performance measurement or testing.

Some of the early virtual machine systems were as follows:

- IBM M44/44X - This was an experimental system designed to run on a highly modified IBM 7044 - that had, among other features, a dynamic address relocation capability. It provided virtual machines similar to the IBM 7044. It was neither a self-virtualizing class machine nor family-virtualizing as it was not a true replica of either the M44 or 7044. The M44 was designed by IBM Yorktown Research for two basic purposes. First, there was a need for a large scale computer which could be used as an experimental tool to observe both hardware and software system levels. Second, they desired to build a paging machine and measure its performance under various loads. The M44 computer had a timesharing system that provided conventional interactive functions as well as batch. Much work was done on this system to study multi-programming, paging, and dispatching algorithms (2, 3, 4).

- System/360 Model 30 Hierarchical Control Program - This was a systems evaluation tool that provided a single virtual System/360 of the family virtualizing type. It was an experimental system that provided a low cost, flexible system testing tool to measure various performance characteristics, to generate simulated error conditions, and to simulate machine devices and features (1,5).

- IBM CP-40 - This system was developed in 1965 - 1966 for the IBM System/360 Model 40 that had been modified to include a 64 word by 16 bit associative memory array. This associative array was used to provide dynamic address translation. The software support for this Model 40 was developed by the IBM Cambridge Scientific Center to study characteristics of both system and application programs, to look at more efficient structures for use in interactive systems, to investigate associative memories for paging of multi-user systems, and to provide an interactive system for the IBM Cambridge Scientific Center. The associative array allowed 16 concurrent memories of 256K each; the control program support exploited this to provide 16 virtual 360s of the family virtualizing type. The Cambridge Monitor System (CMS) was the interactive system developed to provide a single user interface to System 360 program facilities (e.g. compilers, file system, editor, utilities). CMS was run in a virtual machine either under CP-40 or on the real Model 40. This system was the forerunner of CP-67/CMS (6,7,8,9).

- IBM CP-67/CMS - In 1967 this system was designed to run on a System/360 Model 67 that had dynamic address translation as a standard feature. It was an upward growth of CP-40 and provided a System/360 virtual machine architecture, even including a virtual Model 67. It was therefore both a family-virtualizing and a self-virtualizing system. The limit of 16 concurrent virtual machines was removed due to the System/360 Model 67 architecture. CMS was taken over as an entity to CP-67 and ran immediately because its only requirement was a System/360 interface. CMS was further enhanced under CP-67. Batch systems such as Operating System/360 Primary Control Program (OS/360 PCP) were also run under CP-67 for testing and some production work even though there were few performance enhancements made for non-CMS type systems (4,9,10).

- IBM VM/370 - In 1972 this virtual machine system was made available as an enhancement and major rewrite of CP-67/CMS. It provided both System/360 and System/370 virtual machines with basic and extended control modes. It therefore is both self-virtualizing and family-virtualizing. It included many new features such as the bypass of paging and I/O translation (virtual = real capability), preferential treatment for certain virtual machines, and better debugging and operational tools for the virtual machine operator. With VM/370 it became more feasible to run significant batch or teleprocessing systems in virtual machines. CMS became the Conversational Monitor System with many additional enhancements. CMS could no longer run on a real System/360 since it required the control program (CP) to perform certain services for it such as I/O and error recovery. With VM/370 came more direct interfaces to CP from the virtual machine environment via the DIAGNOSE and the STORE CPUID instructions. Consequently an operating system could now be cognizant that it was running in a virtual machine and perform its operating functions differently. This will be discussed later under "handshaking" (11,12,13).

- Michigan Terminal System (MTS) - This operating system developed by the University of Michigan runs on the IBM System/360 Model 67 and the IBM System 370. It optionally provides multiple virtual System/360s and 370s. The virtual machine supervisory function actually runs under the host MTS supervisor and is of the family virtualizing type. MTS was originally designed to provide a full function multi-user interactive facility and this interactive function is not based on the virtual machine architecture (1,4,14). One major use of the virtual machine facility was to run other operating systems such as OS/360 under MTS (15).

Virtual Machine Usage

The architecture of virtual machines can be used for a wide variety of purposes. There is no one typical usage. It is this accommodation of diverse computing environments that make virtual machines so attractive.

The basic architecture allows multiple and diverse operating systems to run concurrently. This includes batch and interactive systems as well as teleprocessing and data base/data communication systems. This can also include the virtual machine control program or supervisor itself, which is extremely useful for development and debugging. This facility allows users not only to run production work but to perform in parallel the maintenance and testing of operating systems or application programs. It also allows users to consolidate multiple operating systems on one processor as well as to migrate or convert from one operating system to another more easily. If installations do not desire to convert all applications to a new system due to the cost of converting programs run infrequently or lost source programs, virtual machines provide an easy solution for multiple cperating systems to coexist. Inherent in the virtual machine architecture is the security to allow this concurrency of dissimilar tasks. The address space isolation minimizes the effects of software failure in either the virtual machine operating system or application program (16).

The architecture of virtual machines allows an installaticn to test new input/output (I/O) devices as well as new configurations. Virtual devices or facilities can be developed which may or may not resemble real ones. Through specially defined interfaces extended function or simulated devices can be created. The virtual channel-to-channel adapter (VCTC) is one example that is available under VM/370 without a real one existing on the hardware. The VCTC is useful for checking out lcosely coupled multi-processor support on one computer instead of dedicating multiple real computers for this purpose. The basic architecture of virtual machines could allow tightly coupled multi-processing to be simulated also.

As stated earlier, virtual machine architecture provides a high degree cf system integrity and security. It is the implementation of various virtual machine systems that allow sharing of data or executing programs, as the basic design implies dedicated or non-shareable resources. Certain installations have gone to a virtual machine system mainly because of the security implications and the ability to insulate programs and data.

A large use of virtual machines today under VM/370 is time-sharing with CMS. This includes program development, problem solving, applicaticn usage by end users, electronic mail, instructional courses, and text processing. Being based cn a virtual machine system allows CMS to be simple, straight fcrward, and easy to use, and to leave the major resource management, paging, and multi-programming to the control program (CP). CMS therefore is oriented toward allowing the user to develcp and manage applications.

A natural by-product of virtual machine architecture is a computer science laboratory. It allows for experimentation at the cperating system level as well as at the application level. It is a natural for colleges and universities teaching ccmputing science. At the IBM Cambridge Scientific Center it is being used to study and develop prototypes of distributed systems. It was also the vehicle used to develop VM/370 attached processor support, to study MVS performance under VM/370, and to do development work on Query-By-Example (17). It has been used within IBM to simulate other non-System/370 processors, both large and small, for program development as well as measurements. Internally in IBM there is a large computer network using the Network Job Interface (NJI)/Network Job Entry (NJE) protocols (18,19,20). A high percentage of these systems are running VM/370 with the VM/370 Networking (VNET) program (20). The architecture and functions available allow the lines of communications to be extended among technologists who may be hundreds of miles apart but can continue to exploit the virtual machine architecture jointly, if required.

As studying systems was a major reason for the conception of virtual machines, it is still being used for that purpose today. Tools have been added to VM/370 over the years to allow the collection of data characterizing individual virtual machine usage as well as system load and to trace events such as I/O, branches, or all instructions. This can be useful for restructuring applications and systems to make them perform better.

Problems/New Developments

Over the years the virtual machine architecture has been very beneficial but certain problems have occurred as a result of it. Both the problems and advancements in solving them, if any, will be discussed below.

Performance is the number one problem that comes to mind in virtual machine systems due to the control program running in a supervisory state, the operating system in the virtual machine running in problem state, and the amount of simulation and interrupt handling required to service the virtual machine. The overhead incurred while running is normally proportional to the number of supervisor or privileged instructions, such as Start I/O, and Supervisor Calls (SVC) issued by the virtual machine operating system. Many of these instructions occur not in the application program but in the supervisor required to run the application program. Therefore, the application developer has little control over this problem.

Several new developments have occurred in this area for VM/370 frcm both the hardware and software standpoint. First there has been a microcode implementation to enhance the execution of privileged instructions and Supervisor Calls associated with the virtual machine operating system. This implementation is known as Virtual Machine Assist or VMA (21). VMA basically takes cver the simulation that CP normally dces for certain privileged instructions shown in Figure 1.

```
        System/360 and
        System/370               System/370 Only


INSERT STORAGE KEY (ISK)   INSERT PSW KEY (IPK)
LOAD PSW (LPSW)            LCAD REAL ADDRESS (LRA)
SET STCRAGE KEY (SSK)     RESET REFERENCE BIT (RRB)
SET SYSTEM MASK (SSM)     SET PSW KEY FROM ADDRESS (SPKA)
                          STCRE CONTROL (STCTL)
                          STORE THEN AND SYSTEM MASK (STNSM)
                          STCRE THEN OR SYSTEM MASK (STOSM)
```

Figure 1. Privileged Instructions Simulated by VMA.

In addition, SVC handling is done by VMA. In some cases such as SVC handling, VMA simulates the CP handling of it almost totally, but in other cases the VMA simulation is partial. The overall result of VMA is to significantly reduce the time spent by the control program managing and servicing the virtual machine thereby decreasing overhead and reducing the elapsed time to perform the work. For example on an IBM System/370 Model 145 with a certain workload running under DOS/VS the reduction in the VM/370 control prcgram supervisor state was 73%, the reduction in elapsed time was 40%, and the reduction in total privileged operations simulated by the software was 86% (21). For a certain workload running under VS1 on the IBM System/370 Model 145 under VM/370 the reduction in VM/370 Supervisor state was 86%, the reduction in elapsed time was 51%, and the reduction in total privileged operations simulated by the software was 94% (21). VMA is therefore a feature that is highly desirable tc improve batch systems performance under VM/370. CMS is not as heavy a user of privileged instructions therefore VMA does not provide as significant an improvement for CMS.

A further utilizaticn of hardware to enhance the virtual machine performance of VM/370 on certain IBM systems (System/370 Models 135-3, 138, 145-3, and 148) is the Extended Ccntrol Program Support or ECPS: VM/370 (21). It works in conjunction with and is an extension to VMA in that it completes the simulation of more supervisor state instructions. In addition, ECPS: VM/370 provides an extension of the assist concept to certain highly used VM/370 control program routines, such as locking and unlocking page frames, decoding and translating I/O sequences, obtaining and returning free space, and dispatching virtual machines. As in VMA, some functions are simulated completely and others partially. As noted with VMA, ECPS: VM/370 also reduces overhead, reduces elapsed time, and therefore improves throughput.

Up until now the virtual machine architecture provided isolation not only between virtual machine but between the virtual machine code and the supervisory control program code. The operating system executed in the virtual machine the same as it did on the real machine. In fact, it assumed it was on a real machine. A new development for performance improvements changed that interface to allow the virtual machine operating system to be cognizant that it is running in a virtual machine and not on a real machine and therefore operate differently. This is called handshaking and is the third new development for performance. Basically handshaking removes redundant operations such as paging and I/O translation from DOS/VS and VS1, as the VM/370 control program automatically does it on their behalf. It is a system generation option for both systems. Handshaking also allows DOS/VS and VS1 to multiprogram tasks or partitions when a VM/370 control program page fault occurs thereby improving their throughput. From the operational standpoint handshaking allows the spooling systems to inform the VM/370 control program that its spool files are now ready to be processed (21).

Handshaking is a programming approach to enhancing a virtual machine's performance and operational effectiveness. It can be used with or without VMA or ECPS: VM/370. In general, assists and handshaking are two different implementations that solve similar problems but VMA preserves the "pure" System 360/370 interface while handshaking extends the interface beyond the basic principles of operation.

To summarize the performance of assists and handshaking, refer to Figure 2 from reference (22). At the time of VM/370 Release 1, virtual storage operating systems such as OS/VS1 did not run as well in a virtual machine as non-virtual storage systems such as OS/MFT did due to a significant increase in privileged instructions used. To

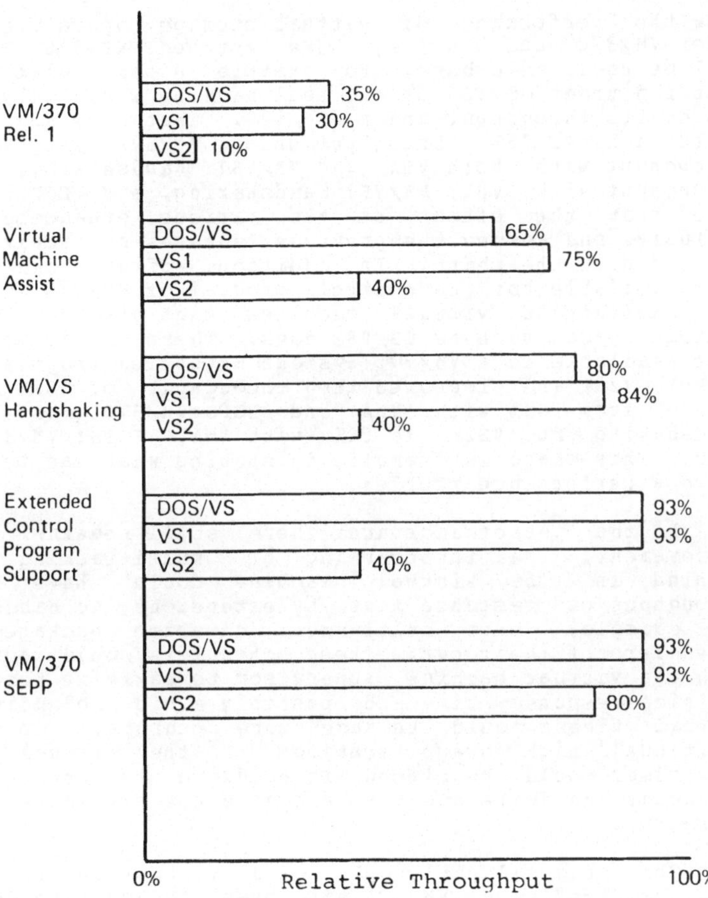

Figure 2.   Performance in Virtual Machine Environment

show the performance of virtual storage operating systems under VM/370 and how they have improved, VM/370 Release 1 will be used as a base. For example a particular workload that ran under OS/VS1 on the real machine would only achieve 30% of its throughput under VM/370. That same VS1 workload would achieve 75% throughput under VM/370 with VMA, 84% throughput with both VMA and VM/VS1 handshaking, and 93% throughput with VMA, VM/VS1 handshaking, and ECPS: VM/370. Note that the effect of the various enhancements are inclusive and assume the previous features are active as you proceed down the chart. In addition, software changes were made available for the control program of VM/370 to improve the handling of virtual machines that utilized multiple address spaces such as OS/VS2 does. These enhancements were made available in a VM/370 Systems Extension Program Product (SEPP) (23) and improved the throughput of OS/VS2 under VM/370 from 40% with VMA and ECPS:VM/370 (there is no handshaking for VS2) to 80% with VMA, ECPS: VM/370, and SEPP. This chart is dramatic in showing what can be done to solve a performance problem.

In the performance area there still remains room for improvement. Multiprogramming or multi-tasking systems running in the virtual machine could have improved throughput or response time by extensions to handshaking. For example, some multi-user database packages have schedulers of their own; these schedulers could communicate with the virtual machine supervisor to maximize throughput, minimize response time and possibly avoid redundant code. Virtual timers could be made more accurate. Conceivably additional high usage routines of the virtual machine supervisor could be placed in hardware to further reduce overhead. Hardware assists are also not available for all computers.

The original philosophy of a virtual machine system such as CP-67 and VM/370 has been to perform only the functions of resource management of the real machine, and to create, manage, and multitask virtual machines within the basic control program. All functions such as access methods, file systems, and networking should reside in the virtual machine, possibly as a subsystem itself. This philosophy keeps the basic control program supervisor small, clean, and efficient but it could possibly hinder the implementation and efficiency of certain functions. One example might be a system-wide file sharing manager. Either partial or total integration of this type of function into the basic control program might be preferred for performance reasons. The trend has been to put new function used by many virtual machines in a service virtual machine or subsystem. Two examples are the Remote Spooling Communication Subsystem (RSCS) of VM/370 which provides remote spooling facilities (12) and the VM/370 Networking (VNET) package which provides a store and forward, peer to peer, networking capability in addition to a remote spooling facility (20,24).

The Virtual Machine Group of GUIDE International has recommended that certain functions be placed in virtual machines to avoid the duplication of code that exists between conventional batch operating systems running in virtual machines and to reduce software development and maintenance costs (25). The implication is that performance would be equal to or better than it currently is. The types of function they see being in virtual machines include data base, data communication facilities, spooling facilities, and access methods. These facilities could and should be shared by both interactive and batch virtual machines.

Subsystems do appear to be a good approach in many cases. Therefore a good inter-virtual machine communication protocol is required to make them perform effectively. VM/370 has a function called Virtual Machine Communication Facility (VMCF) that is a storage-to-storage, inter-virtual machine protocol (12,26). It is very efficient in terms of elapsed time, overhead incurred, and number of interrupts occurring as compared to using spool files for communication (21).

One problem that may occur with subsystems, particularly central service machines, is performance and if it does, must be solved. Should the service machine be dispatched or allowed to run according to a different algorithm than the normal virtual machine? Can the service machine multi-task requests effectively in this environment or does the virtual machine control program need to know that it is multi-tasking? Should there be handshaking? Questions such as these need to be investigated and solutions found if there are problems. Handshaking will probably be required for high usage machines to maximize responsiveness and throughput.

As stated earlier, the virtual machine architecture has implied separation and isolation of machines. Most implementations of virtual systems have addressed the sharing of executing code, some more extensively than others. This is the sharing of nucleus code as well as application code. The sharing of data is not as comprehensive. Read sharing is normally supported to the fullest but write sharing can cause integrity problems in the file or on the device if certain rules are not followed. This is one area that could be solved by a service machine or by placing user function or access methods into the virtual machine control program.

Overall the problems of performance, subsystems, and sharing have had new developments. Performance had been addressed further than the other two but some problems still exist to be addressed in all three areas.

Summary

In conclusion, the System/370 virtual machines have had considerable implementation changes from both the hardware and the software standpoint. This has been advantageous to allow the virtual machine to be taken from the initial stages as an experimental tool to one of a production system with high function, improved performance, and large user acceptance. Virtual machine architecture appears to be an excellent vehicle for distributed systems and solving system problems of the future. Even so, there are still avenues to be explored with the architecture and we in computer science are pursuing just that.

REFERENCES

1. Goldberg, R.P., "Virtual Machine: Semantics and Examples", *Proceedings of the IEEE Computer Society Conference*, Boston, Mass., 141-142 (September 22-24, 1971).

2. Sayre, D., *On Virtual Systems*, IBM Thomas J. Watson Research Center, Yorktown Heights, New York (April 15, 1966).

3. O'Neill, R.W., "Experience Using a Time-Shared Multiprogramming System With Dynamic Address Relocation Hardware", *AFIPS Conference Proceedings, Spring Joint Computer Conference* 30, 611-621 (1967).

4. Parmelee, R.P., Peterson, T.I., Tillman, C.C., and Hatfield, D.J., "Virtual Storage and Virtual Machine Concepts", *IBM Systems Journal* 11, No. 2, 99-130 (1972).

5. Keefe, D.D., "Hierarchical Control Programs for Systems Evaluation", *IBM Systems Journal* 7, No. 2, 123-133 (1968).

6. Adair, R.J., Bayles, R.U., Comeau, L.W., and Creasy, R.J., *A Virtual Machine System for the 360/40*, IBM Corporation, Cambridge Scientific Center, Report No. 320-2007 (May 1966).

7. Hoernes, G.E., and Hellerman, L., "An Experimental 360/40 for Time-Sharing", *Datamation* 1, No. 4, 39-42 (April 1968).

8. Lindquist, A.B., Seeber, R.R., and Comeau, L.W., "A Time-Sharing System Using an Associative Memory", *Proceedings of the IEEE* 52, No. 12, 1774-1779 (December 1966).

9. Meyer, R.A. and Seawright, L.H., "A Virtual Machine Time-Sharing System, *IBM Systems Journal* 9, No. 3, 199-218 (1970).

10. *CP-67/CMS User's Guide*, IBM Systems Library, Order Number GH20-0859, IBM Corporation.

11. *IBM Virtual Machine Facility/370 Introduction*, IBM Systems Library, Order Number GC20-1800, IBM Corporation.

12. *Virtual Machine Facility/370 Features Supplement*, IBM Systems Library, Order Number GC20-1757, IBM Corporation.

13. *IBM Virtual Machine Facility/370: Operating Systems in a Virtual Machine*, IBM Systems Library, Order Number GC20-1821, IBM Corporation.

14. Alexander, M.T., *Time-Sharing Supervisor Programs*, In notes for University of Michigan Engineering Summer Conference, "Advanced Topics in Systems Programming" (June 21 - July 21, 1971).

15. Srodawa, R.J. and Bates, I.A., "An Efficient Virtual Machine Implementation," *AFIPS Conference Proceedings*, Vol. 42, 301-308 (1973).

16. Seawright, L.H., and MacKinnon, R.A., "VM/370 -- A Study of Multiplicity and Usefulness", *IBM Systems Journal* 18, No. 1, 4-17 (1979).

17. *Query-By-Example Availability Notice*, IBM Systems Library, Order Number G320-6062, IBM Corporation.

18. *Network Job Interface (NJI) General Information Manual*, IBM Systems Library, Order Number GH20-1941, IBM Corporation.

19. Crabtree, R.P., "Job Networking", *IBM Systems Journal* 17, No. 3, 206-220 (1978).

20. *VM/370 Networking (VNET) Program Reference and Operations Manual*, IBM Systems Library, Order Number SH20-1977, IBM Corporation.

21. MacKinnon, R.A., "The Changing Virtual Machine Environment: Interfaces to Real Hardware, Virtual Hardware, and Other Virtual Machines", *IBM Systems Journal* 18, No. 1, 18-46 (1979).

22. Reynolds, R.O., "VM/370 System Extensions Program Product - Performance Improvements for MVS in a Virtual Machine Environment," VM/370 Group Minutes, SHARE L, Denver, Co. (March 6-10, 1978).

23. *VM/370 System Extensions General Information*, IBM Systems Library, Order Number GC20-1827, IBM Corporation.

24. Hendricks, E.C., and Hartmann, T.C., "Evolution of a
     Virtual Machine Subsystem", IBM Systems Journal 18, No.
     1, 111-142 (1979).

25. Hutchens, W., "VM/370 in 1978", Proceedings of GUIDE
     International 46, Miami Beach, Florida, 1571-1595 (May,
     1978).

26. Jensen, R.M., "A Formal Approach for Communications
     Between Logically Isolated Virtual Machines", IBM
     Systems Journal 18, No. 1, 71-92 (1979).

SIM-BS1000: FUNKTIONSUMFANG UND ANWENDUNG

Joachim Dorn

Siemens AG, München

Summary

SIM-BS1000 is an integral component of the Siemens operating
system BS2000. It simulates the Hardware/Software interface
of a 4004/35-150, using BS functions as much as posible.

The goal of SIM-BS1000 is to enable the simultaneous running
of BS2000 and BS1000 on one machine. It supports the BS1000 to
BS2000 migration and it allows a limited interplay between
the two systems. A further aim is the interactive testsupport
of BS2000 for BS1000 programs running under SIM-BS1000.

1. Einführung

SIM-BS1000 stellt wahlweise mehreren Betriebssystemen BS1000
die Hardware-/Softwareanschnittstelle einer 4004/35-150 zur
Verfügung. Als integraler Bestandteil des BS2000 nutzt es für
Verwaltungsfunktionen, wie Speicher-, Prozeß-, Gerätever-
waltung sowie die BS1000-Konsolbedienung über Terminal Funktionen dieses Betriebssystems.

Zielsetzung des SIM-BS1000 ist es, auf einer Anlage den gemeinsamen Betrieb des BS2000 und wahlweise mehrerer Systeme
BS1000 zu ermöglichen und dadurch sowohl den BS1000/BS2000 -
Übergang als auch die Koexistens beider Betriebssysteme zu
unterstützen.

Randbedingung für das SIM-BS1000-Konzept war, daß die Hardware und beide Betriebssysteme (bis auf die nur additiven SIM-
Komponenten im BS2000) für den Einsatz des SIM-BS1000 nicht
geändert werden müssen.

SIM-BS1000 ist zur Zeit bei etwa 15 Kunden in überwiegend
temporärem Einsatz. Weitere etwa 30 Einsätze sind geplant.
Die Laufzeitverschlechterung liegt nach bisherigen Messungen
für kommerzielle, d.h. I/O-intensive Anwendungen bei Faktor
1,5-2,5. Sie ist wesentlich von der I/O-Intensität der CPU-
Leistung im Verhältnis zu I/O-Zeiten und von der Anlagenaus-
lastung durch das Gastgebersystem BS2000 abhängig.

2. Funktionsumfang des SIM-BS1000

Die Beschreibung des Funktionsumfangs bezieht sich auf die mit
BS2000 Vers. 4 freigegebene SIM-BS1000-Fassung. Wesentliche
für Vers. 6 bereits realisierte Erweiterungen werden im
letzten Kapitel vorgestellt.

SIM-BS1000 ermöglicht auf einer Anlage neben dem BS2000-Be-
trieb den Einsatz wahlweise mehrerer BS1000-Systeme mit je
mindestens einer Systemresidenz und bis zu 14 simultan ablaufenden Anwenderprozessen pro BS1000.

Der Betrieb unter SIM-BS1000 wird bei der BS2000-Generierung
durch das Einbinden von 6-SIM-Modulen berücksichtigt. SIM-
BS1000 kann nach Vollendung des BS2000-Ladevorgangs zu beliebiger Zeit geladen und wieder beendet werden.
Der für das BS1000 angeforderte virtuelle Speicherbereich kann
wahlweise seitenwechselbar oder aus Effizienzgründen arbeits-
speicherresident (jedoch mit Adressumsetzung) vergeben werden.

Periphere Geräte sind während des Betriebes mit SIM-
BS1000 ausschließlich einem Betriebssystem zugeordnet. Die
dem BS1000 zugeordneten 'Unit Record'-Geräte (Kartenleser,
Stanzer, Drucker) können wahlweise auf BS2000 SAM- oder ISAM-
Dateien abgebildet und somit über die BS2000 SPOOL-Funktionen
bedient werden. Der BS1000-Bedienplatz kann entweder durch den
BS2000-Bedienplatz oder eine Datenstation dargestellt werden.

Das Betriebssystem BS1000 und dessen Anwenderprozesse können
bei Ablauf unter SIM-BS1000 mit Hilfe der interaktiven BS2000-
Testhilfe IDA getestet werden. Dafür ist jedoch ein eigenes
Terminal einem SIM-BS1000-Dialogprozess zuzuordnen, solange
SIM-BS1000 geladen ist.

Mittels eines SVC's (Makroaufruf SETVM) ist es möglich, den
Simulationsmodus ein- und auszuschalten, so daß ein Programm
teilweise im BS1000- teilweise im BS2000-Modus ablaufen kann.

Die Fehlerbehandlung wird bis auf die Klasse Maschinenfehler
(Funktionszustand P4) durch das BS1000 ausgeführt. Dieses gibt
wie im Normalfall eine Fehlermeldung und einen Dump aus.

Zu Fehlern des BS1000 und deren Diagnose gibt SIM-BS1000 eine
Meldung sowie die wichtigsten Registerinhalte aus. (Mehrzweck-
register, Befehlszähler, Unterbrechungszustands, -masken,
Fehlerregister)

Einschränkungen des SIM-BS1000-Betriebes:

. Ein-/Ausgaben dürfen keine programmgesteuerte Unterbrechung
  (PCI) verwenden

. Kanalprogramme dürfen während der Ausführung nicht
  modifiziert werden.

. Programme dürfen nicht 'realtime'-abhängig sein

. BS1000 und Anwenderprogramme sind untereinander nicht
  geschützt.

3. Anwendung des SIM-BS1000

Die Zielsetzung der bisherigen SIM-BS1000 Einsätze erstreckt
sich von der Unterstützung der BS1000/BS2000-Umstellung bis
zur Verbesserung der Koexistenz beider Betriebssysteme in einem Rechenzentrum. Darüber hinaus wird SIM-BS1000 weiter aus-
gebaut, um die Entwicklung und den Test der Betriebssysteme
BS1000 und BS2000 zu verbessern und zu rationalisieren.

3.1. Hilfsmittel bei der BS1000/BS2000-Umstellung

Fast bei jedem BS1000-Anwender existieren eine Reihe von
Assemblerprogrammen,die durch Anwendung betriebssystem-
interner Schnittstellen (z. B. Zugriff auf Systemtabellen,
FCB-Modifikationen) oder 'physikalische' Ein-/Ausgabe nur
mit erheblichem Aufwand im BS2000 umgestellt bzw. völlig neu
entwickelt werden müssen. Derartige Problemaufgabengebiete
können gegebenenfalls längere Zeit unter SIM-BS1000 ablaufen.
Sofern die im BS1000 verbliebenen Aufgabengebiete nur den
kleineren Teil der Gesamtproduktion ausmachen, dürfte mit
dieser Betriebsart trotz des Simulationsoverheads ein höherer
Anlagendurchsatz zu erzielen sein als bei alternierendem
Schichtbetrieb, falls die CPU bei Betrieb mit jeweils nur einem Betriebssystem noch Leistungsreserven besitzt. Dies ist
bei einem Betriebssystemwechsel mit in der Regel vorherigem
Anlagenwechsel der Fall.

Interessante Anwendungsmöglichkeiten sowohl unter dem Um-
stellungs- als auch Koexistenzaspekt ergeben sich durch die
dynamische Umschaltbarkeit des Betriebsmodus der virtuellen
Maschine mit Hilfe des Makroaufrufes SETVM. Bestehen zwischen
bereits ins BS2000 umgestellten und noch im BS1000 verbleiben-
den Aufgabengebieten Verflechtungen durch den Zugriff auf gemeinsame Plattendateien/ Datenbanken, so kann diese Problema-
tik durch Verwendung der Umschaltmöglichkeit in den entsprechenden BS1000-Programmen und anschließendem Zugriff auf die
ins BS2000 umgestellten Dateien/Datenbanken gelöst werden.

Die BS1000/BS2000-Dateikonverter z. B. nutzen diese Funktion,
um im BS1000-Modus Plattendateien zu lesen und ohne den Weg
über Band im BS2000-Modus direkt im aufzeichnungsinkompatiblen
BS2000-Format auf Platte auszugeben.

3.2. Werkzeug zur Verbesserung der Koexistenz beider Systeme

Bei mittleren und großen Anwendern wird zunehmend der
parallele Einsatz beider Betriebssysteme in einem Rechenzentrum auf unterschiedlichen Anlagen praktiziert. Dabei
werden für die noch im BS1000 verbleibende Produktion ebenfalls die Möglichkeiten der interaktiven Programmerstellung/
-wartung mit Hilfe der BS2000 - Editoren EDT oder EDOR genutzt. Durch Einsatz von SIM-BS1000 wird zusätzlich die Anwendung der interaktiven BS2000-Testhilfe IDA für BS1000-
Programme ermöglicht. Allerdings wird dafür eine eigene
Datenstation benötigt. Die im BS2000 erstellten Primärpro-
gramme können über die 'virtuelle' Schnittstelle für 'unit
record' Geräte direkt aus den BS2000 SAM- oder ISAM-Dateien
vom BS1000-Assembler bzw. den Compilern übersetzt, dann gebunden und getestet werden. Dieselbe Möglichkeit ergibt sich
natürlich bei alternierendem Schichtbetrieb beider Betriebssysteme auf einer Anlage.

Bei Betrieb beider Betriebssysteme auf unterschiedlichen Anlagen in einem Rechenzentrum kann mit Hilfe von SIM-BS1000
die Verfügbarkeit der Rechnerkapazität gesteigert werden. Bei
Ausfall der BS1000-Anlage können deren wichtigste Aufgabe zusätzlich auf den BS2000-Rechner verlagert werden.

3.3. Testhilfe für die Betriebssystementwicklung

SIM-BS1000 in Verbindung mit den BS2000-Editoren wird zunehmend für die BS1000-Entwicklung eingesetzt, mit der Zielsetzung, die Vorteile des interaktiven Tests zu nutzen, den
Blockzeitbedarf für den Test des Systemkerns zu reduzieren
sowie Ferntestwartezeiten zu vermeiden. Da SIM-BS1000 zur

Zeit nur das Hardware-/Softwareinterface real adressierender
4004-Anlagen simuliert, ist die Testunterstützung auf BS1000
sowie die ohne Adreßumsetzung ablaufenden System-Initialisie-
rungsroutinen (STARTUP) des BS2000 beschränkt.

4. Weiterentwicklung des SIM-BS1000

Mit BS2000 Version 6 im 1. Quartal nächsten Jahres wird ein
um folgende wesentliche Punkte erweitertes SIM-BS1000 aus-
geliefert:

. Speicherschutz für das BS1000-System und die Anwenderprozesse

. Dynamische Gerätezuordnung für SIM-BS1000 (jedoch jeweils
  ausschließlich für SIM-BS1000 oder BS2000)

. Verbesserte Abbildung des BS1000-Bedienplatzes auf
  Terminal

Entwicklungsschwerpunkte der Folgeversionen sind:

. Simulation der Hardware-/Softwareschnittstelle von
  7.700-Anlagen zur Testunterstützung der BS2000-Ent-
  wicklung.

. Unterstützung der SETVM-Modusumschaltung durch BS1000-
  kompatible Makros zum Zugriff auf BS2000-Dateien.

. Effizienzverbesserung durch Optimierung der Ein-/Aus-
  gabe unter SIM-BS1000.

EIN KONZEPT FÜR DIE LEISTUNGSFÄHIGE
UNTERSTÜTZUNG VIRTUELLER MASCHINEN

G. Dedié, D. Zabel
Siemens AG, 8000 München 70

Abstract

A concept is outlined to virtualize the HW/SW-inter-
face of an interrupt driven machine in order to support a few virtual machines each servicing a set of
multiple users. Part of the physical resources is
allocated statically to the individual virtual
machines.

The virtualization is supported by both new FW within
the processors and by processor resident SW (carrying
the major load of virtualization). The virtual machine
monitor is primarily devoted to static physical resource
allocation to virtual machines.

1. Überblick und Anforderungen

Wir stellen Ihnen ein Konzept zur Unterstüztung
virtueller Maschinen vor, das stark durch einen
Satz von teilweise speziellen Anforderungen geprägt
wird. Die Begriffe Virtuelle Maschine (VM) und
VM-Monitor (VMM) werden dabei im üblichen Sinne
verwendet (vgl. z.B. /1/). Ebenso setzen wir die
Kenntnisse der VM-Anwendungsbereiche als bekannt
voraus.

Das Konzept wird dargestellt auf der Basis einer der
interrupt-getriebenen Architekturen, die heute den
kommerziellen Markt beherrschen. Auf die spezielle
Ausprägung der einen oder anderen Architektur wird
kein Bezug genommen.

Wesentliche Randbedingung ist für uns die Existenz
eines leistungsfähigen, zuverlässigen Dialog-Betriebs-
systems; dies erspart uns z.B. die Ein-Benutzer-VM für
Programmentwicklung am Terminal. Das Konzept wird deshalb nicht auf viele VM mit jeweils einem Benutzer zu-
geschnitten, sondern auf wenige VM mit jeweils vielen
Benutzern. Dies hat, wie im folgenden gezeigt wird,
weitreichende Konsequenzen.

Die Leistungsfähigkeit des Konzepts für Mehrbenutzermaschinen muss einen wirtschaftlichen Einsatz im Feld
garantieren, d.h. die konzeptuellen Reibungsverluste
dürfen 5 - 10 % auch unter ungünstigen kommerziellen
Bedingungen nicht überschreiten. Für andere Einsatz-
fälle wie Systemtest o.ä. steht Leistungsfähigkeit bzw.
optimale Nutzung der Betriebsmittel nicht so stark im
Vordergrund.

Von der HW-Installation her liegt die Untergrenze für
den geplanten wirtschaftlichen Einsatz etwa bei folgen-
der Konfiguration:

        Prozessor   :   1 MOp/sec.

        Speicher   :   2 MByte

        Platten   :   8 - 12 an 2 - 3 Steuerungen

        + Bänder + Papierperipherie + Fernverarbeitungs-HW.

Auf einer derartigen Konfiguration werden typisch 2 - 3
Mehrbenutzermaschinen betrieben.
Im folgenden stellen wir die Anforderungen an unser
Konzept zusammen und geben kurze Erläuterungen dazu:

- optimal für den Einsatz weniger VM mit jeweils vielen
  Benutzern:
  Zuschnitt auf wenige VM ermöglicht einfache und einfach zu realisierende, leistungsfähige Lösungen bei
  nur wenig erhöten Anforderungen an die HW-Konfigura-
  tion (Umfang der Peripherie). Mehrbenutzermaschinen
  garantieren geringe zeitliche Schwankungen des Be-
  triebsmittelbedarfs wegen Mitteilung über viele
  Benutzer.

- Genügend leistungsfähig für Kundeneinsatz:
  · auch unter harter kommerzieller Last (viele I/O,
    viele Systemkontakte) nur 5 - 10 % Leistungsver-
    lust
  · auch für fest gekoppelte Multiprozessoren

- Abschottung der VM gegen zufällige und absichtliche
  gegenseitige Beeinträchtigung bis hinunter auf die
  Benutzungsschnittstelle (BNS) der HW/FW ('HSI').

- Keine Änderung der VM-SW:
  BNS für VM = BNS der 'alten' HW.

- Änderung der HW/FW zulässig, aber sowenig wie möglich:
  · notwendig, um Leistungsziel zu erreichen (möglichst
    nur FW, nicht HW ändern)
  · möglich, da BNS der HW/FW durch ladbare FW-Speicher
    flexibel.

- Höchste Zuverlässigkeit der VM-Unterstützung:
  - neue BNS der HW/FW nicht zu sehr ändern, un HW-Testsysteme weiterbenutzen zu können
  - VMM fuktionell sparsam
  - VMM task-orientiert
- Einfach und schnell zu realisieren:
  - kostengünstig
  - zuverlässig
  - wartungsfreundlich
  - sicher

Nicht gestellt werden folgende Anforderungen:

- BNS oder VM = BNS der 'neuen' HW/FW:
  die Abbildung ist nicht rekursiv, d.h. VMM kann nicht als VM getestet werden.

- Keine Unterstützung von VM's, die Multiprozessoren bedienen (festgekoppelte Systeme).
  Grund: Locks dieser Systeme stellen zu virtualisierende Betriebsmittel dar, die nicht ohne weiteres als Betriebsmittel am HSI erkennbar sind.

2. Konzepte

Das Ziel jedes VM-Konzeptes ist die vollständige Virtualisierung der Betriebsmittel, die normalerweise das Betriebssystem verwaltet. Die Virtualisierung besteht in einer Abbildung des Betriebsmittelzugriffs auf das physikalische Betriebsmittel; dies kann durch Tabellen an HSI oder durch SW-Funktionen erfolgen. Die SW-Funktionen sind normalerweise im VM-Monitor realisiert.

Unser Konzept weicht davon in folgenden Punkten ab:

1. Die abbildenden Funktionen werden teils in HW/FW
   gezogen bzw. durch Veränderung des HSI in FW unterstützt, teils in prozessor-residenter SW realisiert. Kriterium dafür ist die dynamische Häufigkeit des Aufrufs, sowie die Forderung nach möglichst
   geringer Änderung der FW.

2. Deshalb bleibt für den VMM nur die Rolle eines Be-
   triebsmittel-Konfigurators übrig, sowie die Bearbeitung seltener Ergebnisse im VM-Betrieb. Er nimmt
   diese Aufgaben als privilegierte VM wahr, im Bild der
   'Benutzt-Hierarchie' steht er mehr neben, als unter
   den VM.

Im folgenden beschreiben wir unser Konzept und erläutern
grundlegende Begriffe, ohne näher auf die Herleitung des
Konzepts einzugehen. Dabei verifizieren wir die wichtigsten Anforderungen.

Grundlage des Konzepts ist die Kontrolle der 'Aussenkontakte' der VM. Aussenkontakte sind
- Zugriffe auf Betriebsmittel, und
- gewisse Unterbrechungen (Interrupts), die mit Be-
  triebsmittelzugriffen in Zusammenhang stehen.

Bild 1 stellt die Aussenkontakte dar und gibt auch Beispiele für 'Innenkontakte', die rein VM-intern abgewickelt werden.

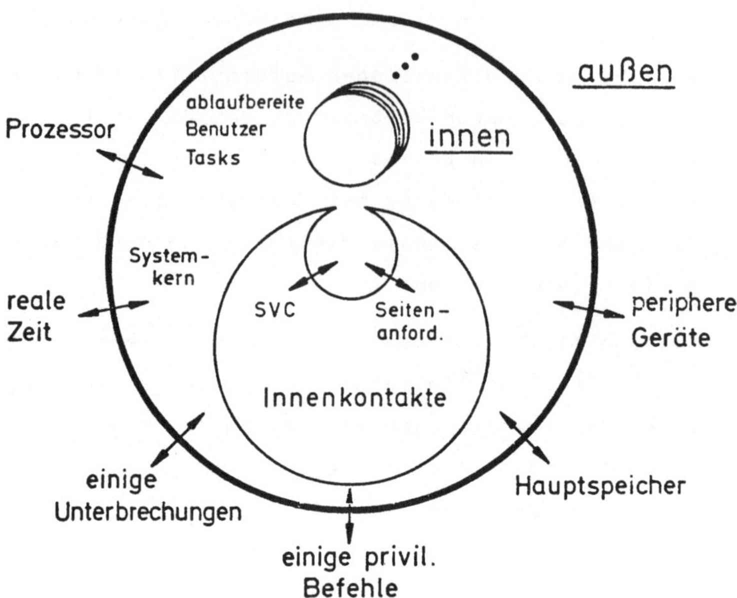

Bild 1: Außenkontakte einer VM

Die Virtualisierung der Aussenkontakte erfordert je
nach Art und Häufigkeit des Kontaktes unterschiedliche Massnahmen:

1. Prozessor:

   Der Prozessor umfasst aus Sicht der VM den eigent-
   lichen Prozessor aus HW/FW und ein kleines Paket
   prozessor-residenter SW, genannt 'Vermittler' (so-
   zusagen die Fortsetzung der HW/FW mit anderen Mitteln). Die BNS dieser Funktionseinheit ist Task-
   orientiert und Message-driven.

Die VM besteht an dieser Schnittstelle aus einer
Task (unter Task verstehen wir die Einheit, an die
ein Prozessor vergeben wird), die einem virtuellen
Prozessor entspricht, dargestellt durch Task-Steuer-
block (TCB), Task-Kontext und Tabellen zur Steuerung
von I/O-Aufträgen und der Intertask-Kommunikation.
Der Kontext umfasst den kompletten Satz der Prozessor-
register der 'alten' HSI (z.B. mehrere Funktionszu-
stände).

2. Hauptspeicher:

Der Hauptspeicher wird der FM als reale Partition
zugeteilt. Die Abbildung der realen Partition auf
den physikalischen Speicher erfolgt einstufig mit
einem Deskriptor am HSI (Basisadresse, Länge).

Die Virtualisierung des Hauptspeichers muss aus
Leistungsgründen von der HW/FW unterstützt werden.
Die Vergabe von Partitionen ist möglich wegen der
geringen Zahl der Mehrbenutzermaschinen und der
Grösse des Hauptspeichers. Dies vermeidet Probleme,
die sich z.B. aus doppeltem Seitenwechsel (in VM und
VMM) bei virtueller Adressierung ergeben können
(siehe /2/).

Die einstufige Abbildung wird auch von I/O-System
unterstützt.

3. Periphere Geräte:

Die Virtualisierung der peripheren Geräte wird in
SW vom 'Vermittler' durchgeführt. Die Geräte werden
den VM als Ganzes statisch zugeteilt. Kanäle und
Steuerungen werden gemeinsam benutzt. Eine Umsetzung
der Kanalprogramme im Vermittler ist nicht erforderlich, da das I/O-System die einstufige Abbildung der
realen Speicherpartitionen unterstützt.
Die Beendigung der I/O-Aufträge wird über den Vermittler der VM als asynchroner Interrupt zugestellt.
Auf die Ein/Ausgabe gehen wir später noch genauer ein.

4. Unterbrechungen und privilegierte Befehle:
Sowohl bei Unterbrechungen als auch bei privilegierten
Befehlen sind Innen- und Aussenkontakte vermischt.
Einige Unterbrechungen und privilegierte Befehle, die
Innenkontakte darstellen, sind so häufig, dass nicht
alle Ereignisse als Aussenkontakte über Vermittler
oder sogar über VMM gezogen werden können.

Bei den Unterbrechungen erfolgt deshalb die Behandlung aufgrund der Einordnung, die in Tabelle 1 dargestellt ist. Mit Ausnahme der Unterbrechung 'I/O-
Beendigung' sind damit die häufigen Unterbrechungen
gleichzeitig Innenkontakte. Die Unterscheidung
zwischen Innen- und Aussenkontakt und die Zustellung
zu VM bzw. Vermittler muss aus Leistungsgründen die
HW/FW vornehmen.

Die privilegierten Befehle, die Aussenkontakte darstellen (z.B. I/O-Initiierung, IDLE), werden von
der HW/FW auf Unterbrechungen vom Typ 'Programmab-
hängiger Fehler' geführt und vom Vermittler ausgeführt oder emuliert. Dadurch können die häufigsten
privilegierten Befehle (Ausnahme: I/O-Initiierung)
als Innenkontakte ohne Verzögerung ausgeführt werden.

Tabelle 1: Unterbrechungen

Typ	Art des Kontakts	Beispiele
Programmabhängige Anforderung	innen	Supervisor Call, Seitenanforderung
Programmabhängiger Fehler	aussen	Ungültiger Befehl, Adressfehler
Programm u n ab- hängiges Ereignis	aussen	I/O-Beendigung, Realzeitgeber

3. Funktionseinheiten und Schnittstellen

Für die Schnittstellenbeschreibung unterscheiden wir
folgende Funktionseinheiten (vgl. Bild 2):

- HW/FW (geändert gegenüber 'alter' HW/FW)
- Vermittler (prozessor-residente SW)
- VM-Monitor (Familie privilegierter VM-Tasks), und
- VM's.

HW/FW und Vermittler bieten gemeinsam, gelegentlich vom
VMM unterstützt, die BNS für die VM, die dem 'alten' HSI
entspricht. Sowohl das alte als auch das neue sind vom
Typ 'interrupt-driven'.

Die VM-BNS ist ein -im Sinne- nichtprivilegierter Teil
der vom Prozessor (HW/FW und Vermittler) angebotenen
BNS. Der privilegierte Teil -die VMM-BNS- ist die Schnitt-
stelle, die nur der VMM zusätzlich zum VM-BNS benutzt.
Die VMM-BNS liegt semantisch höher als die VM-BNS, ist
Task-orientiert und 'message-driven'.

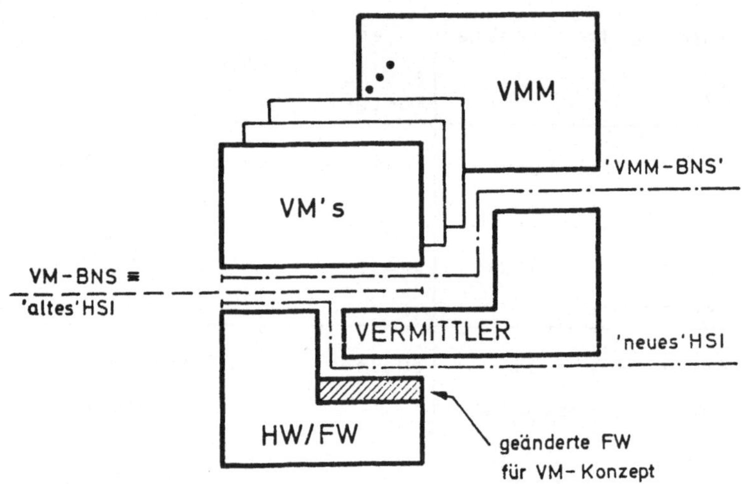

Bild 2: Funktionseinheiten und Schnittstellen

Die VMM-BNS enthält insbesondere Befehle für die Prozessorvergabe und für Task-Kommunikation. Letztere können bei
Bedarf auch in einer erweiterten VM-BNS angeboten werden. Vor Benutzung dieser Befehle ist die Zuweisung von
'Kommunikationspfaden' als Betriebsmittel durch den VMM
erforderlich (vgl. Ausgewählte Details, unten).

Es folgt eine kurze Charakteristik der Funktionseinheiten:

VM   : ein 'interrupt driven' Monoprozessor Be-
             triebssystem, welches für viele Benutzer
             Stapelverarbeitung und/oder Dialogbetrieb
             und/oder Spezialanwendungen (z.B. Trans-
             aktionen) organisiert. Solche Systeme
             sollen ungeändert unter VMM ablaufen können.

VMM   : eine 'message driven' Task-Familie, welche
             multiprozessorfähig ist. Die wichtigsten
             VMM-Aufgaben sind:
             - Partitionieren von Speicher und Peripherie
             - Starten/Überwachen/Beenden der einzelnen
               virtuellen Maschinen
             - Überwachen/Steuern der Maschinenfehler-
               behandlung
             - Entlastung des Vermittlers von dynamisch
               nicht relevanten Funktionen.

             Der VMM ist dynamisch wenig involviert. Er
             steht konfigurierend/überwachend neben den
             arbeitenden Virtuellen Maschinen, allerdings
             bei höchster Zuverlässigkeit.

Ver-   : prozedurorientierte, nicht unterbrechbare,
mitt-   prozessorresidente SW, die dynamisch den
ler   Ablauf von virtuellen Maschinen unterstützt.
             Sie bietet aber auch dem VMM eine semantisch
             höhere BNS. Mit Blick auf die Multiprozessor-
             Unterstützung sind die Vermittler auf den

einzelnen Prozessoren nahezu sperrenfrei
(durch Strukturieren von Daten). Die Zuverlässigkeit des Vermittlers ist mindestens
ebenso hoch wie der HW/FW.

Die wichtigsten Vermittleraufgaben sind die
Bearbeitung der leistungsbestimmenden Aussenkontakte der VM:

- automatische Prozessorvergabe an ablaufbereite VM

- Treiben der Ein/Ausgabe (Abschottung
  zwischen verschiedenen VM's, Multiplexen
  von Kanälen und Controllern, Durchstellen
  der 'Start Device' Befehle, Rückstellen
  der Ein/Ausgabe-Beendigung an die betroffene VM)

- Entgegennahme von Unterbrechungen seitens
  der HW und Zustellung der Unterbrechungen
  an betroffene VM

- Emulieren einiger privilegierter Befehle
  (z.B. IDLE)

- Realisierung des VMM-BNS

- Initiieren der VMM-Fehlerbehandlung bei
  Maschinenfehler oder bei erkennbaren Ver-
  mittler/VMM Fehlern.

HW/FW : Die HW/FW wird in folgenden Punkten zur Unter-
         stützung der VM geändert:

         - einstufige Adresstranslation zur Parti-
           tionierung des physikalischen Speichers

- Führung von Unterbrechungen derart, dass
  der Vermittler für die gewünschten Fälle
  involviert wird

- einige privilegierte Befehle werden ge-
  strichen.

Bemerkung:
Die Entscheidung, welche der für VM benötigten Funktionen im Vermittler anstatt in HW/FW realisiert werden, hängt letztlich von einer Kosten/Nutzen Analyse
ab.

4. Ausgewählte Details

Prozessorvergabe:
Anforderungen an die Prozessorvergabe können in sich
widersprüchlich sein, sie reichen von 'bester Anlagen-
auslastung' bis 'kürzester Reaktionszeit für Real-
zeitanwendungen'. Wir bewerten folgende Anforderungen besonders hoch:

- Anteil einer VM an der verfügbaren Ein/Ausgabe-
  leistung

- Anteil einer VM an der verfügbaren Prozessor-
  leistung

- Antwortzeiten

- Realzeitverhalten

- Auslastung der gesamten Anlage.

Eine Lösung wird erreicht, in dem die Vergabemecha-
nismen dem Vermittler zugeordnet werden (Dispatching),
während dem VMM die Festlegung der Policy, d.h. die
Parameterisierung des Dispatching obliegt (Scheduling).
Es wird unterstellt, dass für die Menge der denkbaren
Anlagenkonfigurationen und VM-Anwendungen eine allge-
meine Lösung, die allen Anforderungen genügt, nicht
möglich ist. Dagegen wird angenommen, dass die Dis-
patchingmechanismen weitgehend unabhängig von der ge-
wählten Schedulerlösung sind. Der Scheduler hingegen
muss ggf. der speziellen Anforderungssituation angepasst werden.

Grundsätzlich wird angestrebt, dass in eingeschwungenem
Zustand Dispatching allein genügt. Der Scheduler des
VMM soll lediglich überwachen und nur dann eingreifen,
wenn der eingeschwungene Zustand nicht erhalten bleibt
bzw. sich überhaupt nicht einstellt. Die gemeinsamen
technischen Mittel für Dispatcher und Scheduler sind
Prioritätensteuerung und Preemption.

Die Scheduler-Aufgaben bestehen in:

- der Freigabe einer VM zum Dispatching (SIGNAL)

- der Rücknahme der Dispatching Freigabe (SUSPEND)

- der Festlegung von VM-Prioritaten; Preemption
  ist abhängig vom absoluten Wert der Priorität

- dem Vergleich der tatsächlichen Prozessorvergabe
  gegen eine Soll-Vorgabe; ggf. wird durch Variieren
  der Prioritäten korrigiert. Innerhalb der Policy-
  Grenzen sollen lange Verweilzeiten der einzelnen
  VM auf dem Prozessor erreicht werden.

Die Dispatcher-Aufgaben bestehen in

(vgl. auch Bild 3):

- ablaufbereite VM nach Priorität auf den Prozessor

  bringen (genauer: dem Vermittler übergeben)

- der Verwaltung von IDLE-VM (zusammen mit Interrupt-

  mechanismen)

- der Unterstützung der Task-Kommunikation

- der Koordinierung mit Dispatchern auf Co-Prozesso-

  ren (falls Multiprozessoranlage)

- der Anwendung von Preemption, sobald eine VM ab-

  laufbereit wird und die Priorität entsprechend hoch

  ist

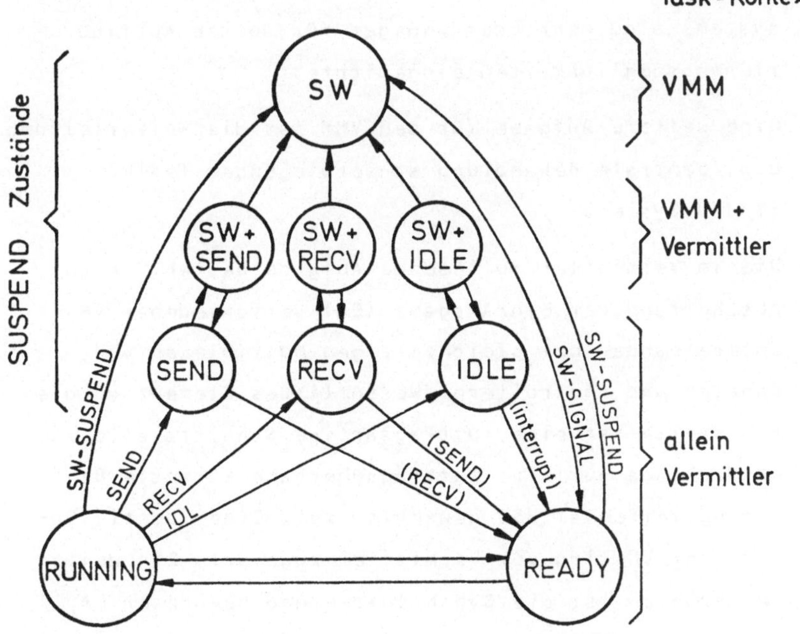

Bild 3: Zustandsübergangs-Diagramm für Tasks

Ein/Ausgabe:

Die Zuordnung der Peripherie zu den einzelnen VM's
obliegt dem VMM. Jede VM erhält eine Konsole, Platten-
geräte, Magnetbandstationen, Papierperipherie, usw.
zugewiesen. Ausser dem Umfang der Konfiguration ändert sich für eine VM im Vergleich zur realen Anlage
nichts. Es ist nicht ausgeschlossen, dass die statische Peripherie-Zuordnung -sofern keine Gegenmass-
nahmen getroffen werden- zu Engpässen in der Konfiguration führen kann. Die Abhilfe besteht darin, dass
der VMM die vorhandene Peripherie umverteilen kann.
Z.B. kann ein Drucker einmal dieser, einmal jener VM
zugewiesen werden. Die in Frage kommenden Betriebssysteme sind mehr oder weniger für solche Konfigu-
rierungsmöglichkeiten eingerichtet.

Eine weitere Aufgabe für den VMM ist die Weiterleitung
bzw. zentrale Behandlung schwerwiegender Fehler
im I/O-System.

Die im Vermittler zu lösende Aufgabe besteht in der
Abschottung der Ein/Ausgabe (EA) verschiedener VM
untereinander bei gleichzeitigem Multiplexen von
Kanälen und Controllern. Wesentliches Element an dieser Stelle ist eine auftragsartige Schnittstelle zum
EA-Werk, da nur eine Auftragsübergabe kürzeste Be-
legungszeiten am HSI gewährleistet. Eine Identifika-
tion der VM wird vom Vermittler zugefügt. Ein weiteres Problem ist die Synchronisierung beendeter EA
mit der VM. Diese kann in der Zwischenzeit vom Prozessor verdrängt oder IDLE-suspendiert sein, oder
auch auf einem anderen Prozessor laufen.

Im letzteren Fall wird eine beendete EA über den VM-Kontext dem anderen Prozessor übergeben, welcher die EA-Beendigung der VM mitteilt, d.h. den entsprechenden Interrupt setzt. In den beiden ersten Fällen wird der Interrupt lediglich in den VM-Kontext geschrieben und die VM ggf. in ablaufbereiten Status gesetzt. Die Prozessorvergabe selbst erfolgt dann wieder nach den Dispatching-Regeln.

Es kommt sehr darauf an, die Nutz-Datenrate zur Peripherie im Vergleich zur realen Maschine nicht zu verringern. Das muss bei der Konfigurierung der VM beachtet werden.

Task Kommunikation:
Die Intensivierung der Taskstruktur ist nach unserer Meinung für zuverlässige und multiprozessor-orientierte SW nicht zu vermeiden. Es stellt sich somit die Frage nach dem Kommunikations-Mechanismus.

Zunächst wird eine Kommunikationslösung zur Verwendung innerhalb des VMM angegeben, eine spätere Ausweitung auf die Betriebssysteme der einzelnen VM ist möglich.

Es wird eine synchrone Übertragung von Messages variabler Längen zwischen Sender und Empfänger gewählt, d.h. beide müssen bereit sein zur Übertragung. Als wesentliche Vorteile gegenüber anderen Kommunikationsmethoden sehen wir an:

- Ausschluss von Asynchronitäten in einer Task
- keine Speicherverwaltung in der Kommunikationsfunktion
  nötig

- sehr leistungsfähige Realisierung möglich.

Jedem Kommunikationspartner wird ein Kommunikations-Raum, bestehend aus Kommunikationspfaden, zugeordnet. Die Übertragung findet nur statt bei Existenz eines gültigen Pfades. Die Synchronisierung von Sender und Empfänger wird gemeinsam von den Vermittlermechanismen für Kommunikation und Dispatching bewirkt (siehe auch Bild 3).

Die angebotene Schnittstelle sieht folgendermassen aus:

$$\text{SEND} \begin{Bmatrix} \text{UNCOND} \\ \text{COND} \end{Bmatrix}$$

$$\text{RECV} \begin{Bmatrix} \text{UNCOND} \\ \text{COND} \end{Bmatrix} \begin{Bmatrix} \text{SPEC} \\ \text{ANY} \end{Bmatrix}$$

wobei bedeuten:

SEND	–	sende
RECV	–	empfange
UNCOND	–	übertrage ohne Nebenbedingungen
COND	–	übertrage nur wenn Partner bereit
SPEC	–	empfange nur auf speziellem Pfad
ANY	–	empfange auf jedem gültigen Pfad.

<u>Literatur</u>

/1/ Goldberg, R.P.:   Survey of Virtual Machine
                     Research; COMPUTER $\underline{7}$, 34 (1974)

/2/ Goldberg, R.P.   The Double Paging Anomaly;
     Hassinger, R. :   AFIPS Conf.Proc., 1974

Wir danken unseren Kollegen von der Systemarchitektur,
besonders den Herren Gümbel, Rettenmaier und Weitzsch,
für wesentliche Beiträge und anregende Diskussion zu
dem vorgestellten Konzept. Unsere Vorgesetzten,
Herr Dr. Donner und Herr Jòkay, haben durch ihre be-
ständige Förderung viel zum Gelingen beigetragen.

VERGLEICH VM370 MIT SIM-BS1000

Günter Kost

Siemens AG, München

Summary

The 'Control-Program' of VM370 acts as a supervisor on the
real hardware. It manges the resources of a single system/360
or /370 computer so that multiple computing systems (virtual
machines) appear to exist. The resourecs that are distributed
to the different virtual machines are virtual cpu-time, virtual memory, virtual channels and devices.
Alternatively SIM-BS1000 is embedded as part of the BS2000
operating system. The distribution of resources and the
treatment of the interrupts are largely controlled by BS2000.
One or more virtual machines, i.e. the functional simulation
of 4004 hardware and a 4004 operating system like BS1000, run
as normal tasks in the BS2000 environment.

1. Funktionen von VM370 und SIM-BS1000

Vor der Erläuterung der SIM-BS1000-Arbeitsweise soll zunächst
der grundsätzliche Unterschied zum Konzept einer der bekann-
testen virtuellen Maschinen , der VM-370 aufgezeigt werden.

Das Kontrollprogramm (CP) der VM370 fungiert als Supervisor
auf der reinen Maschine unter dessen Regie verschiedene
Betriebssysteme (z.B. DOS oder OS) jeweils gesteuert von einer
eigenen Datenstation als Console ablaufen. Dabei werden die
einzelnen virtuellen Maschinen, d.j. jeweils eine funktionelle
Simulation einer /360 oder /370 mit dem dazugehörigen Betriebssystem reihum mit den notwendigen Betriebsmitteln wie CPU-Zeit
(Zeitscheibentechnik), virtuellem Speicher, Kanälen und Geräten versehen.

SIM-BS1000 dagegen ist in Form von 6 System-Modulen (VMEIA,VMINT
VMPARAM,VMIOPH, VMIO und VMDUMP) im BS2000-Betriebssystem ein-
gebunden. Virtuelle Maschinen sind nur zu starten, wenn das
BS2000 geladen ist.

Die Verteilung der Resourcen und Behandlung der Unterbrechungen
werden weitgehend vom BS2000 gesteuert. Eine oder mehrere virtuelle Maschinen, d.h. jeweils die Simulation einer 4004 mit
zugehörigem Betriebssystem , i.a. dem BS1000, laufen jeweils
als normaler Prozeß im Rahmen des BS2000-Systems ab. Verknüpft
mit dem Prozeß einer virtuellen Maschine sind Unterprozesse,
sogenannte Subtasks, die simultane I/O-Verarbeitung erlauben,
und unter deren Regie die Funktion der Unter-System-Console
via Datenstation abläuft.

Das unterschiedliche Konzept der SIM-BS1000 bringt zwar den
Nachteil einer Abhängigkeit von den Versionen des tragenden
Betriebssystems BS2000. Auf der anderen Seite können viele
Funktionen des BS2000 (wie Task Management, Zeitscheiben-
technik, Speicherverwaltung, Device Management und Data
Management) genutzt werden und müssen nicht eigens realisiert
werden.

Die relevanten Daten (wie Gerätekonfiguration und virtuelle
Speichergröße) der einzurichtenden virtuellen Maschinen sind
im VM370-Konzept in Einträgen einer Directory-File enthalten.
Dagegen müssen bei SIM-BS1000 diese Daten bei der aktuellen
Einrichtung einer virtuellen Maschine via ATTACH- und IPL-
Anweisungen versorgt werden, nachdem man sich gegenüber dem
BS2000-System via LOGON-Anweisung als zugelassener Benutzer
erklärt hat. Die Daten werden dann in SIM-BS1000 spezifischen
System-Tabellen abgespeichert. Nach Einrichtung einer
virtuellen Maschine hat man in der jetzigen Ausbaustufe des
SIM-BS1000 so gut wie keine Möglichkeiten die Konfiguration
der virtuellen Maschine zu ändern, im Gegensatz zu VM-370, wo
über umfangreiche CP-Kommandos Einfluß genommen werden kann.

VM370 stellt jeder virtuellen Maschine einen virtuellen
Adreßraum von maximal 16MB zur Verfügung. CP generiert und
wartet jeweils einen Satz von Segment- und Seitentabellen und
realisiert über ein Paging-Verfahren, die Zuordnung zu realen
Seiten im Speicher.

Bei SIM-BS1000 stellt das BS2000 - Betriebssystem jedem Prozeß und damit jeder virtuellen Maschine einen virtuellen Adressraum von maximal 6 MB zur Verfügung und verwaltet den Speicher.

Ein Zeitscheibenmechanismus bei VM370 sorgt dafür, daß jede virtuelle Maschine in periodischen Abständen die Kontrolle der realen CPU erhält. Bei häufigen Console-Anfragen und Terminal-Interrupts wird der Benutzer als interaktiv einge- stuft und erhält kürzere Zeitscheiben und häufigeren Zugriff als ein Batch-Benutzer.

Bei SIM-BS1000 wird die Zuteilung von realer CPU über Warte- schlangen durch die zentrale Prozeßverwaltung des BS2000 gesteuert.Den Prozessen ist eine Mikro- und eine Makrozeit- scheibe zugeordnet. Über den Wert der Mikrozeitscheibe (200ms) hinaus kann kein Prozeß die reale CPU belegen. Nach Ablauf erfolgt das Einreihen in die Warteschlange Q1. Nach Ablauf der prioritätsabhängigen Makrozeitscheiben erfolgt eine Deaktivierung in die Warteschlangen Q5 (Dialog) bzw Q6 (Batch). Auch hier ist die Makrozeitscheibe für den Batch- Benutzer größer als die des Dialogbenutzers. Die Akti- vierungsrate zwischen Batch- und Dialog-Benutzer (Rückführung von Q5, Q6 nach Q1) kann durch den System-Operateur gesteuert werden.

Bei VM370 wie (in begrenztem Rahmen) bei SIM-BS1000 können spezielle virtuelle Maschinen bevorzugt zum Ablauf gebracht werden. So kann bei VM370 einer virtuellen Maschine ein be- liebiger Prozentsatz der gesamten Rechenzeit zugeteilt werden. Bei SIM-BS1000 kann man über die Vergabe einer Priorität be- grenzt Einfluß nehmen. Bei SIM-BS1000 kann man ferner unter Resident-Mode laufen, daß heißt der virtuellen Maschine nicht- seitenwechselbaren Speicher zuordnen. Entsprechend existieren bei VM370 einige Verfahrensvarianten. So können bestimmte Seiten per Lock-Funktion für eine virtuelle Maschine gesperrt werden oder weniger restriktiv seitenwechselbar einer be- stimmten virtuellen Maschine zugeordnet werden. Daneben existiert noch die Option virtuell=real. Mit dieser Option wird einer virtuellen Maschine ein zusammenhängender Speicher- bereich reserviert,in dem der Ablauf ohne Seitenwechsel und die Überwachung durch das CP stattfindet.

Ein Bestandteil von VM370 , das Conversational Monitor System,
mit dessen Hilfe im Dialogmodus Dateien gewartet und Programmentwicklung über einen umfangreichen Kommandokatalog betrieben
werden kann, hat kein entsprechendes Gegenstück im SIM-BS1000.
Es besteht auch keine Notwendigkeit dazu, da entsprechende
Arbeiten vorwiegend im parallel laufenden BS2000-Betrieb er-
ledigt werden. Insbesondere existiert noch die Möglichkeit
von der virtuellen Konsole einer virtuellen Maschine auf den
BS2000-Modus umzuschalten.

2. Arbeitsweise der Virtuellen Maschine in SIM-BS1000

In den Siemens-Anlagen 4004 und 7000 kann sich das System in
4 verschiedenen Programmzuständen befinden. Der Programmzu-
stand P4 ist schwerwiegenden Harware-Fehlern und Netzausfall
vorbehalten. P2 und P3 sind privilegierte Programmzustände
des Systems, wobei P3 vorwiegend bei Unterbrechungsanalyse
belegt ist. P1 ist der unprivilegierte Benutzerzustand.
In der virtuellen Maschine läuft beispielsweise das Betriebssystem BS1000 als Benutzer-Prozeß im P1-Zustand ab. Dadurch
ist gewährleistet, daß neben SVC's, Programmfehlern u.a. auch
jeder privilegierte Befehl (im Zustand virtuell P2 oder P3) zu
einer Unterbrechung führt. Die Programmzustände der virtuellen
Maschine sind virtueller Natur und werden von SIM-BS1000
mittels eines im Hauptspeicher simulierten Scratch-Pad-Memory
ebenfalls simuliert. Virtuelle Programmzustandsübergänge erfolgen bei Unterbrechungen, die an die virtuelle Maschine
weitergegeben werden (virtuell P3) oder bei privilegierten
PC-Befehlen des Untersystems. Durch eine geeignete Schnittstelle der virtuellen Maschine zum BS2000-Betriebssystem
werden spezifische Unterbrechungen ausgesiebt. Diese können
dann an das BS1000-System (virtuelle Maschine) weiterge-
reicht oder von SIM-BS1000 selbst bearbeitet (z.B. Simulation
von privilegierten Befehlen) werden.

3. Unterbrechungsanalyse

Jede Unterbrechung im BS2000-Betriebssystem führt zu einem
Übergang in den realen P3-Zustand und zum Ansprung der
BS2000-System-Komponente EIA. Ist die virtuelle Maschine bei

der Systemgenerierung berücksichtigt worden, so wird von EIA
in den Modul VMEIA (ebenfalls P3) verzweigt. VMEIA siebt dann
die Unterbrechungen heraus, die für die virtuelle Maschine
relevant sind. Zunächst werden asynchrone Unterbrechungen,wie
echte I/O-Termination oder 'Console Interrupt' sofort an das
BS2000 System zurückgegeben. Das gleiche gilt für alle
synchronen Unterbrechungen, die nicht im realen P1-Zustand
erfolgen oder aber von einem Prozeß, der nicht mit einer
virtuellen Maschine verknüpft ist. Für diese Klasse von
Unterbrechungen bleibt das BS2000-Organisationsprogramm
zuständig.

4. Unterbrechungsbehandlung

Die Behandlung der Unterbrechungen wird im wesentlichen vom
Modul VMINT durchgeführt. VMINT untersucht die Art der Unterbrechung und sammelt diese im virtuellen IFR-Register (VMIFR).
Wird als Ursache, der Unterbrechung ein privilegierter Befehl
erkannt, und ist dieser erlaubt (z.B. im Zustand virtuell P2
oder P3), so wird zur Simulation in entsprechende VMINT-Unter-
routinen verzweigt.Bei einem Bearbeitungsdurchlauf von VMINT
können mehrere Unterbrechungen anliegen. So treffen in VMINT
auch asynchron simulierte 'I/O-Termination-Interrupts' und
'Console-Interrupts' von den Subtasks der virtuellen Maschine
ein. Ferner simuliert VMINT selbst (in Zusammenarbeit mit
einem Timer Subtask, der von VMPARAM zum Ladezeitpunkt
generiert wird) 'Timer-Interrupts'. Zur Weitergabe von Unterbrechungen sucht VMINT jeweils den höchstprioren aus und lädt
Register 15 des virtuellen P3-Zustandes mit dem zugehörigen
Unterbrechungsgewicht. Damit wird die Schnittstelle zur Unter-
brechungsroutine des Gastsystems versorgt. Im Anschluß wird in
den virtuellen P3-Zustand geschaltet. Dazu wird der P1-Stack
des Prozesses mit Befehlszähler und Register des virtuellen
P3-Zustandes geladen. Die Register des betroffenen virtuellen
Zustandes können dabei der virtuellen Scratch Pad Memory entnommen werden. Abschließend veranlaßt VMINT den Übergang in
den Zustand 'real P1' und damit in den Zustand 'virtuell P3'.
Der weitere Ablauf bleibt nun dem Gastsystem überlassen.

5. Simulation von privilegierten Befehlen

VMINT simuliert eine Untermenge von privilegierten Befehlen,
sofern sie im Gastsystem im privilegierten Status (d.h. i.a.
im Zustand virtuell P2 oder P3) gegeben werden. Es handelt
sich dabei um die Befehle LSP, SSP, PC, IDL, SDV, TDV, HDV
und CKC. Aus dem Befehlzähler des unterbrochenen Zustands kann
der Operationscode des Befehls ermittelt werden, der dann über
eine Sprungtabelle die zuständige Unterroutine in VMINT
ansteuert.

6. Ein-/Ausgabe für reale und virtuelle Geräte

Im SIM-BS1000 werden reale Geräte für die virtuelle Maschine
aus dem Geräte-Pool des BS2000-Betriebssystems ausschließlich
zugeordnet. Dynamisches Wegnehmen und Zufügen von Geräten
während einer Session wird in einer zukünftigen Version wie
bei VM370 möglich sein. Keine Entsprechung findet das Mini-
Disk-Konzept in SIM-BS1000. Eine Zuordnung einer realen Platte
zu mehreren virtuellen Maschinen ist nicht möglich.
Eine Parallele existiert bei der möglichen Behandlung von Unit-
Record-Geräten. VM370 realisiert eine Spooling-Funktion für
solche Geräte und sichert die Daten in 4K-Blöcken auf einer
VM370 -Platte. SIM-BS1000 erzeugt entsprechend BS2000-Dateien,
deren Verarbeitung dem BS2000-Spool überlassen wird.

Die Ausführung einer Start-I/O- oder SDV-Anweisung weist bei
beiden Konzepten Parallelen bei der Vorbereitung der Kanalprogramme auf, die Realisierung der I/O wird unterschiedlich
ausgeführt. Das CP erhält die Kontrolle bei einer Start-I/O-
Anweisung einer virtuellen Maschine und führt dieser Start-I/O
für diese aus, nachdem es die Kanal-programm-liste in einen
eigenen Arbeitsbereich kopiert hat. Es sorgt dafür, daß die
Anforderungen an virtuellem Speicher in realen Speicher umge-
setzt wird.
Bei SIM-BS1000 wird die Realisierung der I/O einem Unterprozeß
mit BS2000-spezifischen I/O-Operationen überlassen. Dieser
Unterprozeß wartet dazu auf die Beendigung der I/O anstelle
des Hauptprozesses der virtuellen Maschine, der gleichzeitig
für andere Aufgaben frei ist. Im Anschluß simuliert der

Subtask eine Unterbrechung, indem er Register 15 mit dem
Unterbrechungsgewicht des zugeordneten (virtuellen) Kanals
lädt und den Hauptprozeß aufweckt, sofern sich dieser im
Wartezustand befindet. Damit versetzt sich der Subtask dann
gleichzeitig wieder in den Wartezustand für die Bearbeitung
der nächsten Ein-/Ausgabe-Operation.

Erkennt VMINT bei der Unterbrechungsbehandlung die derart simulierte Unterbrechung, so erfolgt eine I-O-Termination-Behand-
lung, so etwa die Versorgung der virtuellen Kanalregister. Im
Anschluß kann dann die (simulierte) Unterbrechung von VMINT
an das Gastsystem weitergegeben werden.
Die Ein-/Ausgabe von realen Geräten wird vom zugehörigen
Unterprozeß der virtuellen Maschine über den Makro $XCPW aus-
geführt. Dazu werden vom Modul VMIOPH Vorarbeiten erwartet.
Zunächst wird vorausgesetzt, daß die CCW-Ketten sich im
nicht-seitenwechselbaren Speicher befinden. Ein Übertragen der
ursprünglichen CCW-Ketten in einen geeigneten Arbeitsbereich
ist erforderlich.
Die angesprochenen I-O-Puffer werden resident gemacht. In
Sonderfällen werden zusätzliche CCW's in die Ketten eingefügt.
Dann nämlich, wenn I-O-Puffer Seitengrenzen überschreiten und
die Ausnutzung einer Page-Chaining-Hardware nicht vorausgesetzt werden kann.

Gelegentlich werden zusätzliche CCW's zur Fehlerbehandlung
eingefügt, wenn nämlich eine mögliche Pufferüberschreitung
von der Länge eines einzulesenden Blockes abhängt.

NACHBILDUNG MASCHINENORIENTIERTER BETRIEBSSYSTEM-SCHNITTSTELLEN FÜR REAL-TIME SYSTEME

Günter Mußtopf
Fachbereich Informatik
Universität Hamburg

Abstract. The concept of virtual machines is successfully used during the design of computer hardware as well as system software (operating systems, compilers, etc.). Therefore it would be very interesting to have a corresponding method for the design and implementation of real-time systems available.

The main characteristics of present real-time systems (multiprocessor, distributed systems) are explained in short. Subsequently the different kinds of the implemention of real-time operating systems are given. The influence of the new electronic components is taken into account. Finally the disadvantages of virtual machines with respect to the design of real-time systems are discussed.

1. Zielsetzung

Das Konzept der virtuellen Maschinen wurde bisher primär für den Entwurf von DV-Systemen eingesetzt. Es hat sich für Großanlagen (Hardware und Software) bewährt. Zu untersuchen ist jedoch, ob dieses Verfahren unverandert auch für künftige Real-Time Systeme verwendet werden kann. In diesem Sinn ist das Ziel dieses Beitrages mehr die Formulierung von Fragen als deren Beantwortung. Ursache für diese "Unsicherheit" sind nicht allein die - zumindestens in der Praxis anhaltende - Software-Krisis, sondern der wachsende Einfluß elektronischer Bauelemente und der (vielfach auch dem "Anwender" zugängigen) Mikroprogramm-Schicht.

Die Begriffe virtuelle Maschine und Real-Time Systeme werden mit unterschiedlicher Bedeutung und in unterschiedlichem Zusammenhang benutzt. Es ist deshalb zum besseren Verständnis der folgenden Diskussion erforderlich, zunächst diese Begriffe zu erläutern.

2. Begriffe

2.1 Virtuelle Maschine

Eine virtuelle Maschine ist eine <u>hypothetische</u> Maschine (1), die als Hilfsmittel zur Verallgemeinerung von Verfahren in verschiedenen Gebieten eingesetzt wird. Allerdings kann heute weitgehend jede virtuelle Maschine ohne Hardware-Entwicklung (im Sinne festverdrahteter Logik) mit Hilfe von Mikroroutinen realisiert werden. Sie wird dadurch zu einer realen Maschine. Die Vielfalt der Anwendungen virtueller Maschinen wird durch einige Beispiele erläutert.

Die Realisierung von Rechnern sehr unterschiedlicher Leistung mit einem einheitlichen Satz von Maschinenbefehlen (Rechnerfamilien) ist ein erstes Beispiel (Abb. 1). Werden identische oder verträgliche Betriebssysteme eingesetzt, so sind die Objektprogramme portabel. Dieses Verfahren wurde für viele Rechner-Familien wie IBM /360 oder DEC PDP 11 (2) erfolgreich eingesetzt.

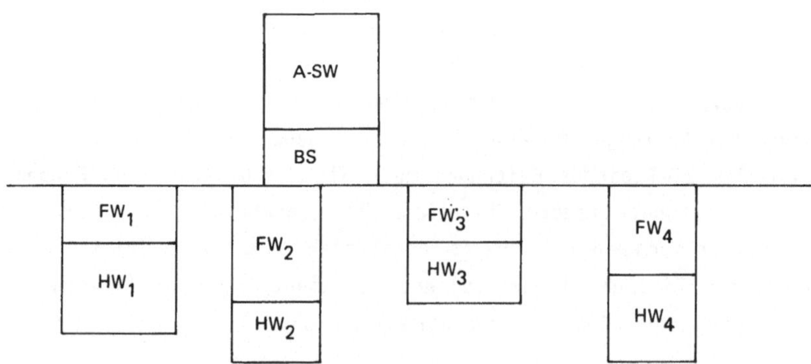

Abbildung 1: Rechnerfamilien

Ein verwandtes Problem liegt im Fall unverträglicher Betriebssysteme (Abb. 2) oder der Nachbildung nicht mehr verfügbarer Rechner vor. In diesem Fall laufen Objektprogramme unter Kontrolle unterschiedlicher Betriebssysteme oder mit einem unterschiedlichen Satz von Maschinenbefehlen quasi-parallel ab. Hier werden im Gegensatz zum ersten Beispiel in die virtuelle Maschine auch die (vorwiegend aus Software bestehenden) Betriebssysteme eingeschlossen. Dieses Verfahren wird z.B. im VM /370 eingesetzt. Charakteristisch für diese Anwendung ist, daß Systeme mit einer einheitlichen Architektur nachgebildet werden.

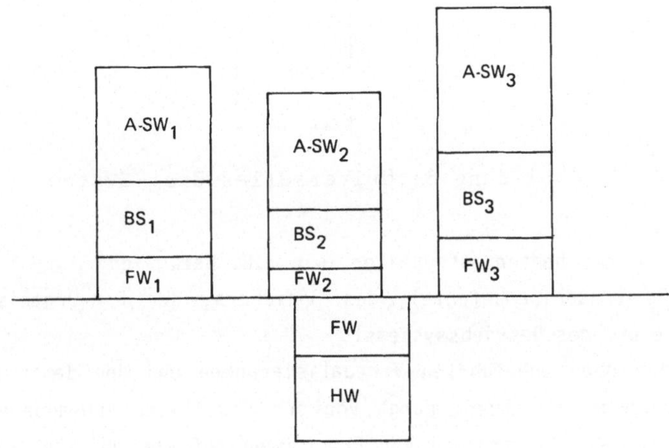

Abbildung 2: Nachbildung von Rechnern mit
verwandter Struktur

Ein ähnliches Ziel wird mit einem universellen Gastrechner (universal host (3)) angestrebt. Dieser besteht aus einem mikroprogrammierbaren System, das die Nachbildung sehr unterschiedlicher Rechnerarchitekturen mit Hilfe von Mikroroutinen ermöglicht (Abb. 3). Ein gutes Beispiel stellt das System Nanodata QM-1 (4,5) dar.

Schließlich werden noch die High-Level Language Computer (6) erwähnt. In diesen Systemen (z.B. B 1700) wird versucht, virtuelle Maschinen auf der Ebene höherer Programmiersprachen zu definieren.

Diese Beispiele zeigen, daß virtuelle Maschinen auf sehr unterschiedlichen Ebenen angesiedelt werden. Weiterhin ist es sinnvoll, virtuelle Ma-

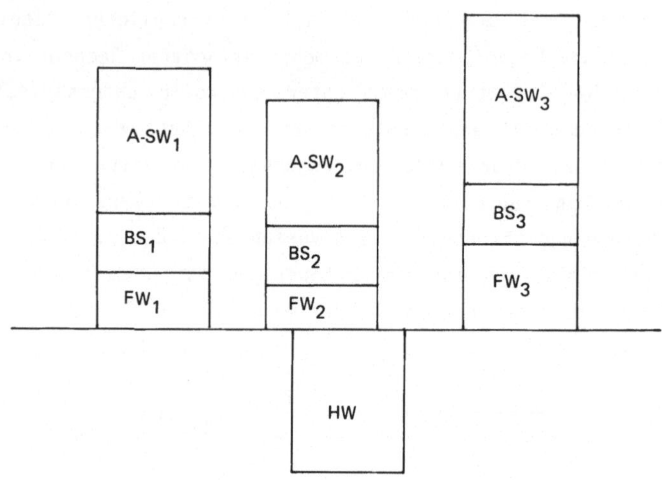

Abbildung 3: Universelles Gast-System

schinen in Komponenten aufzuteilen, wie z.B. bezüglich
  der CPU (Maschinenbefehle), des Speichers, der E/A-Organisation, der
  Konsole und des Betriebssystems.
Welche der oben angeführten Virtualisierungen und den damit verbundenen
Ebenen eingesetzt werden, hängt von den jeweiligen Anwendungen bzw. der
Zielsetzung ab (Übertragung von Programmen auf der Objektebene, Entwick-
lung von Rechnerfamilien, Reduktion des Compileraufwandes, Rationalisie-
rung der Erzeugung von Betriebssystemen usw.).

2.2 Real-Time Systeme
Unter dem Begriff Real-Time Systeme werden hier Hardware und Software als
Ganzes verstanden. Im folgenden werden die wesentlichen Eigenschaften von
Real-Time Systemen aufgezählt.

Funktionelle Eigenschaften: Real-Time Systeme arbeiten ereignisgesteuert.
Zu diesen äußeren Ereignissen zählen nicht nur Signale (z.B. von einem
technischen Prozeß), sondern auch die (absolute und relative) Zeit. Diese
spielt u.a. in Form der Reaktionszeiten für bestimmte Aktivitäten eine
zentrale Rolle. Reagiert ein Real-Time System auf Ereignisse nicht innerhalb der vorgegebenen Reaktionszeit, muß dies als System-Fehler gewertet

werden. Die Fehlerfreiheit eines Real-Time Systems läßt sich also nicht allein aus der formalen Fehlerfreiheit der Software (Algorithmen usw.) und Hardware ableiten.

Eine andere Eigenschaft von Real-Time Systemen besteht darin, daß die Ergebnisse vielfach auch temporäre Signale enthalten (z.B. Schließen eines Ventils, Stellen einer Gleisweiche, Auslösen eines Warnsignals usw.) Schließlich werden sehr hohe Anforderungen an die Zuverlässigkeit und Sicherheit von Real-Time Systemen gestellt (z.B. Steuerung eines Walzwerkes, Transportsysteme, Verkehrssteuerung, Kraftwerke usw.).

<u>Hardware:</u> Durch die Vielfalt der Peripheriegeräte zur Datenerfassung (Meßwertgeber) und zur Prozeßsteuerung und der Anzeigen in Warten bestehen RealTime Systeme meist aus "mixed Hardware". Nach der enormen Leistungssteigerung der Minicomputer werden heute in steigendem Maße Rechnernetze und Multiprozessorsysteme eingesetzt. Dieser Trend wird noch dadurch verstärkt, daß festverdrahtete Logik in Steuereinheiten und Peripheriegeräten durch Mikroprozessoren ersetzt werden. Die Kommunikation Rechner - Peripheriegerät wird dadurch zu einem Rechner-Rechner-Dialog.

<u>Systemstruktur:</u> Real-Time Systeme werden z.B. für die Steuerung von technischen Prozessen eingesetzt. Ihr Aufgabenprofil ist während des Systementwurfs bereits bekannt. Dies gilt ebenso für die einzelnen Systemkomponenten. Die Aufgabenstellung bleibt auch über längere Zeiträume unverändert. Allerdings müssen Modifikationen durchgeführt werden, die beispielsweise der Verbesserung des betreffenden Produktionsprozesses dienen. Weiterhin werden installierte Real-Time Systeme nur sehr selten durch Nachfolgesysteme ersetzt. Aus diesem Grund befinden sich noch heute in einigen Fällen TransistorRechenanlagen der 1. Generation im Einsatz. Schließlich führen der wachsende Umfang und die steigende Komplexität dazu, daß eine Wiederverwendung der Software von Real-Time Systemen und damit auch die Forderung nach Portabilität der Software an Bedeutung verliert. Dagegen gewinnt die Wiederverwendung von in sich abgeschlossenen Systemkomponenten rasch an Interesse. Diese bestehen aus Hardware <u>und</u> statischer Software (ROMs, PROMs o.ä.) auf der Basis von Mikroprozessoren. Die Verteilung von Aufgaben oder Teilaufgaben von einem zentralen Rechner auf

derartige Systemkomponenten (verteilte Systeme) unterstützt diesen Trend. Charakteristisch ist dabei, daß die Systemkomponenten funktionsorientiert sind, d.h. es liegt eine weitgehend feste Aufgabenverteilung vor. Bei Auftreten von Hardwarefehlern werden die Aufgaben nach einer festgelegten Strategie delegiert. Diese Entwicklung führt zu einer wachsenden Spezialisierung der Systemkomponenten.

<u>Real-Time Betriebssysteme:</u> Die historische Entwicklung von Betriebssystemen für Minicomputer weist viele Parallelen zu derjenigen für Großanlagen auf:

o wachsende Universalität (z.B. Betriebsarten),
o steigender Leistungsumfang (z.B. Multiprogramming, Datei-Management, Multiprocessing),
o erheblicher Speicherbedarf (Hauptspeicher und Externspeicher),
o wachsender Verwaltungsaufwand und
o die hohe Flexibilität führt zur Schwerfälligkeit!

Dies hat bei Real-Time Systemen längere Reaktionszeiten zur Folge. Die Forderung nach Verkürzung der Reaktionszeiten und der für die Hardware erkennbare Trend zur Spezialisierung führen auch bei Real-Time Systemen zurück zu dedizierten Betriebssystemen. Die Preisentwicklung von elektronischen Bauelementen hat nur einen erstaunlich schwachen gegenläufigen Einfluß. Die enorme Leistung und Vielfalt integrierter Schaltungen fördern eher die Spezialisierung. Verstärkt wird diese Tendenz noch durch die für Prozeßperipherie erforderliche Vielzahl von Treibern. Schließlich müssen auch für das Taskmanagement alternativ unterschiedliche Strategien zur Verfügung stehen.

3. Realisierung von Real-Time Betriebssystemen

Die Forderung nach dedizierten Real-Time Betriebssystemen regte die Entwicklung von Verfahren zur rationellen Implementierung von Betriebssystemen an. Beispiele dafür sind in den Projekten COPF (7), dem Entwurf eines VDI Arbeitskreises oder des Purdue Europe TC 8 (8) zu finden. Diese Vorschläge beschäftigen sich primär mit der Definition von Basisfunktionen von Betriebssystemen. Diese sollen einerseits unabhängig von der Hardware sein und andererseits als Grundlage für die Realisierung von anwendungs-orientierten Betriebssystemfunktionen dienen (Abb. 4). Diese Strategie entspricht der Definition einer virtuellen Maschine bezüglich der Betriebssysteme (vituelles Betriebssystem). Bemerkenswert, aus der Sicht dieser Diskussion, sind zwei Erfahrungen aus dem Vorhaben COPF. Zum einen war es schwierig, das <u>Niveau</u> der Basisfunktionen festzulegen. Zum anderen zeigte es sich, daß die Bereitstellung von alternativen Basisfunktionen bzw. von Basisfunktionsgruppen empfehlenswert ist. Dies entspricht jedoch der Aussage, daß mehrere Sätze von Basisfunktionen, d.h. unterschiedliche virtuelle Betriebssysteme sinnvoll sind.

Das kurz geschilderte Verfahren zur Realisierung von Betriebssystemen ist jedoch nur ein Lösungsweg. Im folgenden werden die unterschiedlichen Methoden aus der Sicht der Struktur von Real-Time Systemen aufgezählt. Da-

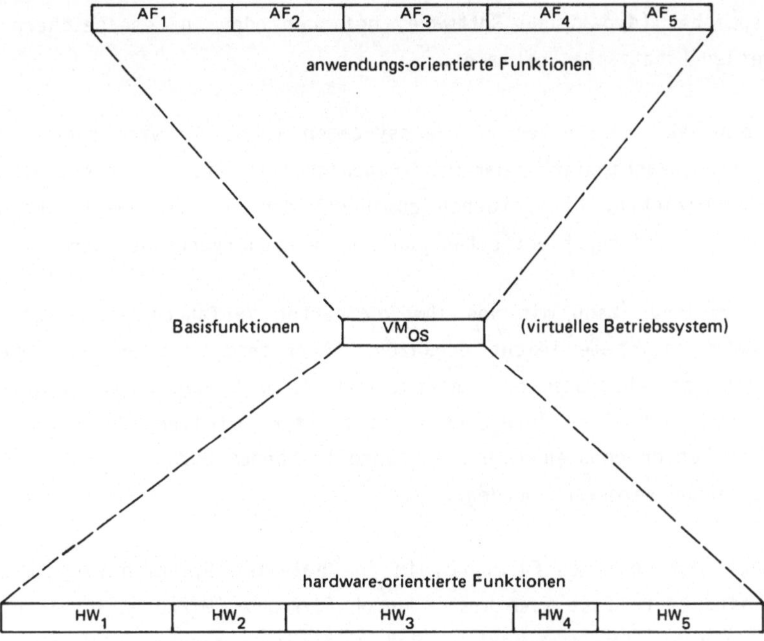

Abbildung 4: Virtuelles Betriebssystem

bei wird davon ausgegangen, daß i.a. Multiprozessorsysteme eingesetzt werden.

3.1 Zentrale Organisation.Real-Time Betriebssysteme mit einer zentralen Organisation enthalten eine hierarchisch orientierte Schichtstruktur. Die zentrale Organisation entspricht im wesentlichen der Verwendung von Basisfunktionen. Charakteristisch ist dabei, daß die Betriebssystemfunktionen im gleichen System (Rechner) ablaufen wie die Anwendungsprogramme bzw. Betriebsmittel, die sie überwachen.

Zu unterscheiden sind jedoch die Arten der Realisierung solcher Betriebssysteme. Zu untersuchen wäre dabei, inwieweit die Art der Realisierung die Struktur der virtuellen Betriebssysteme beeinflußt.

3.1.1 Realisierung durch Software.Die Realisierung von Betriebssystemen durch Software ist das traditionelle Verfahren. Dabei ist zunächst gleichgültig, ob bzw. in welchem Umfang Module sich temporär bzw. resident im Arbeitsspeicher (dynamische Software) befinden oder in Lesespeichern fixiert werden (statische Software).

Das Konzept von virtuellen Betriebssystemen (Abb. 4) wird hier eingesetzt, um unterschiedliche Hardware-Eigenschaften (z.B. Interruptbehandlung) auszugleichen. Damit können zumindest die auf den Basisfunktionen aufbauenden anwendungsorientierten Funktionen wiederverwendet werden.

Der Programmierer kann mit den ihm vertrauten Verfahren und Werkzeugen solche Betriebssysteme leicht ergänzen. Allerdings kann er auch ebenso leicht den Betriebssystemkern ändern, wodurch u.U. die zugrunde gelegte Struktur des virtuellen Betriebssystems zerstört wird und Unverträglichkeiten und Fehler entstehen. Diese Nachteile können durch statische Software weitgehend vermieden werden.

3.1.2 Realisierung durch Firmware.Die in Real-Time Systemen eingesetzten Rechner sind heute fast ausnahmslos durch Firmware (Mikroroutinen) realisiert. Durch die Preisentwicklung von Halbleiterspeichern und den Übergang von Lesespeichern zu Schreib-/Lesespeichern für Mikroroutinen (dyna-

mische Firmware) wird die Verlagerung von Software-Moduln in die Firmware
gefördert. Dadurch kann zweifellos die Effizienz der Betriebssystemfunktionen (Reaktionszeiten) gezielt verbessert werden. Aus der Sicht des
Programmierers entspricht dies der Erweiterung des Befehlsvorrates beispielsweise für die Analyse und Verarbeitung von Signalen (Interrupts).

Dieser Trend wird auch die Definition von virtuellen Betriebssystemen
beeinflussen. Diese sollten sicher oberhalb der Ebene der Maschinenbefehle liegen. Durch die oben erwähnte Verlagerung von Funktionen aus der
Software in die Firmware wird jedoch die Ebene der Maschinenbefehle ange-
hoben. Da bisher nur Vorschläge für Standards im Bereich von Betriebssystemen bestehen, entstehen natürlich auch sehr unterschiedliche Sätze von
betriebssystem-orientierten Befehlen. Dies führt wiederum zu Schwierig-
keiten bei der Definition virtueller Betriebssysteme.

Schließlich soll ein Beispiel für die Rückwirkung auf CPU-orientierte
Maschinenbefehle (virtuelle CPU-Maschine) gegeben werden. Die Forderung
nach dedizierten Real-Time Betriebssystemen führt zu einer sehr starken
Modularisierung und damit zu einer Vielzahl von Prozeduraufrufen. Dies
bringt eine (für Real-Time Systeme nicht zulässige) Verlängerung der Reaktionszeiten mit sich. Spezielle Befehle für Prozeduraufrufe sind also
unbedingt erforderlich. Dieser schließt nicht nur die Rückkehrorganisati-
on, sondern auch das Retten und Rückspeichern von Registern und den Trans-
port von Parametern ein.

3.1.3 Realisierung durch Hardware
Werden von Real-Time Systemen extrem hohe Leistungen gefordert, so muß
festverdrahtete Logik (Hardware) eingesetzt werden. Vielfach wird auch
eine parallele Verarbeitung angestrebt. Dabei ist es zunächst nicht wesentlich, ob dies in einem Chip oder auf einer Platine erfolgt. Beispiele
für derartige Forderungen sind sehr hohe Signalraten oder die Zuordnung
der Zeit zu einem Signal. Der Einsatz spezieller Hardware-Komponenten
kann beispielsweise in speziellen Peripheriegeräten geschehen. Eine andere Möglichkeit zur Erfüllung dieser geforderten Leistungssteigerung bietet die Übertragung der in 3.1.2 genannten Funktionen von Firmware in
Hardware, d.h. beispielsweise die Verwendung von geeigneten Interrupt-

und Prozedur-Werken. Wesentlich ist hier, daß eine Nachbildung solcher Werke durch Firmware nicht möglich ist, da hierdurch die vorgegebenen Zeitbedingungen i.a. verletzt würden.

3.2 Dezentrale Organisation

In Multiprozessorsystemen werden gleiche oder ähnliche Betriebssystem-Module mehrfach gespeichert. Zusätzlich ist für die Synchronisierung eine Kommunikation zwischen den Systemkomponenten erforderlich. Diese Situation ist u.a. ein Motiv, die Verlagerung von Betriebssystemaufgaben zu betrachten. Dabei sind zwei Strategien zu berücksichtigen.

3.2.1 Einsatz spezialisierter Rechner

Eine Reihe von Betriebssystemaufgaben wie z.B. Verwaltung von Betriebsmitteln und Taskmanagement kann in vielen Systemkomponenten in gleicher Weise behandelt werden. Es liegt deshalb nahe, einem "spezialisierten Rechner" (Systemkomponente) diese Managementaufgaben zu übertragen. Dadurch wird auch die Synchronisation zwischen den Systemkomponenten vereinfacht. Für diese Aufgabe können Minicomputer, dedizierte Hardware auf der Basis von Mikroprozessoren oder mikroprogrammierbare Systeme eingesetzt werden.

Die Delegation von Teilen der Betriebssystemaufgaben beeinflußt oder erschwert jedoch die Definition von virtuellen Betriebssystemen!

3.2.2 Einsatz spezieller Prozessoren

Aufgaben, die spezifisch für eine Systemkomponente sind oder sehr kurze Reaktionszeiten fordern, können nicht in andere, abgeschlossene Systemkomponenten verlagert werden. In diesem Fall werden spezialisierte Prozessoren bzw. Controller (Werke) eingesetzt, die in die betreffende Systemkomponente integriert werden. Beispiele dafür sind die Kommunikation mit anderen Systemkomponenten, das File-Management und die Prozeß-E/A. Selbstverständlich beeinflussen solche Strukturen in steigendem Maße ebenfalls die Struktur virtueller Betriebssysteme.

4. Konsequenzen

Der Trend zu dedizierter Hardware ist bei Real-Time Systemen unverkenn-
bar. Dies gilt sowohl für die Struktur des Gesamtsystems als auch für die
der Systemkomponenten. Während des Systementwurfs werden die Aufgaben A_i
($i = 1, 2, \ldots, m$) so in Teilaufgaben aufgeteilt (Abb. 5a), daß Aufgabengruppen A_k ($k = 1, 2, \ldots, n$) mit gleichartigen Problemen gebildet werden
können (Numerik, Verarbeitung von Zeichenketten oder Bitketten usw.).
Diesen Aufgabengruppen können wiederum entsprechend spezialisierte Systemkomponenten HW_k zugeordnet werden (Abb. 5b). Beispiele dafür sind
o 1-bit Prozessoren für Folgesteuerungen,
o Feld"rechner" für schnelle Matrixoperationen,
o Slice-Prozessoren für schnelle Verarbeitung von Zeichenketten,
usw.

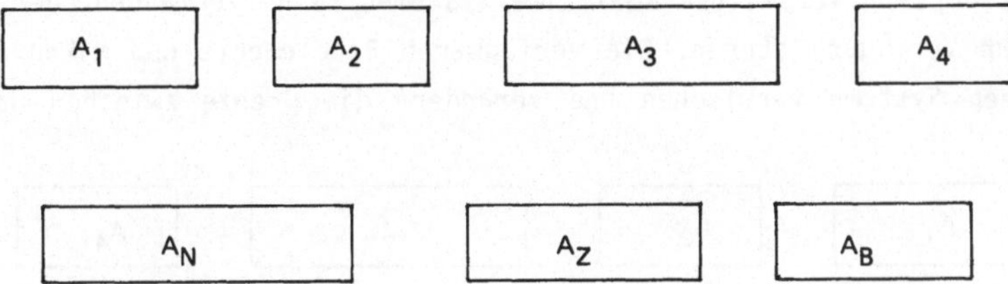

Abbildung 5a: Definition von anwendungs-orientierten
Aufgabengruppen

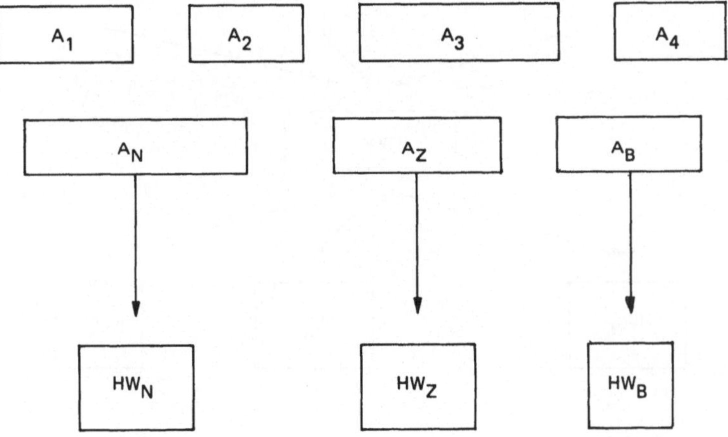

Abbildung 5b: Einsatz dedizierter Hardware

Dieses Verfahren wird (gleichgültig, ob es aus formalen Gründen gut oder schlecht ist) mit großem Erfolg eingesetzt. Nicht zuletzt können derartige oft recht kleine Systemkomponenten, die sich auf einer Platine befinden, unverändert wiederverwendet werden.

Allerdings ist für den Entwurf solcher Systeme die Benutzung virtueller Maschinen in der bisherigen Form wenig sinnvoll (Abb. 5c). Die unterschiedlichen Aufgabengruppen werden zunächst auf eine universelle Maschine abgebildet. Anschließend muß diese wieder auf dedizierte Hardware abgebildet werden. Ein Ausweg aus dieser Situation könnte lediglich die Einführung eines Satzes virtueller Maschinen bieten (Abb. 5d).

Die eigentliche Schwierigkeit in diesem Gebiet liegt darin, daß heute für den Entwurf von verteilten Real-Time Systemen keine Verfahren oder Kriterien zur Verfügung stehen. Die verfügbaren Bauelemente und mikroprogrammierbaren Systeme verwischen und verändern die Grenze zwischen Hardware

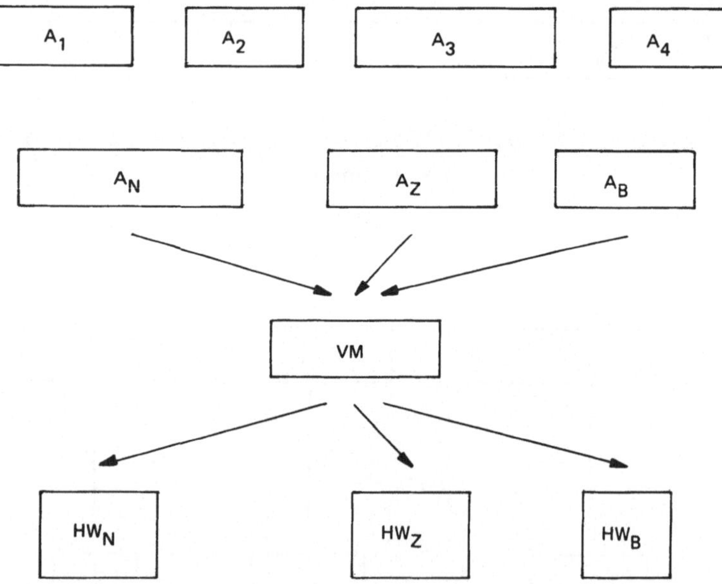

Abbildung 5c: Verwendung einer universellen
virtuellen Maschine

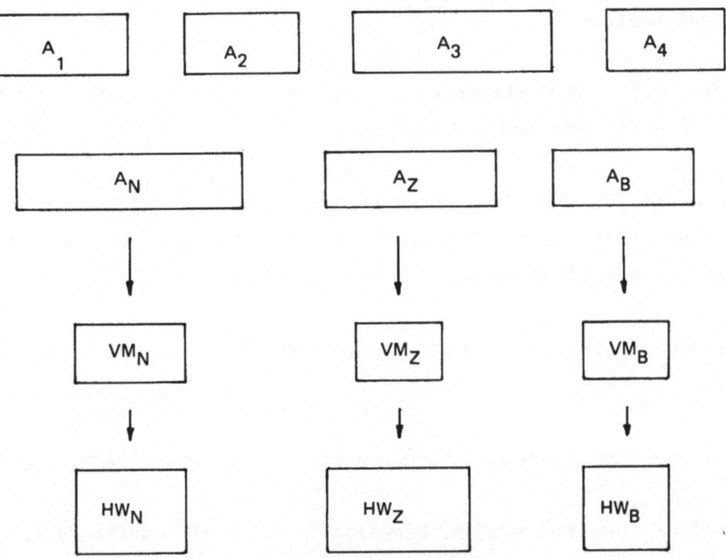

Abbildung 5d: Verwendung von dedizierten
virtuellen Maschinen

und Software (9). Die Frage, ob eine bestimmte Teilaufgabe oder Funktion durch Hardware, Firmware oder Software realisiert werden sollte, kann heute im günstigsten Fall nur für die jeweils vorliegende Anwendung beantwortet werden. Während des Systementwurfs müssen detaillierte Software- und Hardwarekenntnisse und Wissen und Erfahrungen aus den jeweiligen Anwendungsgebieten vorhanden sein. Hilfskonstruktionen wie virtuelle Maschinen sind für ein erfolgreiches Arbeiten unbedingt erforderlich. Allerdings müssen diese entsprechend der Struktur von Real-Time Systemen weiterentwickelt werden.

Literaturhinweise:

(1) Kuck, D.J.: The structure of computers and computation, Vol. I, pp. 356-361. John Wiley & Sons 1978.

(2) O'Loughlin, J.F.: Microprogramming a fixed architecture machine. Infotech State of the Art Report no. 23, Microprogramming and systems architecture, Maidenhead, 1975, pp. 205-224.

(3) Salisbury, A.B.: Microprogrammable computer architectures. Elsevier, 1976.

(4) Nanodata: The microcode. Nanodata Corp., Williamsville N.Y., 1978.

(5) Nanodata: The QM-1 system. Nanodata Corp., Williamsville N.Y., 1978.

(6) Chu, Y.: High-level language computer architecture. Academic Press N.Y. 1975.

(7) Ehrig, J., Hahn, H., Hotes, H.: COPF, ein Satz von Programmbausteinen für Realzeit-Betriebssysteme. KFK-PD 40, 1975.

(8) Purdue Europe: Report of the Technical Committee on Real-Time Operating Systems, 1978.

(9) Musstopf, G. Microprocessor's hardware and software. IFAC/IFIP SOCOCO 1979, Prague.

VIRTUAL MACHINE DISPATCHING
UNDER FAIRNESS CONSTRAINTS

H. Schmutz

H. Eberle

K. F. Finkemeyer

IBM Deutschland GmbH
Scientific Center Heidelberg

Abstract

The paper analyzes the problems of low level dispatching
under predictability constraints, with good responsiveness
and low overhead. It is shown that nonpreemptive and/or
round-robin disciplines fail for the general case. A novel
algorithm is proposed based on sorting at time slice intervals. Simulation results are used to discuss the properties
of the new dispatching algorithm.

1. Introduction

The scheduling of processes in operating systems is
performed at several levels. The lowest level scheduler in
this hierarchy is subsequently referred to as dispatcher.
The dispatcher operates according to objectives set up by
higher level schedulers (operating system components and/or
operator). One important problem is to define the dispatching objectives (i.e. the parameters of the dispatcher) in
such a way that they are meaningful to higher level scheduling and realistically met by the dispatcher implementation.

Requirements

This study was performed for the design of a dispatcher for
virtual machines satisfying the following requirements:

1. The dispatcher should introduce only "small",
   ignorable overhead.

2. The dispatcher should support predictability.

3. The virtual machines should remain responsive.

These requirements will be discussed in more detail subsequently. They may be summarized as follows: the dispatched
virtual machines should not only functionally be equivalent
to, but also performance wise come close to the behaviour of
real machines. The underlying principal idea is that the
resources of the base CPU which are

- the CPU power

- the main memory

- communication paths with the environment such as
  channels

can be distributed over the virtual machines without losses.

Performance

The first requirement will not directly be investigated.
Clearly, any dispatching causes overhead. However, under the
assumption of a simple dispatching algorithm the overhead
can be expected to be small if dispatching does not substantially increase the number of interrupts. For all subsequently discussed dispatching algorithms additional interrupts occur at time slice intervals. The first requirement

will be interpreted such that objectives 2 and 3 above can
be met at long time slice intervals, i.e. at intervals which
do not substantially increase the frequency of interrupts.

Predictability

The notion of predictability deserves some preliminary
considerations. We distinguish between a strong and a weak
form of predictability.

Strong predictability means that variations of the workload
on a virtual machine have no impact on the performance of
the remaining virtual machines on the same base CPU. As a
consequence it may become necessary that the base CPU enters
the wait state although one or more virtual machines are
"running", i.e.dispatchable. Or, in other words, CPU power
is wasted in some situations for the purpose of predictability. This may look strange, however, the requirement for
strong predictability arose in practice.

For major computer installations providing compute service
for several divisions within their organization, the computer center is responsible for providing a guaranteed service
level to satisfy the needs for the day to day operations.
With strong predictability the computer center manager can
make sure that no division is ever tempted to use more
computer resources than it has available in a worst case
situation. Out of a similar motivation, the data processing
manager of a major installation asked for a fifteen percent
growth of CPU power per year, not more! A fifty per cent
growth in one year followed by a zero growth in the two
subsequent years tends to stimulate the growth of applications too much in the first year with the result of an
unextendable, overloaded system towards the end of the three
years period. Since hardware does not offer this level of
granularity for the tuning of CPU power, a software solution

with "strongly" predictable dispatching is a requirement.

Frequently a weak form of predictability is desirable. Here again each virtual machine obtains a guaranteed minimum of CPU service. However, if the workloads of the remaining virtual machines permit, a virtual machine may obtain better CPU service than the guaranteed minimum.

Responsiveness

The third requirement addresses hardware responsetime, i.e. the time between the signal of an external event, also known as an interrupt, and the start of processing of that inter- rupt. Real hardware needs in general as hardware response- time something in the order of the execution time for a couple of instructions. In a virtual machine there may be an additional delay due to dispatching if the base CPU is not .assigned immediately to the virtual machine receiving the interrupt. It is unrealistic to expect a virtual machine to be as responsive as a real machine in all situations. However, in most situations only the total system response- time is critical. For example, for typical batch applica- tions, where the total responsetime is minutes or hours, a hardware responsetime of less than a second is sufficient; or, for interactive timesharing or DB/DC applications, where total responsetime is between .5 and several seconds, a hardware responsetime of less than .1 seconds may be suffi- cient. Clearly, there are other applications such as process control for which a virtual machine approach may be totally inadequate.

The above considerations let it appear desirable that a dispatching algorithm favours the responsiveness of I/O-bound, interactive workloads to the possible disadvan- tage of compute bound workloads.

Storage Allocation

In general, a dispatcher has to cooperate with a storage management algorithm for decisions such as rollout/rollin to determine the right level of multiprogramming. For the purpose of this study it is assumed that main memory is statically assigned to the virtual machines. This permits to ignore the effects of storage management on dispatching - page transfers for a virtual machine may be looked at as any other input/output operation for this machine. It is clear, that this assumption is only realistic for a small n with each VM(i) supporting a multiprogramming operation system. The interaction between storage allocation and dispatching (or, more general scheduling) as it is necessary for example in VM/370 if used with CMS /1/ is not subject of this study.

2. Basic Definitions

CPU Power

Subsequently we assume a real base CPU on which n virtual machines VM(1), VM(2),... VM(n) are dispatched. We introduce a quantitative measure, the CPU power, which is proportional to the instructionrate of a CPU and use a proportionality factor such that the CPU power of the real base CPU becomes 1. Further, we assume, that the CPU power for each VM(i) is a dispatching parameter $p(i)$ with the constraint:

$$\text{SUM } p\ (i)\ \leq\ 1$$
$$i \leq n$$

Conservation of CPU-Power

The behaviour of a virtual machine VM(i) will subsequently be compared with the behaviour of a real CPU with the same CPU power. It will be referred to as the comparator CPU to VM(i). Its instruction rate is $p(i)$ times the instruction rate of the real base CPU. The CPU service granted to a virtual machine under a given dispatching algorithm is, of course, also a function of its workload 1. The conservation

of CPU power requires that the CPU service granted to VM(i)
under dispatching is at least as high as the CPU service
q(i,l) obtained on the comparator CPU for any workload l.
Clearly

$$q(i,l) \leq p(i)$$

The workload on VM(i) is I/O bound if $q(i,l) < p(i)$ and CPU
bound if $q(i,l) = p(i)$.

Predictability
Under a given dispatching algorithm D and for given workloads l(i) the VM(i) obtain fractions f(D,i,l) of the
execution rate of the real base CPU.

A dispatcher S satisfies strong predictability if f(S,i,l)
depends only on the i'th component of l, subject to the
further constraint that

$$f(S,i,l(i)) \geq q(i,l(i)) \tag{1}$$

for all workload vectors l.

A dispatcher W is an extension of S satisfying weak predictability if for all workload vectors l

$$f(W,i,l) \geq f(S,i,l(i)) \tag{2}$$

It is our objective to find dispatching algorithms S and W
which permit maximal CPU usage. However, it is clear from
the discussion in section 1 that predictability is not the
only objective of dispatching. Instead of designing possibly
very complex algortihms which satisfy (1) and (2) above
exactly, we will take the more pragmatic approach of designing simple algortihms and study their performance, predictability and responsiveness behaviour by analysis and simulation.

3. The Workload Model and Analytical Results

3.1 The Workload Model

For the analysis of dispatching algorithms a stochastic model for the workload on a virtual machine is necessary. This model should be as simple as possible, but permit to reflect unoverlapped and overlapped CPU processing. While such a model is certainly not a "true" picture of reality we conjecture that a more complex model would not confront the dispatcher with different situations. With other words, we claim without proof that the simple model is reasonably adequate for a thorough analysis of dispatching.

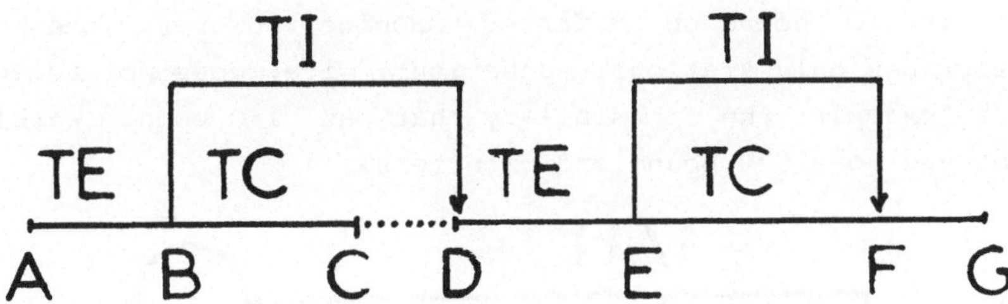

Figure 1: Transaction Sequence

The workload is determined by three independent random variables TE, TC and TI as illustrated in figure 1. Each of these variables is given by a distribution. The workload consists of a sequence of basic transactions. Each transaction is determined by a time TE of unoverlapped processing and a time TC of overlapped processing and a time TI of I/O time. The length TL of a transaction is given by:

$$TL = TE + \max\ (TC, TI)$$

Within a transaction, the CPU is busy for a time period TE + TC and enters the wait state for a period

$$TW = TL - (TE + TC)$$

if $TW > 0$. For the transaction AD of figure 1 the CPU is busy from A to C and waiting from point C to D, while for the subsequent transaction DG the CPU is busy throughout the full period.

Clearly, modelling the same workload on a machine with a different execution rate changes the TE and TC values but leaves the TI values identical. Thus the model reflects well the fact that a CPU bound workload on a slow machine may become I/O bound on a faster machine. However, the model describes only stationary behaviour, i.e. does not reflect, for example, the possibility that an I/O bound workload changes to a CPU bound and vice versa.

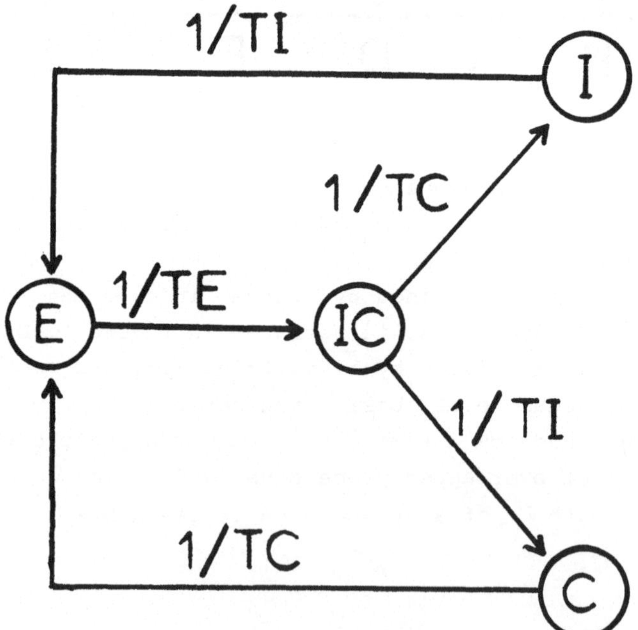

Figure 2:The Workload Model as Semi-Markov Process

If the random variables are exponentially distributed, the
described model corresponds to a semi-Markov model illustrated in figure 2. State E corresponds to periods AB and
DE in figure 1, states I and C correspond to periods CD and
FG, respectively, and state IC corresponds to periods BC and
EF. For this case the equilibrium conditions can easily be
derived:

$$\frac{PE}{TE} = \frac{PI}{TI} + \frac{PC}{TC}$$

$$\frac{PIC}{TC} + \frac{PIC}{TI} = \frac{PE}{TE} \qquad (3)$$

$$\frac{PI}{TI} = \frac{PIC}{TC}$$

$$\frac{PC}{TC} = \frac{PIC}{TI}$$

where

TE, TC, TI   stand for the expected values of the random
variables TE, TC, TI and

PE, PC, PIC, PI   are the probabilities that the CPU is
running unoverlapped before start of the I/O
operation (PE), unoverlapped after completion of the I/O operation (PC), overlapped
with the I/O operation (PIC), or waiting for
completion of the I/O operation (PI).

The probability PB, that the CPU is busy, is given by

$$PB = PE + PIC + PC = 1 - PI \qquad (4)$$

PB can easily be derived from (3) and (4) to

$$PB(ti) = \frac{tc + ti}{tc + ti + ti * 2} \qquad (5)$$

where * denotes exponentiation and tc, ti are given by:

$$tc = \frac{TC}{TE + TC} \qquad ti = \frac{TI}{TE + TC}$$

3.2 Nonpreemptive Round-Robin Dispatching

We introduce now two additional independent random variables, TR and TW, for the length of alternating periods of
time. Consider one virtual machine i: during the R-period
(for Running) the virtual machine i owns the CPU and no
other virtual machine obtains CPU service; during the
W-period (for Waiting) the CPU is allocated to the other
virtual machines only. If TR and TW represent the expected
values of TR and TW, we have

$$p(i) = \frac{TR}{TR + TW} \qquad (6)$$

and TR + TW represent the time slice length.

This model reflects round-robin dispatching in which each
virtual machine obtains the CPU for a time period which is
in length proportional to the CPU power of the virtual
machine. It is immediately clear, that this algorithm

satisfies objective (1) above for very small time slices. We use again a semi-Markov model to study the effect of realistic time slice lengths.

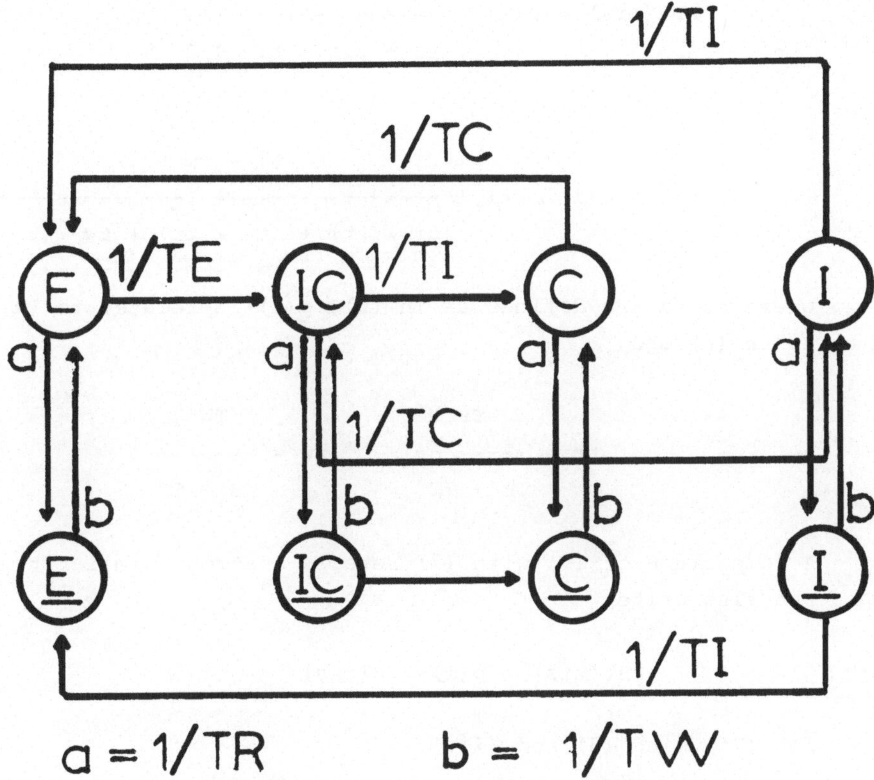

Figure 3:Semi-Markov Model for Round-Robin Dispatching

Figure 3 shows the state transition diagram, assuming again all random variables to be exponentially distributed. States are denoted as in section 3.1 with non underlined symbols for states in the R-period and underlined symbols for states in the W-period.

It is lengthy, but straight forward to compute the probability PBV that the CPU is busy for the considered virtual machine. The result is:

$$PBV(tis) = p(i) \times \frac{tc + tis}{tc + tis + tis * 2} \tag{7}$$

$$tis = p(i) \times ti \times \frac{ti + tw}{(ti \times tr) + (tw \times tr) + tw \times ti} \tag{8}$$

where tc,ti are defined as in (5), p(i) is related to TR, TW as in (6) and

$$tr = \frac{TR}{TE + TC} \qquad tw = \frac{TW}{TE + TC}$$

A comparison of (7) with (5) reveals a strong similarity. We can also write

$$PBV(tis) = p(i) \times PB(tis) \tag{9}$$

for (7) using (5) and (7).

For analysis, consider the two extreme cases for time slice lengths, $tr \to 0$ and $tr \to$ inf for constant p(i):

$$\lim_{tr \to 0} PBV = p(i) \times PB(p(i) \times ti)$$

$$\lim_{tr \to inf} PBV = p(i) \times PB(ti)$$

The effect of time slices greater than zero is equivalent to

an increase in I/O time, which in turn results in a degradi-
tion of CPU usage. Figure 4 shows the ratio between PBV for
tr = 3 and PBV for tr = 0 as a function of tc and ti in the
form of contour lines. There is a minimal plateau at the
level of 0.67 at values of tc = 0.6 and ti = 3.3. For tr = 1
a similar picture arises with a minimal plateau at the level
of 0.86, again a value significantly less than 1.

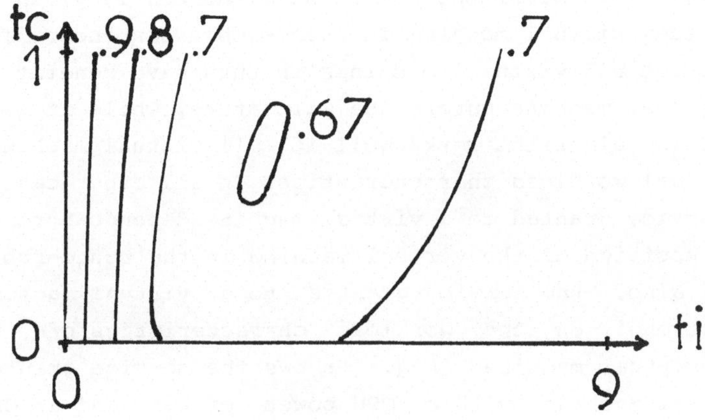

Figure 4: Performance Degradation with Nonpreemptive Round-
          Robin Dispatching

The above analysis illustrates, the general failure of
nonpreemptive dispatching for the special case of nonpreemptive round-robin dispatching with exponential distributions.
Consider a workload with which a virtual machine is
completely CPU - bound if executed on the comparator CPU,
but which is I/O bound on the base CPU. With any nonpreemptive discipline, the base CPU would enter occasionally the

wait state, the algorithm would thus fail to conserve the CPU-power.

3.3 Preemptive Round-Robin Disciplines

The popularity of round-robin disciplines in the literature /2,5/ and in implementations /3/ was a primary motivation for the analysis of a modification. The modified algorithm works as follows: each VM(i) has highest priority during a period which is in length proportional to its CPU power p(i). While VM(i) enters the wait state, the CPU is given to the next ready virtual machine in round-robin sequence. The idea is to let all virtual machines in turn have benefit if another virtual machine enters the wait state, while it owns the CPU. This algorithm works well if all virtual machines have identical workload characteristics. In all other cases, the CPU service granted to a virtual machine depends strongly on the position of the virtual machine in the round-robin sequence. Also, the service granted to a virtual machine depends strongly on the workload characteristics of the remaining virtual machines. Fig. 5 shows the service granted to a virtual machine with a CPU power of 0.5 and a CPU utilization of 0.8 on the comparator CPU dependent on the CPU utilization of a second virtual machine on its comparator CPU. This one example, analyzed with an analytical model with exponential distributions similar to those considered in section 3.1 and 3.2, illustrates that the modified round-robin algorithm fails both, the conservation of CPU power and the predictability requirement.

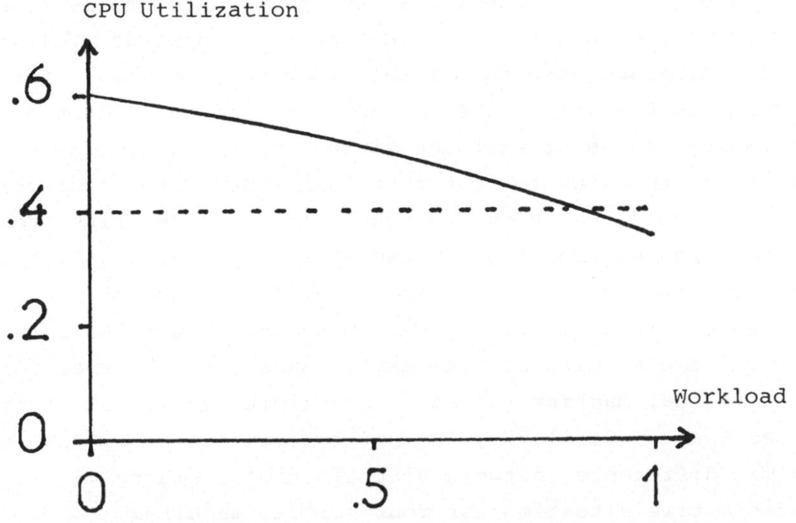

Figure 5: CPU Utilization of VM(1) Dependent on Workload of
         VM(2)

4. Dispatching Based on Sorting

4.1 The Proposed Dispatching Algorithm

The analysis described in section 3 leads to the conclusion
that sorting of the virtual machines dependent on their
workload charasteristics is necessary to cope with asymmetric workload distributions. Two primary questions arise:

(a) which are the sorting criteria, and,

(b) how is it decided that a virtual machine is put
    into a forced wait for the purpose of predictabil-
    ity.

As answer to both questions we propose to collect all sorting criteria into time dependent quantities VT(i,t), 1 ≤ i ≤ n, associated to virtual machine i at real time t. We refer to VT(i,t) as the virtual time of VM(i) at time t. The basic idea is to sort the virtual machines at time slice intervals according to their virtual times into a priority list and to dispatch during the intervals the first ready virtual machine. For the purpose of strong predictability we make sure that the virtual times grow in average at the same rate as the real time. We set an advance limit AL for the maximum time a virtual time may be ahead of the real time. If a virtual machine exceeds this limit it is put into a forced wait. Similarly, we set a lag limit LL for the maximal difference between virtual times. Figure 6 illustrates a time situation for four virtual machines.

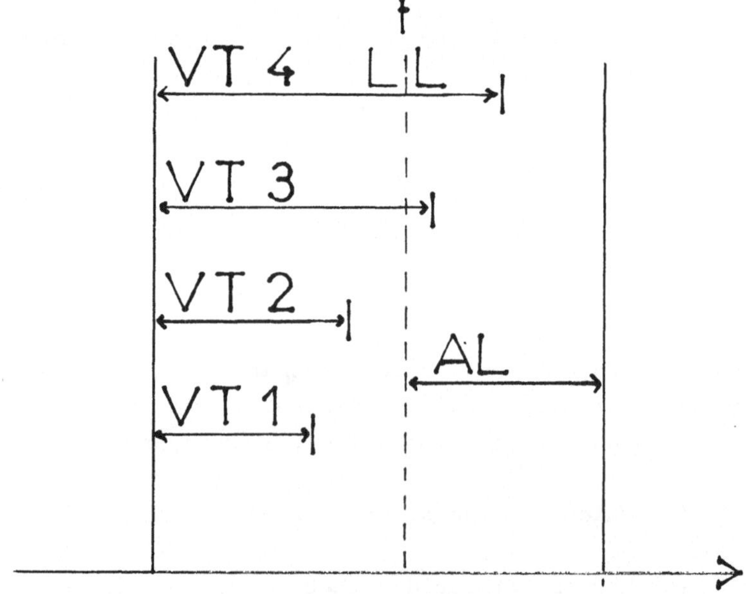

Figure 6: Virtual Times, Lag Limit and Advance Limit

AL and LL are dispatching parameters in addition to the vector p(i) of CPU powers and the time slice length TS. Special cases are infinite or very large values for the ratio of the limits to the time slice length.

It is now well defined, when a virtual machine VM(i) enters a forced wait: if VT(i,t) exceeds t + AL, VM(i) is forced into a wait state for the time period t + AL - VT(i,t).

It is clear how the virtual time should advance during CPU processing: proportional to the real time with the inverse of the CPU power as factor. However, the accounting for wait time deserves some more considerations. The basic idea is, to account less or equal wait time than the same workload would have caused waiting on the comparator CPU. Clearly, it would be unfair to increase the virtual time linearly with the wait time, since the same workload may cause less or no waiting on the slower comparator CPU.

Figure 7 (a) to (c) illustrates the proposed accounting. The virtual machine has a CPU power of 0.5 and starts unoverlapped processing at real time A. At the real time RX it issues an I/O operation which terminates at real time TT. At real time WT it begins waiting for the completion of the I/O operation. The virtual time has reached value VT1 at real time WT (i.e. VT1 = VT(i,WT)). The algorithms has to calculate VT2 = VT(i,TT), i.e. the virtual time after completion of the I/O event.

The quantities WT, TT, VT are the only values known to the dispatcher (in addition to the dispatching parameters). In particular, the value of RX is unknown to the dispatcher. The proposed, and in figure 7 illustrated wait time calculation is as follows:

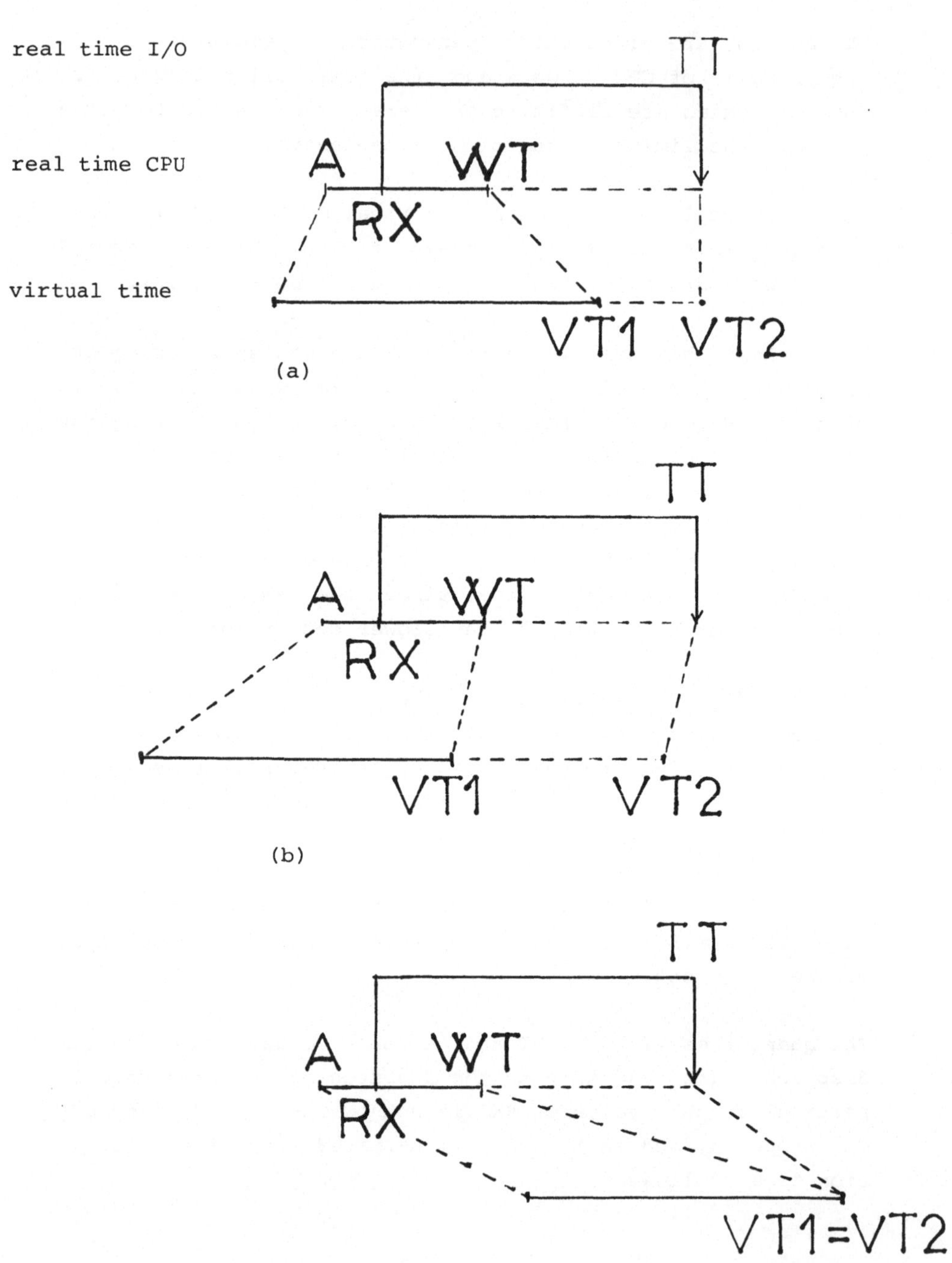

Figure 7: Wait Time Accounting

```
if WT ≤  VT1   then
VT2 = max (VT1,TT)
else
VT2 = VT1 + TT - WT
```

The resulting wait time is exactly as on the comparator CPU
if VT (i,RX) = RX. If VT(i,RX) < RX, the wait time is
greater, if VT(i,RX) > RX the wait time is less than the
wait time on the comparator CPU. It is therefore desirable,
to keep the virtual time ahead of real time by means of an
advance limit AL greater than zero.

To justify the lag limit parameter LL consider the following
situation for infinite LL and large AL. VM(1) enters a very
long wait, say for several minutes, waiting for an external
signal. VM(2) continues processing advancing its virtual
time far beyond real time until the signal for VM(1)
arrives. At this point VM(1) gets priority until VT(1,t) has
become equal to VT(2,t). If VM(1) is CPU bound from now on,
VM(2) will remain without CPU service for several minutes,
in contradiction to the responsiveness requirement. A finite
LL limits the delay of VM(2) in this situation. In particular, a finite LL becomes important for very large values of
AL. Dispatching with very large values of AL avoids forced
waits and satisfies the weak predictability conditions (2)
above.

4.2 Formal Definitions of the Algorithm
The proposed dispatching algorithm is defined by the following rules:

        1. Parameters of the algorithm are:
           TS   the time slice
           AL   the advance limit
           LL   the lag limit
           p(i), 1≤i≤n the vector of CPU powers

2. In addtion two vector variables $VT(i,t)$ and $WT(i,t)$, $1 \leq i \leq n$, are used, the vectors of virtual times and of wait points for machines i at time t. At start time t, these variables are set to:

$$VT(i,t) \leftarrow t + TS \times \underset{j<i}{\text{SUM}} \ p(i)$$

$$WT(i,t) \leftarrow t$$

3. Initially, and at time slice end the following 3 steps are performed in the described sequence:

   3.1 The virtual machines are sorted into a priority list such that $VT(i,t) \leq VT(i+1,t)$ for $1 \leq i \leq n$, where t is the current time.

   3.2 Let T be the maximum virtual time, i.e.

$$T = \underset{1 \leq i \leq n}{\text{MAX}} \ VT(i,t).$$

   The vector $VT(i,t)$ is replaced by:

$$VT(i,t) \leftarrow \max \ (VT(i,t), \ T-LL)$$
$$\text{for } 1 \leq i \leq n.$$

   3.3 Finally, preemptive dispatching is initiated for a period

$$TS \times p(i)$$

   as described in 4.

4. Preemptive dispatching between two time slice

interrupts works as follows:

4.1 Whenever VM(j) runs, i.e. has the base CPU assigned, all VM(i), i<j, are in wait state. If a VM(i), i<j, becomes ready, VM(j) is preempted and the base CPU is assigned to VM(i).

4.2 Whenever a running VM(i), $1 \leq i \leq n$, enters the wait state, the current real time is assigned to WT(i,t), i.e. WT(i,t) $\leftarrow$ t.

4.3 If an interrupt for a waiting VM(i), $1 \leq i \leq n$, occurs at time t, its virtual time VT(i,t) is updated according to the following rules

if VT(i,t) $\geq$ WT(i,t) then
   VT(i,t) $\leftarrow$ max (VT(i,t),t) else
   VT(i,t) $\leftarrow$ VT(i,t) + t - WT(i,t)

4.4 Any VM(i), $1 \leq i \leq n$, is only dispatched at time t if VT(i,t) satisfies

$$VT(i,t) \leq t + AL.$$

If not, VM(i) is put into a forced wait state for a period VT(i,t) - t - AL.

4.5 Whenever a VM(i), $1 \leq i \leq n$, terminates a running period of length Δt (e.g. it enters a wait state, or an interrupt occured), its virtual time VT(i,t) is increased as follows:

$$VT(i,t) \leftarrow VT(i,t) + \Delta t \div p(i).$$

> If the interrupt was a time slice end inter-
> rupt, processing continues as in 3, otherwise
> the hightest priority virtual machine, which
> is not waiting, is dispatched.

4.3 First Discussion of the Algorithm

The described algorithm is simple. Toycoding the algorithm
for a minimal, restricted dispatcher with very little total
overhead has shown that the overhead due to sorting up to
eight virtual machines is only a small fraction. Even for
large n, sorting need not be an obstacle, since in this
case, where responsiveness has to suffer anyhow, an approxi-
mate sorting can be implemented very efficiently in hardware. For example, Chen et al /6, see also 4/ describe a
hardware logic which puts the m highest priority machines on
top of the list (or, if used in the opposite direction, the
m lowest priority machines at the end of the list).

The reader may easily verify, that the initial values for
the vectors VT and WT are not critical for the algorithm.

The subsequent section describes some results obtained by
simulation of the algorithm under workloads given by distributions for the time variables TE, TC and TI. The primary
goal of the simulation was to verify the algorithm. It is
not possible, to report on all obtained simulation results.
The initial experiments showed that workloads, which are
either I/O bound on the comparator CPU or CPU bound on the
base CPU, do not present any problems. Many experiments
have therefore been conducted with workloads which are
(almost) CPU bound on the comparator CPU but clearly I/O
bound on the base CPU.

4.4 Choice of Dispatching Parameters

The subsequently described experiments were conducted to
illustrate the influence of the dispatching parameters on

the results. We investigated a configuration with three
machines VM(1), VM(2), VM(3). All times are exponentially
distributed and therefore determined by their mean values.
The following values describe the configuration.

VM(1): $p(1)$ = .25, TE = 0, TC = 6, TI = 24
VM(2): $p(2)$ = .25, TE = 6, TC = 0, TI = 24
VM(3): $p(3)$ = .5 , TE = 0, TC = 100, TI = 0

All times are in milliseconds and for execution on the base
machine. VM(3) is CPU bound on the base CPU and on the
comparator CPU. Its dispatching is therefore no problem,
VM(3) obtained 50 percent of the base CPU in all runs.

VM(1) uses in average .67 of the CPU if executed on the
comparator CPU, VM(2) uses due to less overlap only .50 of
the CPU on its comparator CPU.

Figure 8 shows the dependency of the thruput on the advance
limit. The Y axis indicates the ratio of the thruput on
the base CPU to the thruput on the comparator CPU. Runs were
made for TS = 120, LL = 240 and AL has been doubled from run
to run from a starting value of 15 milliseconds. Thruput
increases for values of AL which are less than 240. This is
due to the effect described in figure 7. A larger advance
limit reduces the accounting for wait time. AL should
therefore be greater than the majority of I/O times and
also, since in the worst case a virtual time may exceed the
real time by the double of time slice length, AL should be
greater than the time slice length times two for optimal
thruput with strong predictability.

Figure 9 shows the dependency of the thruput on the choice
of the lag limit. Again, a lag limit with less than two
times the time slice length causes increased virtual time
accounting. In summary, we conclude, that for maximal

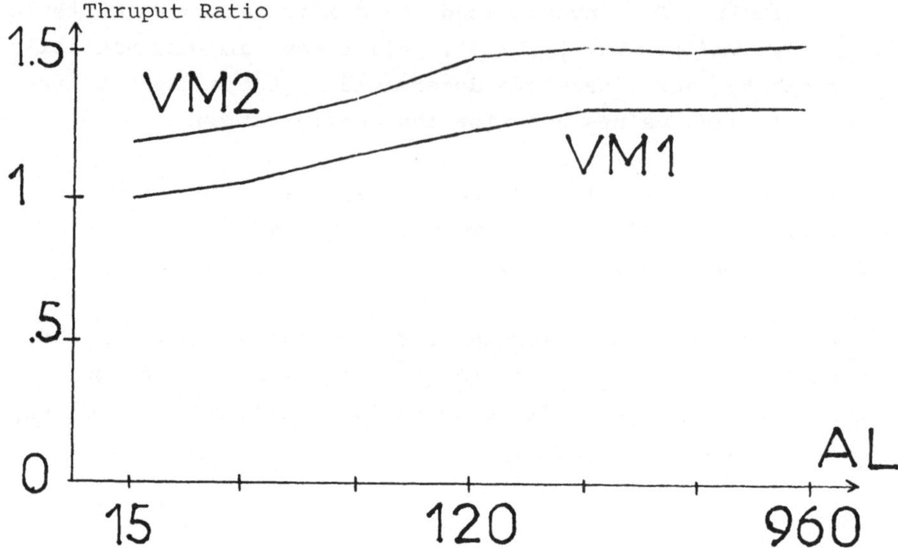

Figure 8: Variation of the Advance Limit

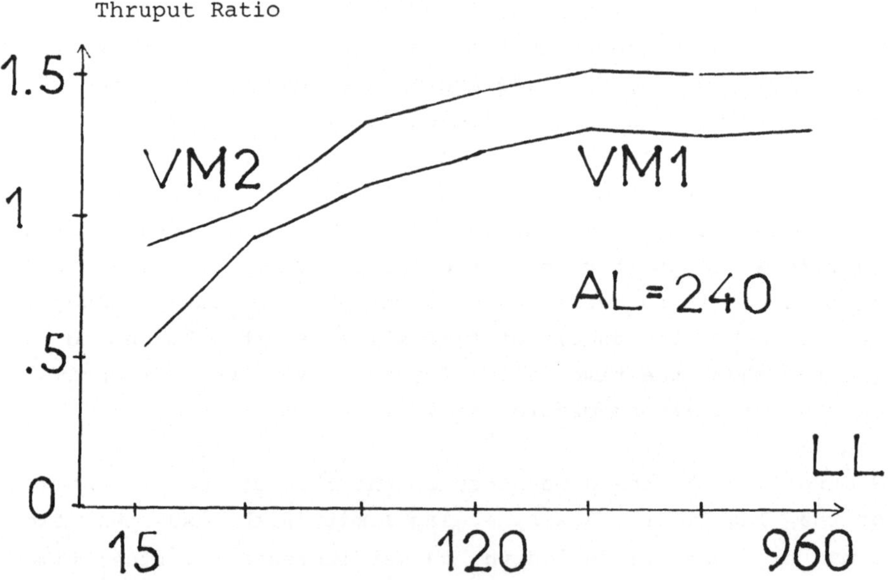

Figure 9: Variation of the Lag Limit

thruput under strong predictability both limits should be
greater than the majority of I/O times and at least two
times the length of the time slice.

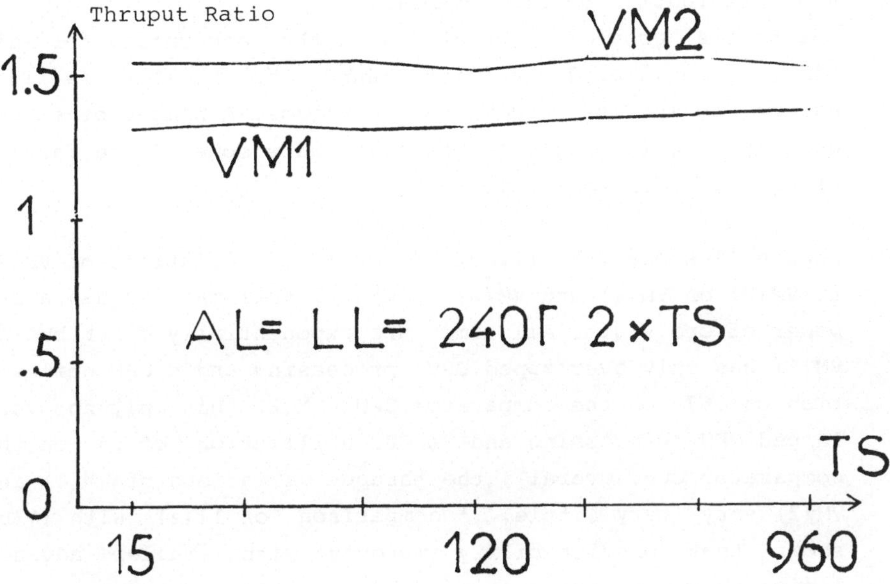

Figure 10: Variation of the Time Slice Length

Figure 10 shows the dependency of the thruput on the time
slice length with the limits set as described above. Inter-
estingly, the thruput is within measurement accuracy independent of the time slice length for stationary behaviour of
the virtual machines. For non-stationary behaviour, i.e. if
workloads switch between I/O bound and CPU bound behaviour,
the length of the time slice is more important, but still
not critical. As a general rule, the time slice length
should be in the same range as the average I/O time. With
this choice, the frequency of interrupts is only marginally

increased and the adaptation to changes of workload characteristics is fast enough to maintain good responsiveness for
I/O bound machines with all workload mixes.

4.5 Varification of Predictability
Due to the problems connected with the accounting for wait
time, strong predictability cannot be ideally realized
except for strictly CPU bound workloads. A number of subsequently described experiments illustrate some of the factors
affecting predictability.

Figure 11 shows the effect of workload variations of VM(3)
to VM(8) on VM(1) and VM(2). Each virtual machine has a CPU
power of one eigth. All times are exponentially distributed.
VM(1) has only overlapped CPU processing and a CPU utilization of .67 on the comparator CPU, VM(2) has only nonover-
lapped CPU processing and a CPU utilization of .5 on the
comparator CPU. Overall, the thruput variations of VM(1) and
VM(2) vary very little. A comparison of 11(a) with 11(b)
shows that predictability improves with smaller advance
limits, however, accompanied by a reduction of thruput.

Figure 12 shows the thruput for the same VM(1), VM(2) as in
figure 11, however, the workloads of VM(3) to VM(8) are
combined into VM(3) with a CPU power of .75. This corresponds to a situation where VM(1) and VM(2) represent two
small machines competing with a large VM(3). If a virtual
machine has a CPU power of .75, variations of workloads on
the remaining virtual machines have little impact. However,
as figure 12 illustrates, variations of workload on VM(3)
have a stronger influence than in the case of 8 virtual
machines with equal CPU power as shown in figure 11.

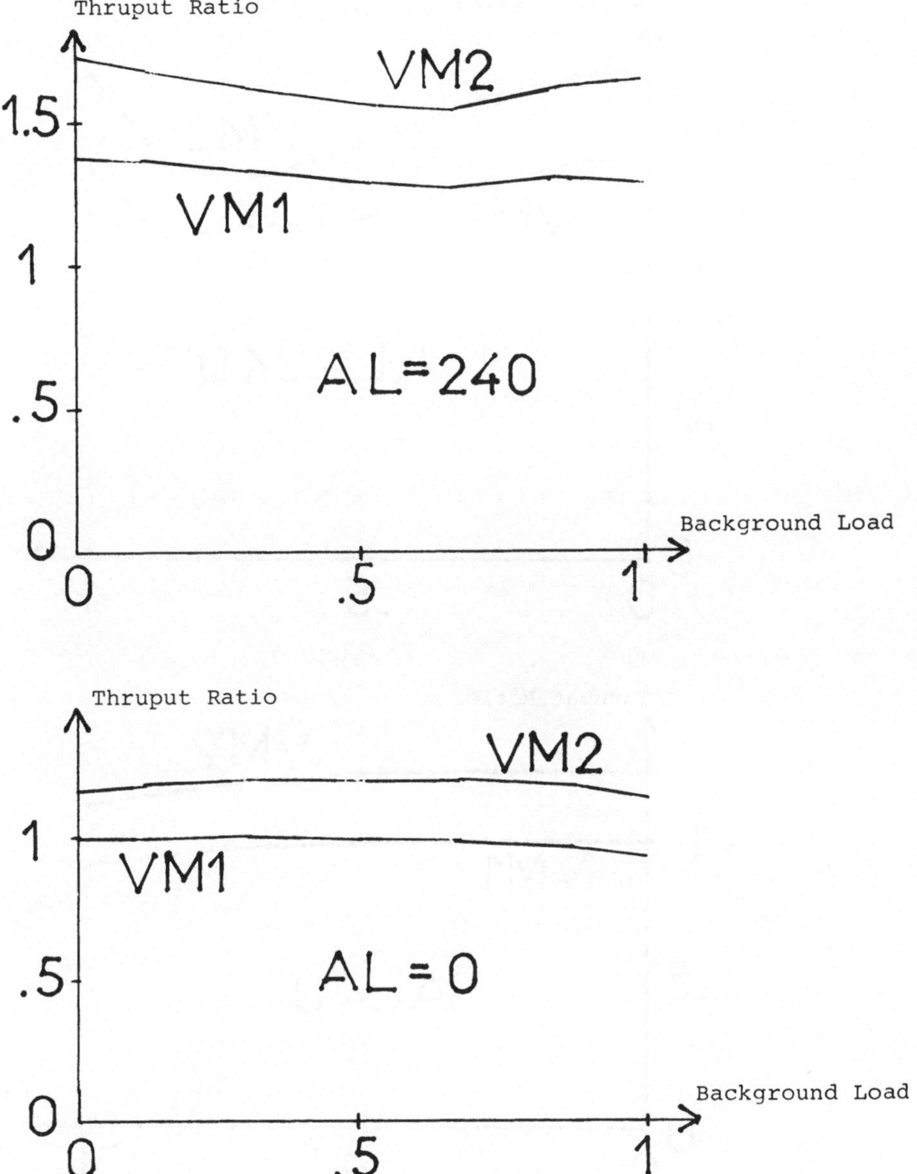

Figure 11: Predictability with 8 Machines

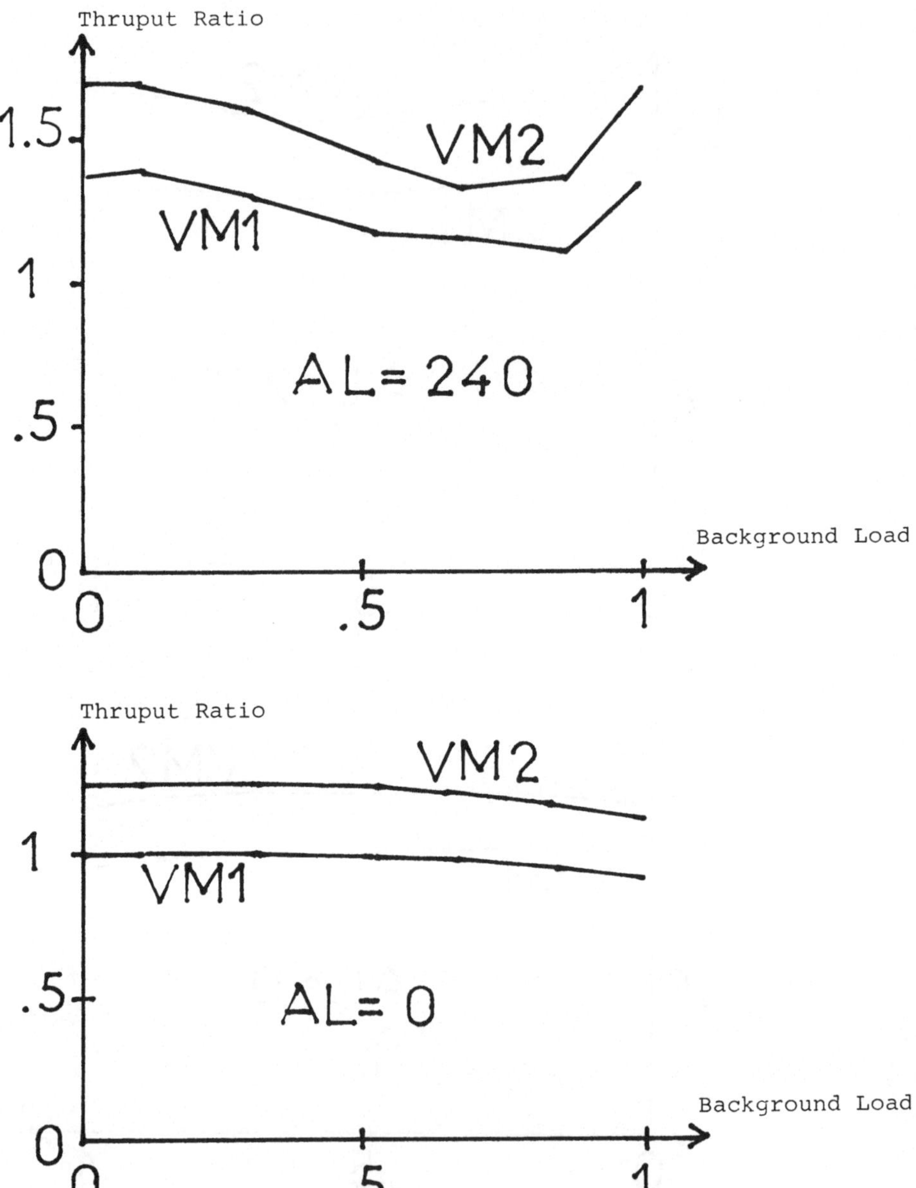

Figure 12: Predictability with 3 Machines,
unequal CPU Power Distrubution

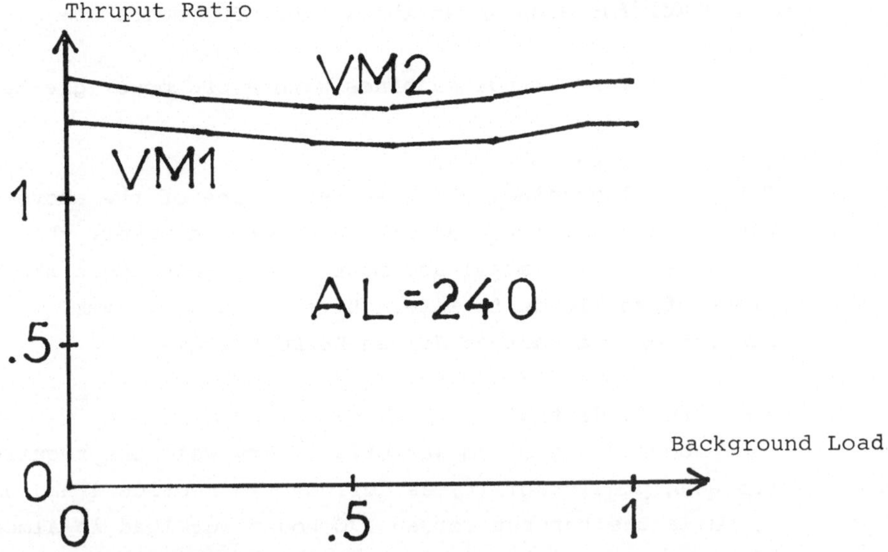

Figure 13: Predictability with 3 Machines, Equal CPU Power
        Distribution

Figure 13 shows again a situation with 3 virtual machines,
now each having a CPU power of one third. VM(1) and VM(2)
behave the same way as in the previous cases on their
respective comparator CPU's. Now we see, that variations of
workload on VM(3) have less effect on the thruput of VM(1)
and VM(2).

To summarize the observations:

    Predictability is good

    (a) for workloads which are CPU bound on the base CPU
        or which use very little CPU on the comparator
        CPU.

(b) for equal distribution of CPU power.

(c) for virtual machines with a CPU power greater than
.7.

For virtual machines which satisfy none of the above criteria, predictability suffers somewhat, however, the variations are still small and most likely less than the variations of workloads in interactively used systems, i.e. time
sharing or transaction driven DB/DC systems.

4.6 Weak Predictability

The proposed algorithm satisfies very well the requirements
for weak predictability as defined in section 1 and section
2. While the thruput for an I/O bound workload is almost not
affected by an infinite advance limit, virtual machines with
a CPU bound workload may draw benefit of up to a factor of
the inverse of the CPU power in this case. No situation has
been identified in which the thruput of the virtual machine
was less than the thruput on the corresponding comparator
CPU.

4.7 Responsiveness

No special runs were made to measure responsivenss. For all
workloads with a CPU utilization of less than .9 on the
comparator CPU, the average responsetime was less than the
average I/O time (assumed as 24 milliseconds). In many
cases, in particular, if I/O bound and CPU bound workloads
were mixed, the average responsetime was between .5 and 5
milliseconds for I/O bound (i.e. less than .9 CPU utilization on the comparator CPU) workloads. In contrast for CPU
bound (.99 utilization) workloads, responsetimes of almost
400 milliseconds have been observed. This corresponds well
with the objectives set up earlier. The good responsetime

behaviour is a direct consequence of sorting at time slice intervals. I/O bound virtual machines tend to obtain highest priority by sorting according to virtual time.

5. Summary and Conclusion

For the purpose of a fair, predictable and CPU power conserving distribution of the CPU among virtual machines, both, round-robin and nonpreemptive dispatching disciplines fail.

A novel dispatching algorithm based upon sorting at time slice intervals has been proposed and analyzed. The algorithm has 3 parameters, a time slice length, an advance limit and a lag limit. It has been shown, that variations of the parameters have within a wide range little impact on dispatching results. Further, the objectives of performance, predictability and responsiveness are well met for most situations, and still "satisfactory" for the remaining less important situations.

The proposed algorithm is currently restricted to dispatching of virtual machines with statically assigned resources. In particular, any interaction between storage management and dispatching has been ignored. It is subject of further research, to investigate storage allocation (i.e. page replacement) algorithms which assign storage to virtual machines dependent on the workload of the machines alone, i.e. independent of the workloads of other virtual machines running concurrently on the same CPU. If this is successful, the proposed dispatching algorithm should become generally applicable to low level dispatching in multiprogramming systems.

Acknowledgements:

The authors are indebted to Peter Silberbusch and Richard Parmelee for helpful suggestions in contents and presentation of the paper as well as for their contributions to the validation of the proposed dispatcher.

Literature:

/1/ IBM Virtual Machine Facility /370: CMS User's Guide. Form-No. GC20-1819, IBM Corporation, White Plains, N. Y.

/2/ Coffman, E.G. and Denning, P.J.: Operating Systems Theory. Englewood CLiffs, New Jersey: Prentice Hall, 1973.

/3/ Hoare, C.A.R. and Perrot, R.H. (eds.): Operating Systems Techniques. Proceedings of a Seminar at Queens University, Belfast, 1971. London and New York: Academic Press, 1972.

/4/ Smith, C.H. and Wittie, L.: Discriminating Content Addressable Memories. In: Feng, T. (ed.): Parallel Processing, Proceedings of the Sagamore Computer Conference, August 20-23, 1974. Lecture Notes in Computer Science 24. Berlin-Heidelberg-New York: Springer, 1975, p. 100-102.

/5/ Sherman, S., Baskett III, F. and Browne, J.C.: Trace-Driven Modeling and Analysis of CPU Scheduling in a Multiprogramming System. Comm. ACM 15, 1063-1069 (1972).

/6/ Chen, T.C., Lum, V.Y. and Tung, C.: The Rebound Sorter: An Efficient Sort Engine for Large Files. IBM Research Laboratory, San Jose, California, Rep. RJ 2204, March 1978.

MESSVERFAHREN BEI VM/370

INTERPRETATION DER AUSWERTUNGS-ERGEBNISSE

Georg Wessling

IBM Deutschland GmbH

Zum Thema VM/370-Messverfahren koennte man natuerlich
stundenlang reden. Eine Eingrenzung des Themas muss deshalb
erfolgen und sie soll in der Form geschehen, dass der
Schwerpunkt in der Interpretation der Messdaten liegt. Ich
will also gar nicht sprechen ueber die Gewinnung der Daten
und nur als Einleitung kurz eingehen auf die Anwendungsmoeg-
lichkeiten der Messverfahren, oder, wie sie auch genannt
werden, der Performance-Tools.

1.0 FRAGESTELLUNG.

Wozu sind Performance-Tools gut? Man kann die medizinische
Terminologie verwenden. Performance-Tools sind keine
Therapiehilfen, sondern Diagnose-Instrumente. Der Einsatz
eines Performance-Tools verbessert nicht automatisch die
Performance eines Systems, sondern liefert Daten ueber die
Betriebsmittel-Auslastung, die eine Analyse der gegenwaerti-
gen Situation erleichtern, was dann hoffentlich zu wirksamen
Therapievorschlaegen fuehrt. Performance-Tools dienen dabei
sowohl einer Art laufender Vorsorgeuntersuchung, wie auch
einer Diagnose im akuten Notfall.

Die Definition der Performance-Tools koennte man also
folgendermassen vornehmen: Sie sind Programme, die die
Leistungsdaten einer EDV-Anlage erfassen und auswerten.

Daraus ergeben sich die gueltigen Fragestellungen:
Wie ist die Betriebsmittel-Auslastung?
Wie wird sie sich tendenziell weiterentwickeln?
Welche Engpaesse sind vorhanden?
Warum also ist die Performance genau so, wie sie ist, und
nicht anders, z.B. besser?

Natuerlich gibt es auch andere wuenschenswerte, durchaus
legitime und vernuenftige Fragen, die aber mit Performance-
Tools nicht beantwortbar sind:
Ist die Performance gut oder schlecht? (Performance als
Antwortzeit oder Durchlaufzeit; der Durchsatz ist eher mit
Performance-Tools messbar.)
Wie gut oder wie schlecht ist sie?
Wie gut wird sie sein, wenn ich ein anderes Daten-Kommunika-
tions-System einsetze, also beispielsweise IMS statt CICS?

Das alles muss man versuchen mit anderen Mitteln in den
Griff zu bekommen.

2.0 WELCHE FRAGEKOMPLEXE SIND BEANTWORTBAR?

2.1 BEI DER NOTFALLDIAGNOSE:

Welche Komponenten bilden einen Engpass?

CPU, Speicher, Ein/Ausgabe, mit oder ohne getrennter Behandlung von Paging-I/O, sind die gesondert betrachtbaren Teile.
Wie wir noch sehen werden, lassen sich die Ursachen fuer
einen eventuellen Engpass meistens bis auf den einzelnen
Benutzer, bzw. auf einzelne E/A-Einheiten herunterbrechen.

Vorhandene Anwendungen einfach unter VM/370 weiterlaufen zu
lassen, bedeutet auf jeden Fall einen Mehrverbrauch an CPU
und Speicher. Wenn dieser Mehrbedarf nicht verfuegbar ist,
sei es durch Aufstockung, sei es durch Ausnutzung bisher
brachliegender Reserven, dann ist auch bei perfektem Tuning
eine Engpass-Situation unvermeidbar.

Der CPU-Mehrverbrauch entsteht in erster Linie durch die
Simulation von privilegierten Instruktionen, die wiederum
dadurch noetig ist, dass aus Sicherheitsgruenden nur der
Control-Program-Teil (CP) von VM/370 im Supervisor-Status
laeuft, alles andere aber im Problemstatus. Jede privilegierte Instruktion in einer virtuellen Maschine fuehrt
deshalb zu einem Program-Check; CP fuehrt dann die Instruktion aus und reflektiert das Ergebnis an die virtuelle
Maschine. Reduzieren von privilegierten Instruktionen ist
deshalb eine wirkungsvolle Tuning-Massnahme.

Der Mehrverbrauch an Speicher ergibt sich einfach aus dem
Platzbedarf des VM/370, wobei bei genauerer Betrachtung
erleichternd hinzukommt, dass der Supervisor eines Gast-Be-
triebssystems unter VM/370 nicht mehr komplett resident ist.

Ein weiterer Fragekomplex ist die Suche nach Komponenten,
die in unueblich hohem Ausmass Betriebsmittel verbrauchen
und deshalb Performance-Suender darstellen. Das koennen
Benutzer, Programme, Betriebssysteme oder sogar Hardware
sein. Hier ist der Uebergang vom Tuning zum Debugging
fliessend. So wurden beispielsweise Mikroprogrammfehler oder
Fehler in der Zeitgeberbehandlung durch Performance-Tools
entdeckt, Fehler also, die auch ein System ohne VM/370
belasten, dort aber u. U. jahrelang unentdeckt vorhanden
sind.

2.2 BEI DER VORSORGEUNTERSUCHUNG:

Dort sind es im wesentlichen die gleichen Fragen, wie bei
der Notfall-Diagnose, projeziert auf die Fortsetzung eines
Trends zur staerkeren Belastung des Systems.
Also: Welche Komponenten werden sich, gleiches Belastungsprofil vorausgesetzt, zuerst zu einem Engpass entwickeln?
Gibt es Komponenten mit besonders hohem Resourcenverbrauch,
der sich bei staerkerer Belastung gravierend auswirken kann?

Alle diese Fragen lassen sich, durch u. U. wiederholte
Messungen und Auswertungen klaeren. Die Analyse der Daten
erfordert einige Erfahrung, da die Ergebnisse oft nur
relativ zu Erfahrungswerten aussagekraeftig sind.

3.0 METHODEN DER PERFORMANCE ANALYSE.

Je nach der Situation ist ein unterschiedliches Vorgehen
empfehlenswert.

3.1 BEI DER NOTFALL-DIAGNOSE:

Zur Entdeckung von Engpaessen ist es sinnvoll, nur in
Spitzenbelastungszeiten, und dann relativ kurz zu messen.
Die Analyse der Auswertungsergebnisse fuehrt meistens
schnell zu Abhilfevorschlaegen.

Die Entdeckung von Performance-Suendern kann wesentlich
laenger dauern. Meist sind mehrere Messungen bei unterschiedlichem Jobprofil noetig. Zwar ist beispielsweise die
virtuelle Maschine, die viel verbraucht, schnell lokali-
siert, nicht aber der Job oder die sonstige Komponente, die
der eigentliche Verursacher ist. Korrelation der Messergeb-
nisse mit Jobtypen anhand von Konsolprotokollen gehoert dann
zu den naechsten Schritten.

3.2 BEI DER VORSORGE-UNTERSUCHUNG:

Performance-Tools stellen hier haeufig zusaetzliche Hilfsmittel zu anderen Verfahren dar. Vorhersagen ueber die
Zukunft, nach gravierenden Aenderungen im Belastungsprofil,
lassen sich leichter durch
 * Benchmarks,
 * Simulationen oder
 * analytische Vorhersageverfahren
machen.

Performance-Tools sind dabei nahezu unerlaesslich, um die
derzeitigen Belastungswerte zu erhalten, von denen bei den
anderen Verfahren ausgegangen wird, bzw. die noetig sind, um
Simulationsmodelle oder analytische Modelle erst einmal zu
verifizieren.

Soll die Vorhersage ausschliesslich durch Verwendung von
Performance-Tools erfolgen, dann ist die Vorgehensweise
aehnlich wie bei der Notfall-Diagnose. Hinzu kommt dann der
Versuch der Hochrechnung. Dabei scheidet einfaches Extrapo-
lieren natuerlich aus. Bei rein mengenmaessiger Ausweitung
der Systemlast unter Beibehaltung des gegenwaertigen
Belastungprofils ist eine qualitative Aussage ueber die Art
der zu erwartenden Engpaesse moeglich. Eine quantitative
Ausage sollte man nur in der Form wagen, dass man Grenzen
aufzeigt, nach deren Ueberschreiten mit Sicherheit ein
vernuenftiger Betrieb auszuschliessen ist, ohne dass garan-
tiert ist, dass es unmittelbar vor der Grenze noch gut geht.

4.0 INTERPRETATION VON MESSERGEBNISSEN.

Ich moechte nun, anhand eines Beispiels zeigen, welche
Informationen zum Entdecken von Engpaessen verfuegbar sind.

Die Daten werden zunaechst ueber eine Standardeinrichtung
des VM/370, den MONITOR-Command gesammelt. Zum Auswerten
dieser Daten gibt es verschiedene Programmpakete. Was ich
Ihnen hier vorstelle ist ein relativ neues und allgemein
verfuegbares Produkt.

Das Deckblatt (Abb. 1) enthaelt unter anderem ein Verzeich-
nis der gesammelten Datenklassen. PERFORM, USER und DASTAP
werden jeweils einmal je waehlbares Beobachtungsintervall
gewonnen und enthalten sowohl Stichproben wie auch aufgelau-
fene Zaehler. Die anderen Klassen enthalten einen Satz je
entsprechendes Ereignis, also z.B. einen SEEK-Record je
Platten-I/O.

Die Anzahl der Datensaetze gibt einen ersten Hinweis auf die
statistische Relevanz.

Die gemessene Maschine, eine IBM /370-158 mit 4 Megabyte
Speicher steht im Servicezentrum. Auf einer virtuellen
Maschine wird ein DOS-Closed-Shop-Betrieb durchgefuehrt. In
ca. 5 weiteren virtuellen Maschinen laufen VS-Betriebssys-
teme, der Rest sind CMS-Benutzer. Es handelt sich um einen
typischen Testbetrieb, bei dem sich die Gast-Betriebssysteme
nicht als Tuningobjekte gewinnen lassen.

4.1 ENGPAESSE GENERELL.

Die Qualitaet der System-Performance muss extern festgestellt werden. Das kann z. B. durch Protokollieren vergleichbarer Antwortzeiten oder durch Definieren eines erforderlichen Durchsatzes geschehen. Es gibt aber einige Indikatoren fuer die Feststellung, ob ueberhaupt wesentliche Engpaesse bestehen, die allerdings als absolute Werte sehr wenig aussagen und auch relativ zu irgendwelchen Erfahrungswerten mit Skepsis zu verwerten sind. Es sind (Abb. 2):

RAI = Resource Availability Index. Er drueckt aus, in wieviel Prozent aller Beobachtungen eine virtuelle Maschine entweder 'Runuser' war (d. h. die CPU zugeteilt bekam) oder sich in freiwilligem 'Wait State' befand. In allen anderen Faellen wartete sie auf irgendwelche Resourcen.
Einwand: Auch ein alleine laufendes Programm muss oft auf die Beendigung eines I/O-Requests warten. Dieser Fall wird mit als 'not available resource' gezaehlt.

EXPF = Expiration Factor. Im Idealfall drueckt er das Verhaeltnis 'Laufzeit im Multiprogramming-Betrieb' zu 'Laufzeit stand-alone' aus. Messbar ist hier aber nur Laufzeit zu CPU-Zeit. Die Verwendung eines festen Wertes je I/O (im Beispiel 20 ms) macht die Zahl wesentlich realistischer.

Die hier ermittelten Werte von RAI = 0,83 und EXPF = 2,89 sind als gut zu bezeichnen.

4.2 CPU-ENGPASS.

Die wichtigsten Indikatoren fuer das Vorhandensein eines CPU-Engpasses sind TOTCPU und CPUQ.

TOTCPU zeigt die CPU-Auslastung insgesamt. Eine Auslastung weit unter 100 % schliesst einen CPU-Engpass aus. Umgekehrt ist aber eine 100-prozentige Auslastung noch kein Beweis fuer einen CPU-Engpass.

CPUQ zeigt, wieviele Benutzer durchschnittlich auf die CPU warten mussten.

Das vorliegende Beispiel laesst auf einen CPU-Engpass schliessen.

Die Ursachen werden in erster Annaeherung durch TVRATIO, PRIVOP und VPGMINT angezeigt.

TVRATIO drueckt das Verhaeltnis des Verbrauchs von 'CPU gesamt' zu 'CPU im Problemstatus' aus. Auf Systemen mit VMA-Mikrocode, aber ohne VM-ECPS-Mikrocode (unser Beispiel)

sind Werte um 2,0 normal. Werte, die wesentlich darueber-
liegen, sind meist durch exzessiven Anfall von privilegierten Instruktionen verursacht.

VPGMINT ist annaehernd identisch mit dieser Zahl.

PRIVOP zeigt die Zahl der nicht per Mikrocode simulierten
privilegierten Instruktionen.
Aus der 'Instruction Simulation Summary' (Abb. 3) ist zu
ersehen, welche Instruktionen vor allem vorkommen. Diese
Liste, in Verbindung mit der TVRATIO der einzelnen Benutzer
in der User-Liste (Abb. 4), gibt Anhaltspunkte fuer das
Tuning der Anwendungen und/oder der Gast-Betriebssysteme.
Unter Produktionsbedingungen waere hier durch Eliminieren
der unter VM/370 ueberfluessigen TCH-Instruktionen ein
deutlicher Effekt erzielbar. In einem Testbetrieb ist das
schlechter durchfuehrbar.

4.3 SPEICHER-ENGPASS.

Die zunaechst sehr direkt verwertbar erscheinenden Werte
STGUTIL (Storage Utilisation) und CORESAT (Core Saturation
Factor) sind in der Praxis wenig brauchbar. Der Grund liegt
in den VM-Algorithmen fuer deren Berechnung.

Der Hauptindikator fuer Speicher-Engpass ist RATIO.
RATIO zeigt das Verhaeltnis der 'aktiven' zu den 'Inqueue'
Benutzern. Aktiv, aber nicht inqueue ist man, wenn man in
einer 'Eligible List' auf das Freiwerden von Speicher warten
muss. Wenn dieser Wert auch nur maessig ueber 1,0 liegt
(etwa 1,2), dann ist bereits ein Speicherengpass aufgezeigt.

Aktiv in diesem Zusammenhang sind die Benutzer, die zum
Beobachtungs-Zeitpunkt in einer 'Queue' oder 'Eligible List'
waren. Im Beispiel war dieser Wert 3,52. Die Variable ACTIVE
dagegen drueckt aus, wieviele Benutzer im Beobachtungsintervall irgendetwas getan haben. Im Beispiel waren das 18,27.

PGBLPGS = Pageable Pages zeigt an, welcher Teil des Speichers als Page-Pool zur Verfuegung steht.

Ursachen fuer einen Speicher-Engpass:

Falls trotz RATIO = 1,0 eine hohe Paging-Rate (PAGERATE)
auftritt, dann liegt die Ursache entweder in einem unguen-
stigem Speicherbelegungsverhalten der einzelnen virtuellen
Maschinen oder in einem Fehler des Page-Managements von
VM/370.

Wenn ein echter Engpass vorliegt (RATIO groesser als 1,0),
dann helfen die Workingset-Zahlen in der User-Liste (Abb. 4)
weiter, um die Verursacher zu finden.

4.4 PAGING- UND E/A-ENGPASS.

Es besteht zwar ein enger Zusammenhang zwischen Speicher-
und Paging-Engpaessen, doch koennen beide auch unabhaengig
voneinander auftreten. Durch optimale Plazierung der
Page-Datasets lassen sich z. B. Speicher-Engpaesse ertraeg-
lich gestalten.

Da aber Paging meistens ueber die gleichen Kanaele, Steuereinheiten und sogar E/A-Einheiten betrieben wird wie die
sonstigen E/A-Aktivitaeten, findet zwangsweise eine gegenseitige Beeinflussung statt. Paging und E/A sind deshalb
immer gemeinsam zu betrachten.

Wesentlicher Indikator fuer das Vorhandensein eines
Engpasses auf diesem Gebiet sind PAGEQ und IOQ. Damit wird
angezeigt, wieviel Benutzer durchschnittlich im Page- oder
I/O-Wait waren. Das Ausmass des Engpasses wird durch PAGE-
WAIT + IOWAIT angezeigt. Dabei ist aber zu beachten, dass
IOWAIT auch bei einer unzureichenden Auslastung des Systems
auftritt und dann eher das Gegenteil ausdrueckt. Die
endgueltige Entscheidung, welcher Fall vorliegt, ist nicht
durch das Ablesen einer einzelnen Variablen moeglich. Eine
kombinierte Betrachtung verschiedener Faktoren ist erforderlich. Als weitere Informationsquellen stehen VIO (virtuelle
I/O-Requests), IOINT (reale I/O-Interrupts) und die Warte-
schlangenwerte an Einheiten und Kanaelen aus der Device-List
(Abb. 5) in Verbindung mit den I/O-Raten der wichtigsten
Einheiten zur Verfuegung.

Alle Indikatoren unseres Beispiels zeigen, dass gegenwaertig
kein Paging- oder E/A-Engpass auftritt. (PAGEQ = 0,26, IOQ
= 0,37, PAGEWAIT + IOWAIT = 0,15, Warten am Kanal bei
maximal 1,9 % aller I/O-Requests.) Einzelne E/A-Einheiten
jedoch sind problemtraechtig. Bei der Einheit 1C5 entstand
in 32 % aller Faelle eine Warteschlange. Das laesst auf eine
unguenstige Plazierung des Page-Datasets schliessen.

Zur weiteren Ursachen-Erforschung stuende noch die Moeglichkeit zur Verfuegung, die SEEK-Daten fuer einzelne, spezifi-
zierbare Zylinder-Bereiche und damit praktisch auf Datei-
ebene auszuwerten. Die in der Standard-Auswertung bereits
gezeigten kurzen durchschnittlichen Sprunggroessen (17
Zylinder fuer die Einheit 1C5) lassen jedoch den Schluss zu,
dass ausser dem Page-Dataset kaum andere Daten angesprochen
wurden, sodass sich dieser Schritt eruebrigt.

4.5 SCHLUSSFOLGERUNG FUER DIESE INSTALLATION.

Falls das vorliegende Belastungsmuster representativ ist, was notfalls durch wiederholte Messungen zu belegen ist, kann man sagen, dass ein stark belastetes, relativ gut ausgelegtes System vorliegt. Die CPU bildet einen Engpass, der etwas gravierender ist, als diese Auswertung allein zeigt. (Annaehernd 100 % TOTCPU selbst bei einer TVRATIO von nur 1,85.)

Um Missverstaendnisse auszuschliessen, sei nochmals darauf hingewiesen, dass Performance-Kriterien extern gewonnen werden muessen. Die Feststellung eines Engpasses sagt allein noch nichts ueber Performance aus. Sie zeigt nur auf, welche von allen moeglichen Verbesserungs-Massnahmen den groessten Nutzeffekt erwarten lassen, naemlich diejenigen, die die als Engpass ermittelten Komponenten betreffen.

Verbesserungs-Moeglichkeiten:

Der Page-Dataset sollte auf mehrere Einheiten verteilt werden, um bei gelegentlichem hoeheren Paging-Anfall keine Wartezeiten zu bekommen.

Auf der Suche nach Verbesserungsmoeglichkeiten im CPU-Bereich stoesst man in der User-Liste auf die Userid N73316. Diese ist in der Reihenfolge des CPU-Verbrauchs der erste Benutzer mit unguenstiger TVRATIO.

Eine Trace-Auswertung (Abb. 6) der Scheduler-Saetze dieses Benutzers zeigt einen verblueffenden Tatbestand: Innerhalb einer Sekunde durchlaeuft dieser Benutzer 20 mal den Scheduler-Algorithmus ohne dass irgendeine E/A-Aktivitaet stattgefunden hat. Der Anstoss zu diesen haeufigen Status-Aenderungen kann nur von der virtuellen Maschine selbst kommen. Erfahrungsgemaess sind Zeitgeber-Unterbrechungen fuer derartige Effekte verantwortlich. Im vorliegenden Falle stellte sich auch ein entsprechender Fehler in der Zeitgeberbehandlung im Gast-Betriebssystem heraus. Performance-Tools sind also auch zum Debugging geeignet.

4.6 EIN WEITERES BEISPIEL:

Abb. 7 zeigt die Messdaten einer anderen Anlage IBM /370-158, di⌐ unter Produktionsbedingungen laeuft. Trotz einer geringfuegig niedrigeren CPU-Auslastung ist die Maschine insgesamt staerker belastet: Mehr aktive Benutzer, mehr Inqueue-User, RATIO = 1,02 und hoehere Werte bei CPUQ, IOQ, PAGEQ und IOINT. RAI ist niedriger. Durch Entfernen der TCH-Instruktionen (hier laufen Produktionssysteme) ist die PRIVOP-Rate guenstiger.

Das System ist gleichmaessiger ausgelastet, d.h. alle Komponenten stellen einen gewissen Engpass dar.

Es ist zu vermuten, dass das Performance-Verhalten im grossen und ganzen zufriedenstellend war.

Die TVRATIO vom Benutzer DOS001 (Abb. 8) ist relativ schlecht. Hier muessten weitere Untersuchungen ansetzen.

<u>5.0</u> <u>LITERATUR</u>:

Tesler, Chuck: Virtual Machine Facility /370, Performance/Monitor Analysis, Program Description/Operations Manual. IBM-Formnummer SB21-2101. 1978

Bard,Y.: Performance analysis of virtual memory time-sharing systems. IBM Systems Journal $\underline{3}$, 366 - 384 (1975).

```
* * * * * * * * *    SUMMARY OF MONITOR RUN    * * * * * * * * * *
                   VM/370 MONITOR ANALYSIS

CREATION DATE                    12/19/78

TIME MONITOR STARTED             13:05:46

FIRST TIME SELECTED              13:05:46

LAST  TIME SELECTED              13:50:59

TOTAL TIME ANALYSED              00:45:13

NUMBER OF SECONDS ANALYSED        2,713

NUMBER OF RECORDS ANALYSED      233,439

NUMBER OF RECORDS BYPASSED            0

NUMBER OF SUSPENSION RECORDS          0


TOTAL NUMBER OF USERS                48

CPU SERIAL NUMBER                510658

CPU MODEL NUMBER                    158  ◄

USER STARTING MONITOR            XD3317


SOFTWARE VERSION                     05

SOFTWARE LEVEL                       00

PTF LEVEL                          0004


MONTAPE VERSION/LEVEL             3.00.0

MONTAPE OPTIONS SPECIFIED

    PAGTYP= 3330, NPAGDEV=  1, NPAGCYL= 100

    PERF UTIL PAGE SIM SERV RESMGR MIGRATION STM RESP CMND USER SEEK IO


MONITOR CLASSES ENABLED     # RECORDS
                              ▼
    00   PERFORM    1          275
    01   RESPONSE   0            0
    02   SCHEDULE   1       139554
    04   USER       1         5861
    05   INSTSIM    0            0
    06   DASTAP     1           91
    07   SEEKS      1        87657
    08   SYSPROF    0            0
```

Abb. 1

```
FIRST DATE 12/19/78   TIME 13:05:46     MONITOR STATISTICAL SUMMARY     PAGE  1
LAST  DATE 12/19/78   TIME 13.50.46
```

VARIABLE	AVERAGE	MINIMUM	MAXIMUM	TIME OF MINIMUM	TIME OF MAXIMUM	STD DEV	# OBS	DESCRIPTION
LOGGED	56.62	54.00	59.00	13.06.16	13.48.16	1.48	90	# OF USERS LOGGED ONTO SYSTEM
ACTIVE	18.27	9.00	41.00	13.18.46	13.42.16	7.10	90	# USERS ACTIVE IN A SAMPLE INTERVAL
INQUEUE	3.52	2.42	6.89	13.38.16	13.29.16	0.89	46,577	# USERS IN DISPATCH & ELIGIBLE QUEUES
DIALED	1.59	1.00	2.00	13.06.16	13.24.16	0.49	90	# USERS DIALED TO MULTI-ACCESS SYSTEM
RAI	0.83	0.63	0.94	13.50.16	13.42.16	0.06	90	RESOURCE AVAILABILITY INDEX
PCTCPUQ	11.54	0.00	47.36	13.08.16	13.27.16	9.02	90	PCT OF ACTIVE USERS IN CPU WAIT
PCTSTGQ	0.00	0.00	0.00	13.06.16		0.00	90	PCT ACTIVE USERS WAITING FOR MAIN STG
PCTPAGEQ	1.40	0.00	26.66	13.06.16	13.14.46	4.17	90	PCT OF ACTIVE USERS IN PAGE WAIT
PCTIOQ	2.11	0.00	16.66	13.06.16	13.25.16	3.92	90	PCT OF ACTIVE USERS IN I/O WAIT
PCTDEFRQ	0.00	0.00	0.00	13.06.16		0.00	90	PCT OF ACTIVE USERS IN SYSLOCK WAIT
PCTPSWAIT	62.99	50.00	71.18	13.27.16	13.48.46	4.62	90	PCT OF LOGGED USERS IN VOLUNTARY WAIT
TVRATIO	1.84	1.24	3.04	13.45.16	13.37.16	0.37	90	RATIO OF TOTAL TO VIRTUAL CPU UTIL.
TOTCPU	99.83	94.34	100.00	13.49.46	13.06.16	0.76	90	CPU TOTAL PCT UTILIZATION
CPCPU	43.66	19.91	67.11	13.45.16	13.37.16	10.39	90	CPU CP STATE PCT UTILIZATION
VIRTCPU	56.17	32.88	80.08	13.37.16	13.45.16	10.50	90	CPU PROBLEM STATE PCT UTILIZATION
IDLE	0.00	0.00	0.37	13.06.16	13.36.16	0.04	90	CPU PCT IDLE
PAGEWAIT	0.01	0.00	0.34	13.06.16	13.49.16	0.06	90	CPU PCT PAGE WAIT
IOWAIT	0.14	0.00	5.62	13.06.16	13.49.46	0.70	90	CPU PCT I/O WAIT
STGUTIL	25.64	16.08	50.46	13.38.16	13.31.16	7.24	46,577	PCT MAIN STORAGE UTILIZATION
CORESAT	0.93	0.52	1.90	13.44.16	13.32.16	0.26	90	MAIN STORAGE SATURATION FACTOR
WKSET	170.77	118.10	245.19	13.21.46	13.17.16	27.85	90	AVERAGE WORKING-SET SIZE PER USER
RATIO	1.00	1.00	1.00	13.06.16	13.06.16	0.00	90	CONTENTION RATIO (AS IN INDICATE CMD)
PGBLPGS	800.00	800.00	800.00	13.06.16	13.06.16	0.00	90	# SYSTEM PAGEABLE PAGES AVAILABLE
SHRPGS	25.00	17.00	29.00	13.06.46	13.26.46	2.96	90	# PAGES BEING SHARED AMONG USERS
RESPGS	0.00	0.00	0.00	13.06.16		0.00	90	# PAGES RESERVED FOR SPECIAL USERS
PAGERATE	7.88	0.63	49.26	13.19.16	13.21.46	7.65	90	PAGING RATE PER SECOND
CHAINPCT	7.04	0.00	33.43	13.07.46	13.29.16	7.75	90	PCT PAGE I/O CHAINED ON ONE SIO
STEALPCT	11.00	0.00	43.47	13.07.46	13.20.16	10.72	90	PCT PAGES STOLEN DUE TO PAGE FAULTS
STEALRATE	0.91	0.00	5.19	13.07.46	13.13.46	1.16	90	# PAGE STEALS PER SECOND
DRUMUTIL	62.44	52.70	76.08	13.22.46	13.48.46	8.22	90	PCT OF PRIMARY PAGING AREA NEEDED
VIO	149.67	51.03	362.29	13.38.16	13.49.46	74.39	90	# VIRTUAL I/O REQUESTS SIMULATED/SEC
IOINT	67.70	33.16	122.06	13.17.46	13.21.46	21.09	90	# REAL I/O INTERRUPTS PER SECOND
CCWTRANS	18.88	6.46	49.96	13.40.16	13.30.46	11.03	90	# CCW CHAINS TRANSLATED PER SECOND
EXPF	2.89	1.00	7.18	13.10.46	13.27.46	1.15	22,053	EXPANSION FACTOR FOR MAJOR COMMANDS
Q1	1.02	0.40	3.21	13.42.16	13.29.16	0.45	46,577	# USERS IN INTERACTIVE QUEUE (Q1)
Q2	2.50	1.78	4.74	13.08.16	13.33.46	0.58	46,577	# USERS IN BATCH QUEUE (Q2)
E1	0.00	0.00	0.00	13.06.16		0.00	46,577	# USERS WAITING FOR INTERACTIVE QUEUE
E2	0.00	0.00	0.00	13.06.16		0.00	46,577	# USERS WAITING FOR BATCH QUEUE
Q1Q2	3.64	1.00	10.00	13.08.16	13.27.16	1.86	90	# USERS NOW IN DISPATCH LISTS
E1E2	0.00	0.00	0.00	13.06.16		0.00	90	# USERS WAITING FOR MAIN STORAGE

Abb. 2.1

```
FIRST DATE 12/19/78   TIME 13:05:46      MONITOR STATISTICAL SUMMARY        PAGE  2
LAST  DATE 12/19/78   TIME 13.50.46
```

VARIABLE	AVERAGE	MINIMUM	MAXIMUM	TIME OF MINIMUM	TIME OF MAXIMUM	STD DEV	# OBS	DESCRIPTION
Q1E1	0.89	0.00	6.00	13.07.16	13.27.16	1.22	90	# ACTIVE INTERACTIVE USERS
Q2E2	2.74	1.00	6.00	13.08.16	13.30.46	1.09	90	# ACTIVE NON-INTERACTIVE USERS
CPUQ	2.00	0.00	9.00	13.08.16	13.27.16	1.58	90	# RUNNABLE USERS WAITING FOR CPU
STGQ	0.00	0.00	0.00	13.06.16		0.00	90	# USERS WAITING FOR MAIN STORAGE
PAGEQ	0.26	0.00	4.00	13.06.16	13.14.46	0.77	90	# USERS IN PAGE WAIT
IOQ	0.37	0.00	3.00	13.06.16	13.25.16	0.66	90	# USERS IN I/O WAIT
PSWAIT	35.68	29.00	42.00	13.27.16	13.48.46	3.05	90	# LOGGED ON USERS IN VOLUNTARY WAIT
Q1WAIT	0.00	0.00	0.00	13.17.16	13.49.16	0.00	814	SECONDS DELAY WAITING TO ENTER Q1
Q2WAIT	0.00	0.00	0.00	13.22.16	13.32.16	0.00	735	SECONDS DELAY WAITING TO ENTER Q2
Q1RATE	9.04	2.49	15.70	13.47.46	13.06.16	2.48	90	# ADDITIONS PER SECOND TO QUEUE 1
Q2RATE	8.16	0.53	25.46	13.47.46	13.07.46	5.95	90	# ADDITIONS PER SECOND TO QUEUE 2
FREEPGS	25.52	0.00	254.00	13.14.46	13.15.16	42.37	90	# PAGES ON THE FREELIST
PSWAP	0.46	0.00	11.00	13.06.16	13.29.16	1.72	90	# PAGES SWAPPING IN FROM PAGE DEVICE
NOFREE	0.54	0.00	8.93	13.06.16	13.13.16	1.41	90	# TIMES FREELIST WAS EMPTY
RECLAIM	0.15	0.00	0.83	13.07.46	13.12.46	0.17	90	# PAGES FLUSHED BUT RECLAIMED
STEALCK	4.40	0.00	19.19	13.07.46	13.13.16	4.53	90	# PAGES CHECKED IN MAKING PAGE STEALS
FLUSHSWAP	0.00	0.00	0.00	13.06.16		0.00	90	# PAGES SWAPPED OFF FLUSHLIST
STEALSCANS	0.00	0.00	0.03	13.06.16	13.31.16	0.01	90	# COMPLETE SCANS WHILE PAGE STEALING
INTTIMER	9.98	0.79	25.99	13.27.46	13.07.46	5.29	90	# VIRT INTVL TIMER INTERUPT SIMULATED
CPUTIMER	0.02	0.00	0.13	13.06.46	13.22.46	0.02	90	# VIRT CPU TIMER INTERUPTS SIMULATED
CLOCKCOMP	0.00	0.00	0.00	13.06.16		0.00	90	# CLOCK COMPARATOR INTERUPT SIMULATED
PRIVOP	294.48	105.59	546.45	13.45.46	13.27.16	110.76	90	# PRIVILEGED INSTRS SIMULATED/SECOND
EXTINT	23.60	14.26	38.76	13.26.46	13.07.46	5.10	90	# REAL EXTERNAL INTERRUPTS PER SECOND
VSVC	0.39	0.00	22.13	13.06.16	13.10.46	2.53	90	# VIRTUAL SVC SIMULATIONS PER SECOND
VPGMINT	489.95	204.86	849.42	13.45.46	13.37.16	130.74	90	# VIRTUAL PGM INTERRUPTS PER SECOND
PFAULT	6.06	0.59	28.59	13.11.46	13.21.46	4.52	90	# PAGE FAULTS PER SECOND
PREAD	4.50	0.39	26.16	13.20.16	13.21.46	3.81	90	# PAGE READS REQUESTED PER SECOND
PWRITE	3.37	0.00	23.09	13.07.46	13.21.46	4.17	90	# PAGE WRITES REQUESTED PER SECOND
PREQ	8.59	0.63	50.69	13.19.16	13.21.46	7.92	90	# PAGE I/O REQUESTS PER SECOND
PSIO	7.85	0.63	47.73	13.19.16	13.21.46	7.30	90	# PAGING SIO COMMANDS/SECOND
STEALS	27.31	0.00	155.99	13.07.46	13.13.46	35.02	90	# PAGES STOLEN PER INTERVAL
DSPCH	347.85	157.26	504.42	13.48.46	13.35.16	75.80	90	# CALLS/SECOND TO (MAIN) DISPATCHER
DSPCHREF	135.90	63.86	332.54	13.38.16	13.32.46	56.68	90	# DISPATCHER FAST REFLECTS PER SECOND
DSPCHPSW	64.34	11.19	248.09	13.45.46	13.27.16	55.64	90	# DISPATCHER NEW PSW PER SECOND
SCHED	108.23	43.69	207.89	13.50.16	13.29.46	35.49	90	# CALLS PER SECOND TO SCHEDULER
DEADLINE	2.26	2.15	4.90	13.08.16	13.06.46	0.51	90	SYSTEM-WIDE TIME-SLICE DEADLINE (SLC)
ETIME	0.00	0.00	0.00	13.06.16		0.00	90	SYSTEM-WIDE SECONDS IN ELIGIBLE LISTS
FAIRCPU	21.90	5.79	33.60	13.49.46	13.08.16	6.94	90	FAIR-SHARE OF CPU PER USER (SECS)
FAIRPAGES	263.24	200.00	400.00	13.30.16	13.19.46	47.80	90	FAIR-SHARE # PAGES PER USER
PROJCPU	4.09	2.41	7.59	13.50.16	13.06.16	0.94	90	PROJECTED CPU MS OVERHEAD/PAGE READ
OVHDCPU	4.24	3.53	4.96	13.50.16	13.15.46	0.30	90	ACTUAL CPU MS OVERHEAD/PAGE READ

Abb. 2.2

DATE 12/19/78   TIME 13:05:46   SUMMARY OF PRIVILEGED INSTRUCTION SIMULATION SUMMARY   PAGE 1

RATES PER SECOND

TIME	SSK	ISK	SSM	L PSW	DI AG	SIO	SIO F	TIO	CLR IO	HIO	HDV	TCH	STN SM	STO SM	LRA	ST IDP	ST IDC	SCK	SC KC	ST CKC	SPT	ST PT	SP KA	IPK	PT LB	RRB	ST CTL	L CTL	CDS	DIAG DISK I/O
13.10	2	0	0	32	16	47	0	3	0	0	0	86	0	44	0	0	0	0	0	0	104	0	0	0	5	0	0	0	0	14
13.15	12	0	0	34	17	24	0	4	0	0	0	75	0	7	0	0	0	0	0	0	76	0	0	0	9	0	0	0	0	16
13.20	2	0	0	23	22	12	0	2	0	0	0	70	0	2	0	0	0	0	0	0	89	0	0	0	1	0	0	0	0	21
13.25	11	0	0	48	18	39	0	3	0	0	0	73	0	8	0	0	0	0	0	0	86	0	0	0	8	0	0	0	0	15
13.30	13	0	0	88	20	83	0	3	0	0	0	77	0	14	0	0	0	0	0	0	36	0	0	0	1	0	0	0	0	16
13.35	4	0	0	43	19	83	0	3	0	0	0	148	0	67	0	0	0	0	0	0	38	0	0	0	0	0	0	0	0	17
13.40	2	0	0	26	7	53	0	2	0	0	0	62	0	62	0	0	0	0	0	0	81	0	0	0	2	0	0	0	0	6
13.45	13	0	0	23	21	12	0	2	0	0	0	53	0	1	0	0	0	0	0	0	61	0	0	0	0	0	0	0	0	16
13.50	11	0	0	40	12	42	0	2	0	0	0	126	0	9	0	0	0	0	0	0	54	0	0	0	4	0	0	0	0	8
13.50	1	0	0	59	6	64	0	1	0	0	0	265	0	4	0	0	0	0	0	0	10	0	0	0	0	0	0	0	0	2
13.50	8	0	0	40	17	44	0	3	0	0	0	88	0	23	0	0	0	0	0	0	68	0	0	0	3	0	0	0	0	14

Abb. 3

DATE 12/19/78   FROM 13:05:46 TO 13:50:59   USER RESOURCE UTILIZATION SUMMARY   # SECONDS: 2713   PAGE   1

		CPU					STORAGE WKSET K BYTES		PAGING PAGE I/O THOUSANDS		PGDEV SLOTS THOUSANDS PRIMARY		OFLO	I/O DISK+TAPE THOUSANDS	PRINT	SAMPLES		RUNNING STATUS PCT DELAYS DUE TO						
RANK	USERID	REL PCT	CUM PCT	TOTAL	VIRT	TOT VIRT RATIO	AVG	MAX	READ	WRITE	AVG	MAX	OFLO MAX	DISK+TAPE	PRINT LINES	NO. OBS	PCT IVE	CPU	STG	PAG	I/O	AP LOK	VOL WAIT	RAI
1	ZD3317	37	37	973	927	1.1	125	312	0	0	996	996	0	3	1	91	100	52	0	0	0	0	0	.48
2	N73316	17	54	444	143	3.1	341	452	1	1	127	128	0	7	0	91	100	61	0	3	0	0	22	.36
3	RD3315	13	67	328	107	3.1	449	880	1	1	575	596	0	15	10	91	99	21	0	2	0	0	63	.76
4	OS3749	9	76	234	107	2.2	181	220	0	0	126	127	0	12	21	91	63	23	0	0	0	0	74	.77
5	ZN3317	7	83	196	15	13.5	96	132	0	0	61	62	0	10	11	91	100	12	0	3	0	0	81	.84
6	CB0425	3	86	66	42	1.6	205	280	1	0	66	110	0	5	0	91	90	2	0	2	6	0	88	.89
7	J85714	2	88	61	35	1.7	130	1164	0	0	27	131	0	10	0	91	39	0	0	3	23	0	90	.74
8	EX5666	2	90	46	16	2.9	45	100	1	0	22	23	0	1	10	91	33	17	0	0	0	0	92	.83
9	OQ0878	1	91	37	10	3.8	525	1024	1	1	218	256	0	4	0	81	38	0	0	0	0	0	95	1.00
10	E33749	1	92	31	15	2.1	130	200	0	0	29	53	0	3	3	91	74	1	0	0	12	0	90	.87
11	K23660	1	93	27	11	2.4	180	556	0	0	36	146	0	3	1	91	47	0	0	2	5	0	91	.93
12	IK3382	1	94	23	9	2.7	139	380	0	0	24	98	0	2	0	57	93	4	0	0	4	0	93	.92
13	DIRECT	1	95	22	16	1.4	56	636	0	0	41	54	0	2	0	91	42	0	0	5	8	0	92	.87
14	HU0406	1	96	19	7	2.8	165	380	0	0	50	92	0	3	0	91	61	2	0	2	4	0	93	.93
15	C40843	1	96	16	11	1.5	203	400	1	1	114	114	0	1	0	91	77	1	0	4	0	0	83	.94
16	F00843	1	97	16	9	1.8	363	536	1	1	163	163	0	0	0	91	69	2	0	3	2	0	96	.94
17	FX5709	0	97	10	5	2.2	148	176	0	0	25	41	0	1	0	71	83	0	0	0	0	0	94	1.00
18	RL3784	0	98	9	3	2.9	96	96	0	0	96	96	0	1	1	91	16	0	0	0	0	0	99	1.00
19	DZ0425	0	98	7	2	3.0	89	156	0	0	25	39	0	0	0	91	69	2	0	3	0	0	97	.95
20	I67899	0	98	7	4	2.0	33	76	0	0	17	19	0	0	0	59	88	6	0	0	0	0	95	.94
21	K03784	0	99	7	3	2.5	118	272	0	0	29	59	0	1	2	91	41	0	0	3	0	0	99	.97
22	F35851	0	99	5	2	2.4	115	176	0	0	28	28	0	1	0	91	19	0	0	0	6	0	99	.94
23	F25851	0	99	4	2	2.3	71	168	0	0	30	44	0	0	0	91	40	0	0	0	3	0	98	.97
24	ZH3317	0	99	4	0	17.1	10	12	0	0	13	13	0	0	0	91	100	1	0	0	0	0	99	.99
25	IH0409	0	99	4	1	2.7	87	232	0	0	29	64	0	0	0	36	69	0	0	0	0	0	100	1.00
26	KG7889	0	99	3	1	2.4	98	152	0	0	9	15	0	0	0	12	82	11	0	0	0	0	82	.89
27	ZZ3317	0	99	3	1	3.7	57	64	0	0	20	20	0	0	0	91	71	2	0	0	2	0	98	.97
28	NA3752	0	99	2	1	4.6	184	212	0	0	901	901	0	0	0	27	62	0	0	0	0	0	100	1.00
29	FV3665	0	100	2	0	4.5	69	100	0	0	20	24	0	0	0	91	23	0	0	0	0	0	100	1.00
30	KS3315	0	100	2	1	2.9	112	248	0	0	14	52	0	0	0	34	64	0	0	0	0	0	97	1.00
31	FH0843	0	100	2	1	2.3	68	144	0	0	17	20	0	0	0	91	17	0	0	0	0	0	99	1.00
32	KF5711	0	100	2	1	2.2	116	148	0	0	5	7	0	0	0	4	100	0	0	0	0	0	100	1.00
33	E93665	0	100	2	1	3.0	60	72	0	0	18	18	0	0	0	91	12	0	0	0	0	0	100	1.00
34	XM3317	0	100	1	1	2.1	124	192	0	0	25	28	0	0	0	17	44	0	0	0	0	0	94	1.00
35	JN5714	0	100	1	1	2.0	202	236	0	0	41	58	0	0	0	9	75	0	0	0	0	0	100	1.00
36	BO3924	0	100	1	0	3.0	31	56	0	0	18	18	0	0	0	91	14	0	0	0	0	0	100	1.00
37	XD3317	0	100	0	0	4.4	62	68	0	0	25	25	0	0	0	91	17	0	0	0	0	0	100	1.00
38	DEM4	0	100	0	0	0.0	143	256	0	0	64	64	0	0	0	91	10	0	0	0	0	0	100	1.00
39	BH3924	0	100	0	0	0.0	68	68	0	0	0	0	0	0	0	3	100	0	0	0	0	0	100	1.00
40	ZL3317	0	100	0	0	0.0	44	44	0	0	26	26	0	0	0	91	14	0	0	8	0	0	99	.92
41	KD3924	0	100	0	0	0.0	136	136	0	0	45	45	0	0	0	91	8	0	0	0	0	0	100	1.00
42	AF3316	0	100	0	0	0.0	60	60	0	0	15	15	0	0	0	91	8	0	0	0	0	0	100	1.00
43	TA7081	0	100	0	0	0.0	44	44	0	0	17	17	0	0	0	91	9	0	0	0	0	0	100	1.00
44	AM0843	0	100	0	0	0.0	64	64	0	0	16	16	0	0	0	91	9	0	0	0	0	0	100	1.00
45	ZO3317	0	100	0	0	0.0	52	52	0	0	17	17	0	0	0	91	9	0	0	0	0	0	100	1.00
46	DM5555	0	100	0	0	0.0	172	172	0	0	43	43	0	0	0	91	9	0	0	0	0	0	100	1.00
47	KZ3924	0	100	0	0	0.0	76	76	0	0	18	18	0	0	0	91	9	0	0	0	0	0	100	1.00
48	KY3924	0	100	0	0	0.0	0	0	0	0	0	0	0	0	0	6	0	0	0	0	0	0	0	1.00
TOTALS		100	100	2,619	1,507	1.7	128	1164	11	9	90	996	0	85	60	3601	46	10	0	1	2	0	90	.86

Abb. 4

DATE   12/19/78   FROM 13:05:46 TO 13:50:59   DISK AND TAPE I/O ACTIVITY SUMMARY   # SECONDS   2713   PAGE   1

| DEVICE | | | NO. OF SAMPLE | PCT ACTIVITY | TOTAL I/O | TOTAL RATE | ACTIVE RATE | <PCT OF IO> | | NUMBER OF NON-ZERO | SEEK LEN | | <I/O REQUESTS QUEUED FOR DEV> | | | |
ADDR	TYPE	VOLSER	OBS	LEVEL	ISSUED	/SEC	/SEC	ON CHAN	IN SYS	LEN SEEKS	AVG	NON-ZERO	AVG	AVG IF Q NON-ZERO	MAX	PCT OBS WITH Q
188	3340	IFBRES	90	14.4	2,446	0.9	6.3	7.1	4.2	971	45	113	0.0	0.0	0	0.0
189	3340	CICS01	90	35.6	1,785	0.7	1.9	5.2	3.1	1,068	53	89	0.0	0.0	0	0.0
18A	3340	SCHL00	90	6.7	656	0.2	3.7	1.9	1.1	308	35	75	0.0	0.0	0	0.0
18C	3340	ETSNEU	90	73.3	4,526	1.7	2.3	13.2	7.8	1,514	42	126	0.0	0.0	0	0.0
18D	3340	XXXCOS	90	16.7	10,190	3.8	22.6	29.8	17.6	161	7	459	0.0	0.0	0	0.0
18E	3340	IFB340	66	12.1	757	0.4	3.2	2.2	1.3	22	9	312	0.0	0.0	0	0.0
1C3	3340	003790	90	3.3	26	0.0	0.3	0.0	0.0	5	36	139	0.0	0.0	0	0.0
1C4	3340	VMINI6	90	95.6	1,176	0.5	0.5	3.4	2.0	666	3	6	0.0	1.0	1	1.3
1C5	3340	VMPAGA	90	100.0	12,539	4.6	4.6	36.7	21.7	9,608	13	17	0.6	1.9	9	32.2
250	3330	VMINI8	90	41.1	3,500	1.3	3.2	16.9	6.1	798	17	77	0.0	0.0	0	0.0
251	3330	DOS349	90	10.0	124	0.1	0.5	0.6	0.2	78	72	115	0.0	0.0	0	0.0
252	3330	VMINI1	90	68.9	3,521	1.3	1.9	17.0	6.1	853	20	84	0.0	0.0	0	0.0
253	3330	VMINI4	90	46.7	4,432	1.6	3.5	21.4	7.7	946	21	99	0.0	0.0	0	0.0
254	3330	DOS341	90	22.2	1,283	0.5	2.1	6.2	2.2	696	92	173	0.0	0.0	0	0.0
257	3330	VMINI3	90	96.7	7,755	2.9	3.0	37.6	13.4	2,924	21	57	0.0	1.0	2	0.4
585	3420		90	100.0	3,024	1.1	1.1	99.8	5.2							
58B	3420		90	1.1	2	0.0	0.1	0.0	0.0							
58C	3420		90	1.1	2	0.0	0.1	0.0	0.0							

CHANNEL ACTIVITY SUMMARY

| CHANNEL | TOTAL I/O | RATE /SEC | PCT OF SYSTEM | <I/O REQUESTS QUEUED FOR CHAN> | | | |
				AVG	AVG IF Q NON-ZERO	MAX	PCT OBS WITH Q
1	34,101	12.6	59.1	0.0	1.0	2	1.9
2	20,615	7.6	35.7	0.0	1.0	1	0.1
5	3,028	1.1	5.2	0.0	0.0	0	0.0
TOTALS	57,744	21.3	100.0				

Abb. 5

DATE 12/19/78   TIME 13:05:46   INTENSIVE ACTIVITY TRACE ON USERID   N73316   PAGE   5

RECORD NO.	TIME	USEC	REC	Q	DELTA TOD	DELTA CCPU	DELTA VCPU	Q1	Q2	E1	E2	WKSET	VSIO	PREAD	PREF	PSTEAL	PRES
3,105	13.06.18	105423	E	2	0.024063			1	2	0	1	105					
3,106	13.06.18	105711	A	2	0.000287			1	3	0	0	105					
3,108	13.06.18	126047	D	2	0.020336	0.010881	0.003250	0	2	0	0	105					105
3,110	13.06.18	150975	E	2	0.024928			0	2	0	1	105					
3,111	13.06.18	151263	A	2	0.000287			0	3	0	0	105					
3,112	13.06.18	163455	D	2	0.012191	0.010664	0.003224	0	2	0	0	105					105
3,116	13.06.18	183599	E	2	0.020143			0	2	0	1	105					
3,117	13.06.18	183887	A	2	0.000287			0	3	0	0	105					
3,118	13.06.18	195951	D	2	0.012063	0.010880	0.003228	0	2	0	0	105					105
3,120	13.06.18	219791	E	2	0.023839			0	2	0	1	105					
3,121	13.06.18	220079	A	2	0.000287			0	3	0	0	105					
3,128	13.06.18	267503	D	2	0.047423	0.011436	0.003324	0	2	0	0	105					105
3,130	13.06.18	287855	E	2	0.020351			0	2	0	1	105					
3,131	13.06.18	288175	A	2	0.000319			0	3	0	0	105					
3,132	13.06.18	302767	D	2	0.014592	0.011104	0.003383	0	2	0	0	105					105
3,134	13.06.18	326287	E	2	0.023519			0	2	0	1	105					
3,135	13.06.18	326575	A	2	0.000287			0	3	0	0	105					
3,136	13.06.18	338719	D	2	0.012143	0.010531	0.003265	0	2	0	0	105					105
3,138	13.06.18	362223	E	2	0.023504			0	2	0	1	105					
3,139	13.06.18	362511	A	2	0.000287			0	3	0	0	105					
3,140	13.06.18	374927	D	2	0.012416	0.010829	0.003358	0	2	0	0	105					105
3,143	13.06.18	395167	E	2	0.020239			1	2	0	1	105					
3,144	13.06.18	395455	A	2	0.000287			1	3	0	0	105					
3,149	13.06.18	424575	D	2	0.029119	0.010845	0.003231	0	2	0	0	105					105
3,153	13.06.18	448767	E	2	0.024192			0	2	0	1	105					
3,154	13.06.18	449039	A	2	0.000272			0	3	0	0	105					
3,155	13.06.18	461775	D	2	0.012736	0.010527	0.003230	0	2	0	0	105					105
3,156	13.06.18	481951	E	2	0.020175			0	2	0	1	105					
3,157	13.06.18	482239	A	2	0.000287			0	3	0	0	105					
3,161	13.06.18	503903	D	2	0.021663	0.010826	0.003369	0	2	0	0	105					105
3,165	13.06.18	527471	E	2	0.023567			1	2	0	1	105					
3,166	13.06.18	527791	A	2	0.000319			1	3	0	0	105					
3,168	13.06.18	564271	D	2	0.036479	0.010962	0.003374	0	2	0	0	105					105
3,170	13.06.18	581199	E	2	0.016927			0	2	0	1	105					
3,171	13.06.18	581503	A	2	0.000303			0	3	0	0	105					
3,172	13.06.18	593983	D	2	0.012479	0.010880	0.003330	0	2	0	0	105					105
3,173	13.06.18	614351	E	2	0.020368			0	2	0	1	105					
3,174	13.06.18	614655	A	2	0.000303			0	3	0	0	105					
3,175	13.06.18	627599	D	2	0.012943	0.010557	0.003273	0	2	0	0	105					105
3,176	13.06.18	644399	E	2	0.016800			0	2	0	1	105					
3,177	13.06.18	644687	A	2	0.000287			0	3	0	0	105					
3,178	13.06.18	657679	D	2	0.012991	0.010874	0.003291	0	2	0	0	105					105
3,181	13.06.18	678015	E	2	0.020336			1	2	0	1	105					
3,182	13.06.18	678303	A	2	0.000287			1	3	0	0	105					
3,184	13.06.18	704079	D	2	0.025775	0.010576	0.003273	0	2	0	0	105					105
3,185	13.06.18	720991	E	2	0.016912			0	2	0	1	105					
3,186	13.06.18	721279	A	2	0.000287			0	3	0	0	105					
3,190	13.06.18	741615	D	2	0.020336	0.011030	0.003587	0	2	0	0	105					105
3,191	13.06.18	758543	E	2	0.016927			0	2	0	1	105					
3,192	13.06.18	758831	A	2	0.000287			0	3	0	0	105					
3,196	13.06.18	777967	D	2	0.019135	0.010876	0.003368	0	2	0	0	105					105
3,197	13.06.18	801679	E	2	0.023711			0	2	0	1	105					
3,198	13.06.18	801983	A	2	0.000303			0	3	0	0	105					
3,205	13.06.18	849647	D	2	0.047664	0.011279	0.003465	0	2	0	0	105					105
3,206	13.06.18	869935	E	2	0.020287			0	2	0	1	105					
3,207	13.06.18	870223	A	2	0.000287			0	3	0	0	105					
3,208	13.06.18	882271	D	2	0.012047	0.010523	0.003230	0	2	0	0	105					105

Abb. 6

FIRST DATE 12/05/78   TIME 11:40:59   MONITOR STATISTICAL SUMMARY   PAGE 1
LAST DATE 12/05/78   TIME 12.37.13

ABB. 7.1

VARIABLE	AVERAGE	MINIMUM	MAXIMUM	TIME OF MINIMUM	TIME OF MAXIMUM	STD DEV	# OBS	DESCRIPTION
LOGGED	54.51	54.00	56.00	12.06.13	11.51.13	0.66	56	# OF USERS LOGGED ONTO SYSTEM
ACTIVE	22.69	16.00	30.00	12.34.13	12.22.13	2.79	56	# USERS ACTIVE IN A SAMPLE INTERVAL
INQUEUE	7.11	3.73	11.56	12.36.13	11.46.13	1.46	14,384	# USERS IN DISPATCH & ELIGIBLE QUEUES
DIALED	1.30	1.00	2.00	11.42.13	11.54.13	0.46	56	# USERS DIALED TO MULTI-ACCESS SYSTEM
RAI	0.72	0.55	0.84	11.46.13	12.08.13	0.06	56	RESOURCE AVAILABILITY INDEX
PCTCPUQ	13.30	0.00	39.13	12.14.13	11.44.14	8.94	56	PCT OF ACTIVE USERS IN CPU WAIT
PCTSTGQ	0.89	0.00	9.52	11.42.13	11.59.13	2.21	56	PCT ACTIVE USERS WAITING FOR MAIN STG
PCTPAGEQ	2.87	0.00	17.39	11.43.13	11.42.13	4.51	56	PCT OF ACTIVE USERS IN PAGE WAIT
PCTIOQ	5.51	0.00	20.00	11.44.14	12.20.13	5.21	56	PCT OF ACTIVE USERS IN I/O WAIT
PCTDEFRQ	0.00	0.00	0.00	11.42.13		0.00	56	PCT OF ACTIVE USERS IN SYSLOCK WAIT
PCTPSWAIT	86.74	80.00	94.44	11.44.14	12.35.13	3.19	56	PCT OF LOGGED USERS IN VOLUNTARY WAIT
TVRATIO	2.06	1.45	2.82	12.16.13	12.24.13	0.25	56	RATIO OF TOTAL TO VIRTUAL CPU UTIL.
TOTCPU	96.98	74.43	100.00	12.24.13	11.47.13	5.57	56	CPU TOTAL PCT UTILIZATION
CPCPU	49.25	31.33	61.15	12.16.13	11.59.13	5.95	56	CPU CP STATE PCT UTILIZATION
VIRTCPU	47.73	26.35	68.66	12.24.13	12.16.13	6.83	56	CPU PROBLEM STATE PCT UTILIZATION
IDLE	0.00	0.00	0.00	11.42.13		0.00	56	CPU PCT IDLE
PAGEWAIT	0.83	0.00	12.59	11.46.13	12.21.13	2.08	56	CPU PCT PAGE WAIT
IOWAIT	2.17	0.00	21.97	11.47.13	12.24.13	4.25	56	CPU PCT I/O WAIT
STGUTIL	81.08	37.86	97.09	12.08.13	11.55.13	10.97	14,384	PCT MAIN STORAGE UTILIZATION
CORESAT	1.16	0.92	1.54	12.07.13	11.58.13	0.14	56	MAIN STORAGE SATURATION FACTOR
WKSET	169.83	120.13	228.90	12.22.13	11.58.13	25.06	56	AVERAGE WORKING-SET SIZE PER USER
RATIO	1.02	1.00	1.26	11.42.13	11.56.13	0.06	56	CONTENTION RATIO (AS IN INDICATE CMD)
PGBLPGS	816.35	815.00	818.00	11.59.13	11.51.13	0.40	56	# SYSTEM PAGEABLE PAGES AVAILABLE
SHRPGS	28.57	17.00	38.00	12.28.13	11.49.14	4.26	56	# PAGES BEING SHARED AMONG USERS
RESPGS	0.00	0.00	0.00	11.42.13		0.00	56	# PAGES RESERVED FOR SPECIAL USERS
PAGERATE	22.15	9.14	56.52	12.07.13	12.23.13	11.05	56	PAGING RATE PER SECOND
CHAINPCT	4.79	0.28	14.00	11.58.13	11.44.14	3.44	56	PCT PAGE I/O CHAINED ON ONE SIO
STEALPCT	29.29	6.43	49.23	12.08.13	11.50.13	8.59	56	PCT PAGES STOLEN DUE TO PAGE FAULTS
STEALRATE	6.86	0.61	21.29	12.08.13	12.25.13	4.81	56	# PAGE STEALS PER SECOND
DRUMUTIL	11.82	10.57	13.02	12.09.13	11.52.13	0.55	56	PCT OF PRIMARY PAGING AREA NEEDED
VIO	130.60	54.92	200.93	12.23.13	11.48.13	37.44	56	# VIRTUAL I/O REQUESTS SIMULATED/SEC
IOINT	108.78	58.10	154.77	12.19.13	12.25.13	22.20	56	# REAL I/O INTERRUPTS PER SECOND
CCWTRANS	38.83	12.40	65.31	12.19.13	11.46.13	13.03	56	# CCW CHAINS TRANSLATED PER SECOND
EXPF	7.07	2.86	13.99	12.13.15	11.47.13	2.74	1,552	EXPANSION FACTOR FOR MAJOR COMMANDS
Q1	1.78	1.00	3.21	12.16.13	12.25.13	0.58	14,384	# USERS IN INTERACTIVE QUEUE (Q1)
Q2	5.12	2.51	9.74	12.36.13	11.46.13	1.30	14,384	# USERS IN BATCH QUEUE (Q2)
E1	0.00	0.00	0.05	11.42.13	11.51.13	0.00	14,384	# USERS WAITING FOR INTERACTIVE QUEUE
E2	0.19	0.00	1.89	11.42.13	11.59.13	0.42	14,384	# USERS WAITING FOR BATCH QUEUE
Q1Q2	5.94	2.00	10.00	12.35.13	11.44.14	1.68	56	# USERS NOW IN DISPATCH LISTS
E1E2	0.19	0.00	2.00	11.42.13	11.55.13	0.48	56	# USERS WAITING FOR MAIN STORAGE

FIRST DATE 12/05/78 TIME 11:40:59   MONITOR STATISTICAL SUMMARY   PAGE 2
LAST DATE 12/05/78 TIME 12.37.13

VARIABLE	AVERAGE	MINIMUM	MAXIMUM	TIME OF MINIMUM	TIME OF MAXIMUM	STD DEV	# OBS	DESCRIPTION
Q1E1	0.78	0.00	4.00	11.44.14	12.20.13	1.05	56	# ACTIVE INTERACTIVE USERS
Q2E2	5.35	1.00	10.00	12.29.13	11.44.14	1.84	56	# ACTIVE NON-INTERACTIVE USERS
CPUQ	3.00	0.00	9.00	12.14.13	11.44.14	2.04	56	# RUNNABLE USERS WAITING FOR CPU
STGQ	0.19	0.00	2.00	11.42.13	11.55.13	0.48	56	# USERS WAITING FOR MAIN STORAGE
PAGEQ	0.67	0.00	4.00	11.43.13	11.42.13	1.08	56	# USERS IN PAGE WAIT
IOQ	1.26	0.00	5.00	11.44.14	12.20.13	1.22	56	# USERS IN I/O WAIT
PSWAIT	47.28	44.00	52.00	11.44.14	11.53.13	1.73	56	# LOGGED ON USERS IN VOLUNTARY WAIT
Q1WAIT	0.00	0.00	0.03	12.33.13	11.45.13	0.00	212	SECONDS DELAY WAITING TO ENTER Q1
Q2WAIT	0.41	0.00	7.93	11.49.14	12.01.13	1.22	25	SECONDS DELAY WAITING TO ENTER Q2
Q1RATE	3.80	1.83	7.51	11.48.13	12.24.13	1.30	56	# ADDITIONS PER SECOND TO QUEUE 1
Q2RATE	0.46	0.14	1.08	12.28.13	12.25.13	0.15	56	# ADDITIONS PER SECOND TO QUEUE 2
FREEPGS	6.75	2.00	24.00	12.28.13	12.05.13	3.83	56	# PAGES ON THE FREELIST
PSWAP	0.80	0.00	3.00	11.44.14	11.42.13	0.96	56	# PAGES SWAPPING IN FROM PAGE DEVICE
NOFREE	0.84	0.00	7.50	11.48.13	11.42.13	1.69	56	# TIMES FREELIST WAS EMPTY
RECLAIM	0.28	0.04	0.64	11.49.14	12.20.13	0.15	56	# PAGES FLUSHED BUT RECLAIMED
STEALCK	33.49	8.64	82.99	12.08.13	12.23.13	17.69	56	# PAGES CHECKED IN MAKING PAGE STEALS
FLUSHSWAP	0.00	0.00	0.00	11.42.13		0.00	56	# PAGES SWAPPED OFF FLUSHLIST
STEALSCANS	0.03	0.00	0.10	12.08.13	12.24.13	0.02	56	# COMPLETE SCANS WHILE PAGE STEALING
INTTIMER	0.18	0.00	2.88	11.47.13	12.19.13	0.42	56	# VIRT INTVL TIMER INTERUPT SIMULATED
CPUTIMER	0.00	0.00	0.03	11.42.13	12.34.13	0.00	56	# VIRT CPU TIMER INTERUPTS SIMULATED
CLOCKCOMP	0.00	0.00	0.00	11.42.13		0.00	56	# CLOCK COMPARATOR INTERUPT SIMULATED
PRIVOP	277.69	121.93	488.99	12.26.13	12.13.15	78.00	56	# PRIVILEGED INSTRS SIMULATED/SECOND
LXTINT	2.07	1.01	6.31	12.24.13	12.19.13	0.90	56	# REAL EXTERNAL INTERRUPTS PER SECOND
VSVC	0.01	0.00	0.06	11.42.13	11.49.14	0.01	56	# VIRTUAL SVC SIMULATIONS PER SECOND
VPGMINT	337.52	195.87	550.13	12.26.13	12.13.15	74.11	56	# VIRTUAL PGM INTERRUPTS PER SECOND
PFAULT	15.08	7.04	33.90	12.07.13	12.23.13	6.71	56	# PAGE FAULTS PER SECOND
PREAD	12.28	4.50	31.87	12.06.13	12.24.13	6.06	56	# PAGE READS REQUESTED PER SECOND
PWRITE	9.87	3.70	25.33	11.58.13	12.23.13	5.17	56	# PAGE WRITES REQUESTED PER SECOND
PREQ	23.25	9.98	56.72	12.08.13	12.23.13	10.92	56	# PAGE I/O REQUESTS PER SECOND
PSIO	21.89	9.74	50.10	12.08.13	12.23.13	9.45	56	# PAGING SIO COMMANDS/SECOND
STEALS	412.05	36.99	1,278.99	12.08.13	12.25.13	288.96	56	# PAGES STOLEN PER INTERVAL
DSPCH	378.28	262.26	495.32	12.16.13	12.25.13	53.57	56	# CALLS/SECOND TO (MAIN) DISPATCHER
DSPCHREF	79.52	33.68	150.50	12.19.13	12.01.13	31.69	56	# DISPATCHER FAST REFLECTS PER SECOND
DSPCHPSW	99.47	41.86	221.01	12.08.13	12.06.13	44.94	56	# DISPATCHER NEW PSW PER SECOND
SCHED	154.48	80.12	234.72	12.16.13	11.44.14	40.23	56	# CALLS PER SECOND TO SCHEDULER
DEADLINE	10.33	7.62	12.56	12.37.13	11.49.14	1.14	56	SYSTEM-WIDE TIME-SLICE DEADLINE (SEC)
ETIME	0.29	0.00	1.31	11.42.13	12.01.13	0.30	56	SYSTEM-WIDE SECONDS IN ELIGIBLE LISTS
FAIRCPU	5.50	4.36	7.45	12.24.13	12.01.13	1.17	56	FAIR-SHARE OF CPU PER USER (SECS)
FAIRPAGES	143.00	116.00	163.00	11.48.13	11.42.13	15.67	56	FAIR-SHARE # PAGES PER USER
PROJCPU	19.73	4.84	44.87	12.15.13	12.27.14	13.75	56	PROJECTED CPU MS OVERHEAD/PAGE READ
OVHDCPU	5.63	5.17	6.26	12.20.13	11.51.13	0.30	56	ACTUAL CPU MS OVERHEAD/PAGE READ

Abb. 7.2

DATE 12/05/78   FROM 11:40:59 TO 12:38:00   USER RESOURCE UTILIZATION SUMMARY   # SECONDS: 3420   PAGE   1

RANK	USERID	CPU REL PCT	CPU CUM PCT	CPU SEC TOTAL	CPU SEC VIRT	TOT: VIRT RATIO	WKSET K BYTES AVG	WKSET K BYTES MAX	PAGE I/O READ	PAGE I/O WRITE	PGDEV PRIMARY AVG	PGDEV PRIMARY MAX	PGDEV OFLO MAX	DISK+ TAPE	PRINT LINES	SAMPLES NO. OBS	ACT IVE	PCT CPU	STG	PAG	I/O	AP LOK	VOL WAIT	RAI
1	DOS002	28	28	851	414	2.1	628	1820	4	3	731	1074	0	70	9	57	100	63	0	13	0	0	11	.25
2	DOS001	20	48	606	242	2.5	456	1216	4	3	678	978	0	44	24	57	100	38	4	5	27	0	7	.27
3	NEMETZ	12	60	381	267	1.4	489	928	4	4	197	233	0	9	14	57	100	61	0	9	9	0	18	.21
4	HAHN	9	69	261	224	1.2	629	1396	7	6	452	484	0	4	0	57	89	60	2	18	10	0	14	.10
5	SIEBENH	4	73	113	93	1.2	402	752	2	1	178	385	0	4	4	57	66	59	5	5	8	0	48	.22
6	DOS005	4	76	110	35	3.2	194	1044	3	2	780	848	0	11	1	57	100	21	4	2	0	0	66	.73
7	KOCH	3	79	97	61	1.6	185	688	1	1	77	223	0	7	2	57	66	27	0	5	8	0	70	.59
8	DOS007	2	82	72	37	1.9	225	404	1	0	576	612	0	4	3	57	38	57	0	5	0	0	75	.38
9	NES	2	84	66	47	1.4	113	632	1	1	48	230	0	3	0	57	63	17	0	0	6	0	86	.77
10	STENGL	1	85	43	17	2.6	97	188	0	0	26	56	0	8	0	25	46	18	0	0	27	0	75	.55
11	CIHAK	1	87	39	15	2.6	53	124	1	1	23	32	0	6	0	57	82	0	0	0	11	0	91	.89
12	SCHMIDTG	1	88	38	17	2.3	107	672	1	1	75	316	0	5	0	57	70	3	3	0	13	0	88	.82
13	BAYER	1	89	35	17	2.1	100	444	1	0	26	109	0	3	1	57	52	3	0	3	10	0	93	.83
14	HOLLER	1	90	33	11	3.0	78	120	1	1	24	32	0	2	2	57	64	3	0	0	6	0	95	.92
15	SUBMIT	1	91	33	12	2.8	66	76	0	0	24	24	0	2	0	57	45	0	0	4	8	0	93	.88
16	PUHL	1	92	32	18	1.8	51	92	1	0	24	31	0	3	0	57	45	0	0	0	12	0	91	.88
17	WEISSM	1	93	27	8	3.5	92	456	1	1	42	107	0	4	0	57	55	0	0	3	10	0	91	.87
18	MEIER	1	94	23	10	2.4	74	240	1	1	30	61	0	2	0	57	54	0	0	3	3	0	95	.93
19	REISSER	1	95	22	7	3.0	89	788	0	1	24	104	0	3	0	57	43	4	0	0	0	0	96	.96
20	ZELLER	1	95	19	8	2.5	50	260	1	0	20	34	0	2	2	57	64	0	3	0	0	0	98	.97
21	GOEHR	1	96	19	10	1.9	79	392	0	0	24	29	0	2	0	57	45	0	0	0	12	0	93	.98
22	SCHMITTW	1	96	19	8	2.3	85	168	0	0	52	188	0	2	5	57	34	0	0	0	16	0	93	.84
23	HHEIN	1	97	18	7	2.5	74	296	1	0	56	82	0	2	0	57	59	0	0	0	3	0	98	.97
24	ZOTT	0	97	13	4	3.5	44	136	0	0	25	42	0	1	3	57	57	0	0	0	0	0	100	1.00
25	STARK	0	98	11	3	3.0	44	88	1	1	25	28	0	0	0	57	77	0	0	0	2	0	96	.98
26	FIDYKA	0	98	11	4	2.7	76	280	0	0	25	67	0	0	0	57	25	0	0	7	7	0	96	.80
27	MAINT	0	98	9	1	6.1	45	80	1	1	24	24	0	0	0	57	91	0	0	0	4	0	93	.96
28	M3286/1	0	99	8	1	14.4	13	16	0	0	6	6	0	1	0	57	100	0	0	2	0	0	98	.98
29	LEDERER	0	99	5	2	2.3	56	84	0	0	17	25	0	0	0	57	16	0	0	11	0	0	98	.89
30	M3286/2	0	99	5	0	15.4	12	16	0	0	6	6	0	0	0	57	100	0	0	0	0	0	100	1.00
31	SCHALAND	0	99	5	2	2.4	285	404	0	0	229	229	0	1	2	57	4	0	0	0	0	0	100	1.00
32	KASERER	0	99	4	1	3.6	81	100	0	0	21	31	0	0	0	57	14	0	0	0	0	0	100	1.00
33	HOELLMUE	0	99	4	1	5.8	59	108	0	0	21	26	0	0	0	57	38	0	0	0	0	0	100	1.00
34	CHRISTL	0	100	4	1	3.8	69	100	0	0	21	27	0	0	0	57	43	0	0	0	0	0	100	1.00
35	SCHMIDTM	0	100	3	1	4.2	48	100	0	0	19	19	0	0	0	57	14	0	0	0	0	0	100	1.00
36	M3286/3	0	100	3	0	18.2	12	16	0	0	5	6	0	0	0	57	98	0	0	0	0	0	100	1.00
37	POTTLER	0	100	2	1	3.9	73	80	0	0	21	28	0	0	0	57	9	0	0	0	0	0	100	1.00
38	MORSCHH	0	100	2	1	2.9	99	116	0	0	26	32	0	0	0	57	7	0	0	0	0	0	100	1.00
39	HEINDEL	0	100	2	0	5.8	61	76	0	0	22	30	0	0	0	57	9	0	0	0	0	0	100	1.00
40	AZUBI2	0	100	1	0	6.8	66	88	0	0	19	21	0	0	0	5	100	0	0	0	0	0	100	1.00
41	ROESCH	0	100	1	0	5.4	92	96	0	0	24	34	0	0	0	57	5	0	0	33	0	0	98	.67
42	OPERATOR	0	100	0	0	0.0	16	16	0	0	13	13	0	0	0	57	79	0	0	0	0	0	100	1.00
43	HOFMANN	0	100	0	0	0.0	24	100	0	0	24	26	0	0	0	57	11	0	0	0	0	0	100	1.00
44	MUELLER	0	100	0	0	0.0	71	72	0	0	29	29	0	0	0	57	2	0	0	0	0	0	100	1.00
45	KRESINSZ	0	100	0	0	0.0	132	376	0	0	481	481	0	0	0	57	4	0	0	0	0	0	100	1.00
46	EDVINFO	0	100	0	0	0.0	42	60	0	0	15	15	0	0	0	57	4	0	0	0	0	0	100	1.00
47	WOITONIK	0	100	0	0	0.0	11	64	0	0	19	19	0	0	0	57	4	0	0	0	0	0	100	1.00
48	OSIANDER	0	100	0	0	0.0	80	80	0	0	19	19	0	0	0	57	2	0	0	0	0	0	100	1.00
49	BERTHOLD	0	100	0	0	0.0	0	0	0	0	0	0	0	0	0	57	0	0	0	0	0	0	0	1.00

Abb. 8.1

DATE 12/05/78 FROM 11:40:59 TO 12:38:00   USER RESOURCE UTILIZATION SUMMARY   # SECONDS: 3420   PAGE   2

		RELATIVE		CPU		TOT:	STORAGE WKSET		PAGING PAGE I/O		PGDEV SLOTS			I/O THOUSANDS		SAMPLES	PCT	RUNNING STATUS PCT DELAYS DUE TO						PCT	
			CUM	SECONDS	VIRT	VIRT	K BYTES		THOUSANDS		PRIMARY		OFLO	DISK+	PRINT	NO.	ACT		WAITING FOR				AP	VOL
RANK	USERID	PCT	PCT	TOTAL	VIRT	RATIO	AVG	MAX	READ	WRITE	AVG	MAX	MAX	TAPE	LINES	OBS	IVE	CPU	STG	PAG	I/O	LOK	VOL WAIT	RAT
50	AZUBI3	0	100	0	0	0.0	0	0	0	0	0	0	0	0	0	57	0	0	0	0	0	0	0	1.00
51	EDVBO1-3	0	100	0	0	0.0	0	0	0	0	0	0	0	0	0	57	0	0	0	0	0	0	0	1.00
52	STOCKH	0	100	0	0	0.0	0	0	0	0	0	0	0	0	0	57	0	0	0	0	0	0	0	1.00
53	DOS006	0	100	0	0	0.0	0	0	0	0	0	0	0	0	0	57	0	0	0	0	0	0	0	1.00
54	TRAUTV	0	100	0	0	0.0	0	0	0	0	0	0	0	0	0	57	0	0	0	0	0	0	0	1.00
55	RICHTER	0	100	0	0	0.0	0	0	0	0	0	0	0	0	0	57	0	0	0	0	0	0	0	1.00
	TOTALS:	100	100	3,050	1,607	1.9	110	1820	40	33	97	1074	0	209	73	3051	42	15	1	3	6	0	75	.7(

Abb. 8.2

RECHENZENTRUMSBETRIEB UNTER VM370

V. Haller

Messerschmitt-Bölkow-Blohm GmbH, Augsburg

Der Vortrag soll den Betriebsablauf im Rechenzentrum bei MBB Augsburg
als Beispiel einer 100 %-igen VM 370-Anwendung darstellen. Dabei
bilden die organisatorischen und wirtschaftlichen Aspekte den Schwerpunkt des Vortrages.

This Paper may illustrate the computer-centre of MBB Augsburg as a
100 % - VM 370-customer. It will concentrate on the organizational
and economical points of view.

1. <u>Einleitung</u>

Vor einem Auditorium von Betriebssystemdesignern möchte ich zu Be-
ginn meines Vortrages darauf hinweisen, daß ich selbst RZ-Leiter
bin und das Konzept der virtuellen Maschinen daher im wesentlichen
aus der Sicht der organisatorischen und wirtschaftlichen Aspekte
sehe. Diese Sicht hindert mich nicht daran, das VM sehr positiv zu
beurteilen, was bezüglich der organisatorischen Aspekte noch ver-
ständlich sein mag, aber bezüglich der wirtschaftlichen Aspekte
vermutlich zur Verwunderung führt. Zur Begründung meiner Einstel-
lung möchte ich die Anwendung der Möglichkeiten des Betriebssystems
VM von der IBM in unserem Rechenzentrum bei MBB Augsburg darstellen.

Dazu überschlage ich vorerst alle Angaben über Hardware, Personal-
einsatz und Anwendungsgebiete und beginne mit einer Darstellung
der virtuellen Maschinenebene. Zur groben Einordnung nur die Angabe, daß wir eine IBM 370/158 AP, also eine Doppelprozessoranlage,
mit einem Onlinesystem von ca. 150 Bildschirmen betreiben. Diese
Anlage wird ca. Mai d.J. gegen eine IBM 3032 ausgetauscht werden.

2. Virtuelle Maschinenebene

Die Abbildung Nr. 1 zeigt den Zusammenhang aller bei uns installierten virtuellen Maschinen. Insgesamt sind bei uns ca. 11 virtuelle Batchmaschinen, von denen 6 vom Operating gesteuert werden,
42 virtuelle CMS-Maschinen und 7 virtuelle Spoolmaschinen instal-
liert. Zum Verständnis der Abbildung beginne ich mit Erläuterungen
zu den verwendeten Symbolen.

Unter einer v i r t u e l l e n B a t c h m a s c h i n e verstehen wir eine mit einem DOS oder OS-Betriebssystem laufende virtuelle Maschine oder eine mit einem Sondersystem ausgestattete
Maschine mit der Fähigkeit Jobstreams zu verarbeiten.

Eine v i r t u e l l e C M S - M a s c h i n e   ist eine Dialog-
orientierte, virtuelle Maschine, die mit dem Conversational-Monitor-
System (CMS) von der IBM ausgestattet ist. Dies ist ein interaktives
im wesentlichen Editier-System, das in etwa dem TSO entspricht.

Unter einer S p o o l m a s c h i n e verstehen wir eine stark
abgerüstete CMS-Maschine, die lediglich mit einem virtuellen Kartenleser ausgestattet ist und die zur Übertragung und Ablage von Aufträgen an das Rechenzentrum dient.

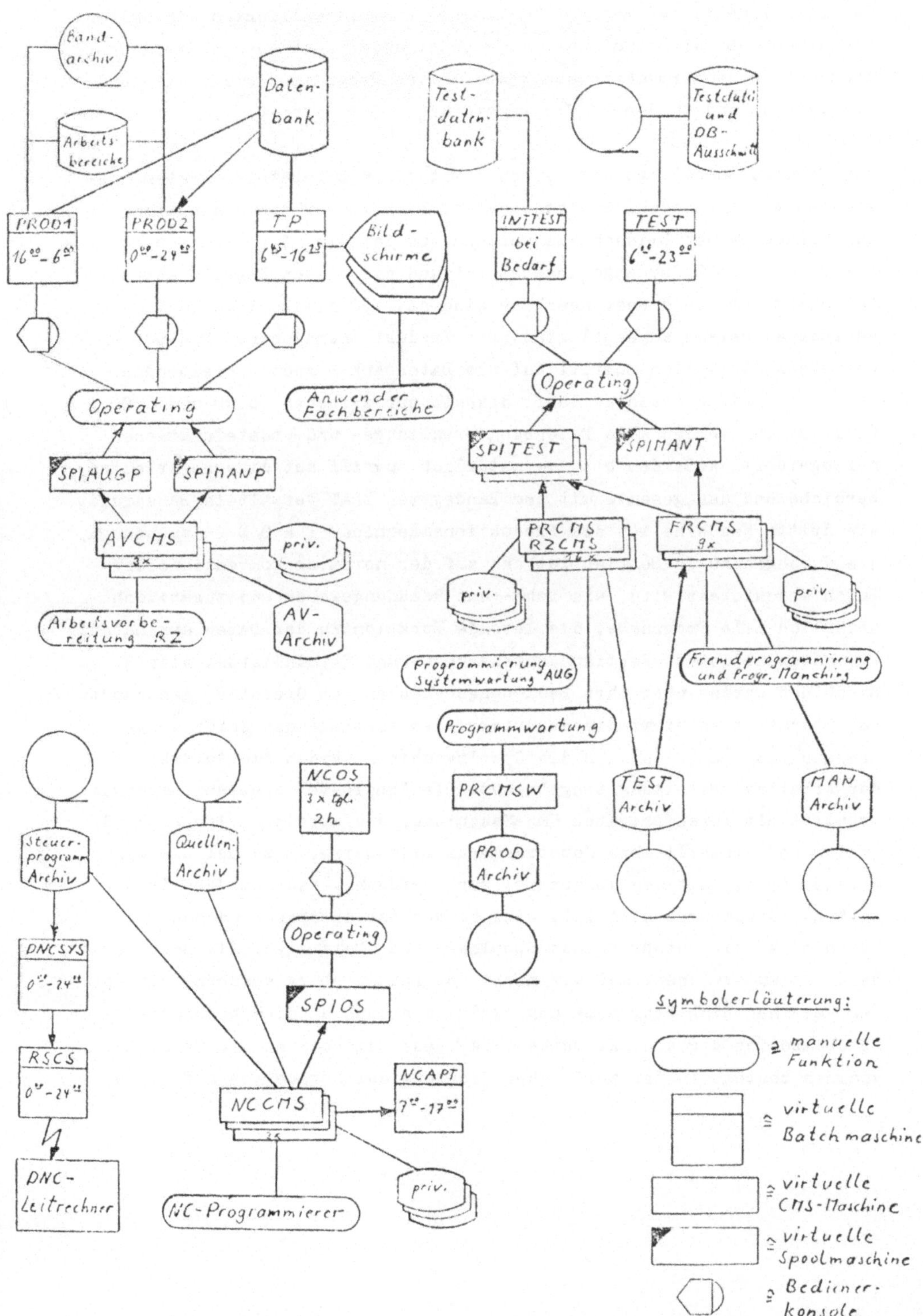

Abb. 1 Virtuelle Maschinenebene

Das funktionelle Zusammenspiel aller bei uns installierten virtuellen
Maschinen läßt sich zumindest in 3 voneinander unabhängige Bereiche
trennen, in den Produktionsbetrieb, in den Programmentwicklungs- und
Testbetrieb und in den NC-Programmierung + DNC-Betrieb.

Der Produktionsbetrieb wird durch 3 mit einem DOS-Betriebssystem ausgestattete Batchmaschinen abgewickelt. Eine dieser Maschinen dient
zur Steuerung der Bildschirmanwendung, es ist die T P - Maschine, die
von 7.00 - 16.00 Uhr angeschaltet ist und die vollen Zugriff auf die
Datenbank hat. An dieser Maschine sind ca. 150 Bildschirme in verschiedenen Werken angeschlossen. Die Produktionsmaschine P R O D 1
hat ebenfalls vollen Zugriff auf die Datenbank - auch schreibenden
Zugriff -. Diese Maschine läuft deshalb nur zwischen 16.00 und 6.00
Uhr. Auf ihr werden alle Datenbankverwaltungs- und Updatefunktionen
durchgeführt. Außerdem hat sie natürlich Zugriff auf diverse Arbeits-
bereiche und das gesamte mit dem Bandsystem EPAT verwaltete Bandarchiv.
Als dritte Maschine ist die Produktionsmaschine P R O D 2 zu nennen,
die durchgehend in Betrieb ist und auf der normaler konventioneller
Batch abgewickelt wird, wie Lohn- und Rechnungswesen und zusätzlich
natürlich alle Programme, die lesende Funktion in der Datenbank haben,
wie Materiallisten, Fertigungssteuerungs- und Terminlisten. Alle 3
Maschinen werden über ihre Bedienungskonsolen vom Operating gesteuert.
Das Operating entnimmt die abzuwickelnden Aufträge den dafür vorgesehenen Spoolmaschinen. In die Spoolmaschinen werden die Aufträge von
der Arbeitsvorbereitung eingebracht. Die Arbeitsvorbereitung wiederum
arbeitet mit ihren privaten CMS-Maschinen; sie arbeitet also am Bildschirm und erstellt ihre Jobstreams am Bildschirm. Dazu hat sie ein
eigenes Archiv mit dem Jobcontrol zur Verfügung. Nachdem jeweils ein
Auftrag zusammengestellt ist, wird er von der entsprechenden CMS-
Maschine an die entsprechende Spoolmaschine übertragen. Als Besonder-
heit ist zu erwähnen, daß wir nicht nur für Augsburg sondern auch für
das Werk Manching Programme abwickeln, die dann an eine besondere
Spoolmaschine abgeschickt werden. Der wesentliche Sinn der Spoolmaschinen besteht in der zeitlichen Trennung der Abgabe von Aufträgen

durch die Arbeitsvorbereitung und der Durchführung der Aufträge durch
das Operating. Ein weiterer Sinn besteht in der räumlichen Trennung
der Funktionen Arbeitsvorbereitung und Operating, denn das Übertragen
von den Räumen der Arbeitsvorbereitung in den Maschinensaal geschieht
ja auf maschinellem Wege.

Ich komme nun zum Programmentwicklungs- und Testbetrieb. Im wesentlichen wird der Testbetrieb abgewickelt auf 2 ebenfalls vom Operating
bedienten Batchmaschinen, der Testmaschine T E S T und der Integrationstestmaschine I N T T E S T . Die Testmaschine ist fast ständig
in Betrieb. Auf ihr werden in 2 Partitions parallel zueinander Tests
durchgeführt und in der 3. Partition werden Dialogtests durchgeführt.
Für die Zeit dieser Dialogtests werden entsprechende Bildschirme in
den Räumen der Programmierung an die Maschine virtuell angeschlossen.
Die Integrationstestmaschine wird bei Bedarf bei Einführung größerer
Anwendungssysteme ausgerüstet für diese speziellen Integrationstests
und dann ebenfalls bei Bedarf betrieben. Beide Maschinen haben - außer
natürlich auf die Bibliotheken - Zugriff auf Testdateien, Testdatenbank oder Ausschnitte der Testdatenbank. Diese, durch das Operating
bedienten Maschinen,werden wiederum durch entsprechende Spoolmaschinen
gefüttert, wobei hier mehrere Spoolmaschinen zur Verfügung stehen, um
z.B. Prioritätsaufträge von normalen Aufträgen zu unterscheiden. Die
Programmierung hat genauso wie die Systemwartung, die Datenbankgruppe,
die Fremdprogrammierung und die Manchinger Programmierung jeweils ihre
eigenen virtuellen CMS-Maschinen mit dem privaten Plattenbereich zur
Verfügung. Des weiteren sind 3 Archive im Zugriff, 1 Archiv für in
Produktion befindliche Programme, das nur von einer speziellen Wartungs-
gruppe in Zugriff ist, dann das Testarchiv, das für alle Augsburger
Programmierer im Zugriff ist und 1 Archiv für die Manchinger Programmierung.

Nun zum NC-Programmier- und DNC-Betrieb. Die in unserem Hause tätigen
NC-Programmierer haben ebenfalls wieder ihre privaten CMS-Maschinen,
auf denen sie ihre in APT-AC geschriebenen Programme entwickeln. Für
eine APT-Compilierung wird eine NC-APT-Batchmaschine benutzt, in der

der APT-Compiler zur Verfügung steht. Dieses ist die erste Batchmaschine, die nicht vom Operating bedient wird sondern direkt von
den NC-Programmierern gefüttert werden kann. Wir haben hier das
Operating nicht eingeschaltet, weil wir aufgrund der dort statt-
findenden Arbeiten keine Beeinträchtigung einer gleichmäßigen Ma-
schinenauslastung befürchten mußten. Hier stehen wiederum 2 Archive
zur Verfügung, das Quellenarchiv für die APT-Source-Programme und
das Steuerarchiv, in dem die von den Postprozessoren erstellten
Steuerprogramme für die NC-Maschinen gespeichert sind. Diese Steuerprogramme werden von einem DNC-Leitrechner abgerufen, und zwar auf
dem Wege über 2 virtuelle Batchmaschinen. Die DNC-SYS-Batchmaschine
liest auf Anforderung die entsprechenden Programme aus dem Archiv
und gibt sie an die RSCS-Maschine weiter. Die RSCS-Batchmaschine ist
ein spezielles IBM-System, das dazu dient, eine Datenfernübertragung an
den DNC-Leitrechner zu ermöglichen, der in einer anderen Halle steht.

3. Hilfsmittel zur Bewertung und Kontrolle des Betriebes

Ausfallursachenreport

Der monatlich aufgestellte und in dem Monatsbericht eingefügte Ausfallursachenreport (Abb. 2) enthält Ausfall- und Wiederholzeiten nach Ursachen gruppiert in Form einer Matrix. Der Report entsteht aus täglich manuell erstellten Abbruchzetteln, die in einer Produktionsbesprechungsrunde erstellt werden.

Ursache	Anzahl System-Ausfälle	System-ausfall-zeit (h)	Anzahl TP-Abbrüche	TP-Ausfall-zeit(h)	Anzahl Verlust-zeiten	Verlust-zeiten (h)	Gesamt-Anzahl
HW	10	4,4	6	2,0	10	51,0	11
HT							
OP			1	0,25			1
BS	7	2,25	7	2,5	7	21,5	7
DS							1
AV							1
PR			1	0,75	8	23,0	12
FA							1
DE							1
Summe	17	* 6,66	15	* 5,45	25	* 95,5	35

* übertragen in Betriebsdatenblatt

HW = Hardwarefehler
HT = Haustechnik (Klima, Strom)
OP = Bedienungsfehler
BS = Betriebssoftwarefehler

DS = Datenbanksoftwarefehler (incl. GENA)
AV = Jobcontrol bzw.Einsteuerungsfehler
PR = Programm-/Datenfehler
FA = Fachabt.fehler
DE = Datenerfassung

Abb.2 Ausfallursachenreport

Online-Verfügbarkeit

Diese Grafik entsteht ebenfalls aus den Abbruchzetteln und Stör-
meldungen der Anwender. Sie ist nach Standorten und Anwendungsgebieten gegliedert und zeigt die Verfügbarkeit auf Wochen- und
Monatsbasis.

VM-Accounting

Diese Auswertung entsteht maschinell aus dem VM-Accounting und
zeigt Anschaltzeiten, CPU-Zeiten, SIO's usw. für jede virtuelle
Maschine (Listbild siehe Anhang).

Fakturierung der RZ-Leistungen

Bei Online-Anwendungen, die bei uns in etwa 50 % der gesamten Produktion ausmachen, wird nach Transaktionspreisen fakturiert. Die
Fakturierung wird maschinell erstellt aufgrund vom TP-Monitor ge-
lieferter Angaben und Auswertung durch selbst erstellte Programme.
Die Batchproduktion, der Test und NC-Betrieb werden nach CPU-Nutzung
fakturiert. Die dafür notwendigen Angaben entstehen sowohl aus VM-
Accounting als auch aus GRASP-Auswertung. Dabei werden die Preise
für Online-Anwendungen als ein Summenbetrag unter der Bezeichnung
FEMAT ausgewiesen. Die Aufschlüsselung dieses Betrages nach Bild-
schirm und Transaktion wird gesondert ausgewiesen (Listbilder siehe
Anhang).

Grafik-Monitor

Dieser Grafik-Monitor ist ein IBM-Produkt. Es gibt in Minutenrhythmus
auf einem Bildschirm relevante Daten über den VM-Betrieb aus, z.B.
Zugriffe zu einzelnen Platten, CPU-Nutzung der einzelnen virtuellen
Maschinen und von diesen Einzelmaschinen abgesetzte Start I/O's
oder Pageraten (Listbild siehe Anhang). Er ist ständig angeschaltet
und sein Bildschirm steht zur Betriebsüberwachung neben den anderen
Bedienerkonsolen.

4. Bewertung des VM 370-Nutzens

Bei der Argumentation über Für und Wider von virtuellen Betriebssystemen kommt immer wieder der sogenannte "Overhead" ins Gespräch;
wir müssen daher zuerst einmal die Größe dieses Overheads ermitteln.
Hierzu folgende Rechnung, die sich natürlich nur auf unser RZ bezieht.

Die zur Verfügung stehende 100 % CPU-Kapazität verteilt sich auf
20 % CMS und ähnliche Aktivitäten und 80 % für DOS und OS-Anwendung
in virtuellen Batchmaschinen. Das Verhältnis der User-CPU zur Be-
triebssystem-CPU in diesen virtuellen Batchmaschinen beträgt bei
uns etwa 1 : 1. Man kann also sagen, 40 % von den 100 % CPU-Kapazität werden für Betriebssystem-Aktivitäten verbraucht. Von diesen
40 % werden wiederum ca. 10 % für Paging-Aktivitäten verbraucht,
die ja das VM den DOS/VS bzw. OS-Systemen abnimmt, so daß in etwa
30 % sogenannter Overheads übrigbleiben. Was bieten diese 30 % Overhead? Was steht diesen 30 % CPU-Verlust an Nutzen gegenüber?

a) Durch den Einsatz vieler virtueller Maschinen auf einem Hardware-
   system ergeben sich Personaleinsparungen im Operating und geringerer
   Raumbedarf. Wir betreiben z.B. einen Rund-um-Betrieb unserer Anlage
   mit nur 12 Personen im Operating.

b) Durch die Möglichkeit, periphere Hardware flexibel dort zuzuordnen,
   wo der Bedarf ist, ergeben sich Einsparungen an Peripheriegeräten.

c) Durch das Konzept der nach Aufgabengebieten geteilten virtuellen
   Maschinen und der damit quasi programmierten und maschinell kon-
   trollierten funktionalen Trennung ergibt sich erhöhte Sicherheit
   in der Verarbeitung.

d) Die Verfügbarkeit der Online-Anwendungen wird erhöht. Um den Online-
   Betrieb zu stören, müssen entweder die virtuelle TP-Maschine oder

die Hardware oder das VM selber zusammenbrechen. Alles andere hat
keinerlei Einfluß. Allein dieser Gesichtspunkt ergibt nach unseren
Schätzungen eine Erhöhung der Online-Verfügbarkeit von ca. 2 %,
was sehr viel ist, wenn man sich in der Gegend von 96 % bewegt.

e) Die Systemwartungsgruppe und die Datenbankgruppe haben die ganz
normale Arbeitszeit des Tages. In diesen Gruppen können fast alle
Systemarbeiten am Tage durchgeführt bzw. vorbereitet werden. Selbst
die Umstellung auf neue Releases des VM selbst kann unter dem
laufenden VM vorbereitet werden. Hierdurch ist eine wesentlich
effektivere Arbeitsweise mit diesen beiden Gruppen gewährleistet,
was wiederum zu Personaleinsparungen führt.

Wir glauben, daß die anfallenden 30 % Overhead durch VM durch die
eben genannten Vorteile voll ausgeglichen werden. Aber es gibt
noch andere Aspekte, die die Verwendung von VM-Systemen zum Teil
sogar erzwingen. So z.B. der Bedarf DOS und OS-Betriebssysteme
parallel gleichzeitig zu betreiben. Eine Notwendigkeit, die bei
uns ebenfalls gegeben ist. Des weiteren ist zu erwähnen die Flexibilität bei Einführung neuer Anwendungssysteme als auch bei Umstellung von Hard- und Software.

USERID	DURATION	CPU-TIME	V.CPU-TIME	PAGES	PAGERAT	SIO	PUNCH	LINES	READER
OOSPRD1	432,0491	97,5226	42,0381	200.553	0,12	28.689.787	267.015	714.608	152.35
OOSPRD2	439,5916	126,5913	63,2313	220.820	0,13	34.533.524	33.737	892.264	128.83
OOSTPMT	219,4478	54,5873	23,4295	228.299	0,28	14.852.892	0	614.243	183.84
	1091,0885	278,7012	128,6989	649.672	0,16	78.076.203	300.752	2.221.115	465.03
RARVM	1,8299	0,1200	0,0267	869	0,13	100.146	0	2.478	
RCMS91	23,0791	0,0956	0,0196	13.229	0,15	19.866	33.492	3.015	7.55
RCMS92	132,2647	0,3050	0,0646	34.267	0,07	31.540	40.199	15.309	1
RCMS93	178,0808	0,2483	0,0642	29.382	0,04	57.640	110.307	20.838	7.11
RCMS94	1,1462	0,0036	0,0004	748	0,18	489	0	159	
RCMS96	25,0000	0,2568	0,1149	12.464	0,13	89.566	137.221	1.375	
RCMS98	41,0769	0,1576	0,0483	22.810	0,15	41.936	37.752	2.092	61
RCMS99	65,9082	0,3668	0,1328	39.515	0,16	120.184	106.301	1.045	2.72
	468,3858	1,5537	0,4715	153.284	0,09	461.417	465.272	46.311	18.03
ICAPT	428,8827	0,0045	0,0001	3.077	0,00	1.351	0	0	39
ICARVQ	8,1291	1,5159	0,7152	3.992	0,13	717.195	0	44.135	
ICARVS	1,8045	0,2648	0,0976	1.590	0,24	144.580	0	6.965	
ICCMSA	141,3964	2,2437	1,2113	100.696	0,19	546.031	55.393	585.549	20.00
ICCMSB	123,4610	0,9378	0,3144	74.415	0,16	344.965	102.098	24.612	32.31
ICCMSC	91,3399	0,7989	0,2440	77.939	0,23	293.731	68.159	16.978	2.04
ICCMSS	28,2356	0,3908	0,1052	40.352	0,39	125.380	31.619	28.021	56
ICDNCSYS	389,0538	0,1655	0,0540	9.466	0,00	27.650	0	65.796	60
ICOS	275,8701	9,4322	6,0864	532.144	0,53	1.082.327	80.856	2.087.571	236.37
ICRSCS	333,8112	3,8809	0,8750	506.903	0,42	1.703.846	75.430	1.353	
	1821,9843	19,6350	9,7032	1.350.574	0,20	4.987.056	413.555	2.860.980	292.30
RARCHIV	14,6347	2,1043	0,6213	2.065	0,03	1.631.053	0	36.188	15
RARVPRD	1,5886	0,0121	0,0001	712	0,12	3.487	0	0	
RCMS	93,2650	0,1280	0,0356	15.071	0,04	29.625	12.374	9.347	43
RCMSIN	26,3799	0,0049	0,0006	1.067	0,01	799	383	0	
PCMSW01	17,0212	0,1213	0,0494	12.691	0,20	29.010	1.137	2.226	
RCMS10	14,4084	0,0253	0,0053	4.190	0,08	4.621	779	1.950	25
RCMS11	127,3443	0,5839	0,1923	49.333	0,10	186.857	97.820	34.772	25.65
RCMS12	15,8828	0,1770	0,0580	12.569	0,21	65.292	49.902	2.152	9.95
RCMS13	25,4869	0,6600	0,2661	41.262	0,44	245.566	207.666	50.232	
RCMS14	163,0569	0,3386	0,0902	36.834	0,06	63.384	7.703	9.621	4.55
RCMS20	175,0058	0,5430	0,1730	53.066	0,08	128.878	41.823	137.931	2.11

MONATLICHE COMPUTERBELASTUNG IN DM   - P R O D U K T I O N -

BEGIN DATE - 02/10/78
END DATE   - 31/10/78

RUN DATE - 08/11/78
PAGE 019

DIE RECHNERKOSTEN DER LISTE BASIEREN AUF DREI KOSTENEINHEITEN:
   1. DM 1400,00 PRO CPU-STUNDE
   2. DM 0,12 PRO ANZEIGE-EINGABE FEMAT
   3. DM 0,50 PRO VERWALTUNGS-EINGABE FEMAT
DIE CPU-ZEITANGABE IST AUFGRUND DER DURCH DAS BETRIEBSSYSTEM
VORGEGEBENEN MESSMETHODE UM DEN FAKTOR 0,57 ZU KLEIN.

GRUPPEN	BEZEICHNUNG	VERWEILZT. HH.MM.SS	CPU-ZEIT HH.MM.SS.	CPU-BETRAG DM	GESAMTBETRAG DM	KOSTEN %
FF11						
F	FERTIGUNG					
F1	FERTIGUNGSPLANUNG	01.27.28	00.23.17	953.08	958.29	.193
F7	F E M A T			.00	55,868.36	11.278
F	FERTIGUNG	01.27.28	00.23.17	953.08	56,826.65	11.471
K	KCNSTRUKTION					
K3	STUECKLISTENWESEN	14.14.44	03.13.26	8,122.58	8,130.07	1.639
K5		00.04.55	00.02.46	113.25	113.25	.023
K	KONSTRUKTION	14.19.39	03.21.12	8,235.83	8,243.32	1.662
M	MATERIALWIRTSCHAFT					
M2	MATERIALBESTANDSFHRG	00.03.26	00.00.31	21.15	21.15	.004
M	MATERIALWIRTSCHAFT	00.03.26	00.00.31	21.15	21.15	.004
N	NC-TECHNIK					
N2	TEILEPROGRAMMIERUNG			.00	13,368.74	2.701
N3	NC-SOFTWARE			.00	6,594.56	1.332
N	NC-TECHNIK			.00	19,963.30	4.033
R	RECHNUNGSWESEN					
R5	ANGEBOTS-/AUFTRAGSW.	02.10.01	01.28.30	3,622.59	3,623.73	.732
R	RECHNUNGSWESEN	02.10.01	01.28.30	3,622.59	3,623.73	.732
FF11	P R O D U K T I O N	18.00.34	05.13.30	12,832.65	88,678.15	17.902
FF11	T E S T	06.51.40	02.09.34	5,303.60	5,358.80	5.027

Abb. 2 RZ-Leistungen für die Hauptabteilung FF11

```
T R A N S A K T I O N S K O S T E N   PRO   B I L D S C H I R M
    ZEITRAUM: 02.11.78 - 30.11.78

 LISTE FUER HERRN HALLER

    LISTE FUER FOLGENDE BILDSCHIRME:
    ALLE BILDSCHIRME
```

BS-NR.	PROGR.	KOSTEN/TRAN.	ANZAHL-TRAN.	KOSTEN S
001	START	12	195	23,40
001	ALPHA	12	41	4,92
001	TSS-A	12	35	4,20
001	TSS-V	50	7	3,50
001	ESK-A	12	5	0,60
001	ESF-A	12	37	4,44
001	TVK-A	12	6	0,72
001	ESF-V	50	3	1,50
001	LAB-V	50	6	3,00
001	LAB-A	12	648	77,76
001	AMW-A	12	2	0,24
001	EEW-V	50	102	51,00
001	BEW-A	12	54	6,48
001	TAGB-B	50	2	1,00
				182,76 *
002	START	12	1124	134,88
002	ALPHA	12	138	16,56
002	AFO-A	12	1	0,12
002	LAB-V	50	571	285,50
002	LAB-A	12	1680	201,60
002	AMW-A	12	2	0,24
002	BEW-V	50	4443	2221,50
002	BEW-A	12	495	59,40
002	WE-V	50	1	0,50

Abb. 3 Kosten für Online-Anwendung an Bildschirm Nr. 1 und Nr. 2

130

USERID	VIRT	SUPR	PGRD	PGWR	VSIO
RZCMSS	2	8	8	1	27
DOSTPMT	*147	181	0	0	1975
DOSPRO1	*I		26	0	096
AVCMS2	0	2	8	0	0
NCAPT	I		25	0	18
HCOPY	0	1	1	2	0
AVCMS	1	5	2	2	10
PPCMS10	I		18	0	25
NCCMSB	0	1	6	0	15
PRCMS22	0	1	5	0	0
NCCMSC	1	5	6	35	0
RSCS	1	5	1	0	69
MAINT	0	2	17	11	0
RZCMSG3	2	8	29	10	114

USERID	VIRT	SUPR	PGRD	PGWR	VSIO
OPERATNS	I		15	0	16
OPERATOR	I		26	0	1
DOSPRO2	* 3	9	16	1	53
PRCMS23	I		25	0	23
DNCSYS	I		4	0	15
HCPRT	0	1	1	1	0
AVCMS3	I		10	0	19
RZCMSG2	I		5	0	79
PRCMS14	I		24	0	17
FRCMS93	I		26	0	17
RZDOSI01	*I		12	0	150
RZDOST01	* 138	266	0	6	2847
NCCMSA	34	47	5	6	782

ADR	VOLSER	SIOCNT	ADR	VOLSER	SIOCNT	ADR	VOLSER	SIOCNT	ADR	VOLSER	SIOCNT
140	D34TP1	175	141	DB015A	114	142	DB001A	14	143	DB005A	16
144	DB009A	1	145	DB013A	14	146	WORK26	0	147	DB020A	17
142	DB002A	502	143	DB006A	185	144	DB010A	218	145	DB018A	2
146	DB002X	0	147	DB017A	17	14A	DB003A	69	14B	DB007A	0
14C	DB011A	0	14D	DB012A	0	14E	DB005X	0	14F	WORK29	4
142	DB004A	14	143	DB008A	24	144	DB016A	7	145	DB014A	25
146	DB006X	0	147	DB019A	26	240	VMRS41	56	241	DBWRK2	0
242	D34P11	0	243	DB012X	0	244	DB011X	0	245	DB012Y	0
246	DSRES2	0	247	D34TS1	0	242	D34P12	0	243	DB010Y	0
244	DB011Y	0	245	DB017X	0	246	DSRES1	0	247	DB014X	0
24A	D34PR3	0	24B	D34RS4	0	24C	VMRES7	26	24D	D34TS3	0
24E	VMRES6	29	24F	D34RS1	0	242	VMRES2	21	243	VMRES3	21
244	DB01CX	0	245	INTTST	0	246	TEST01	0	247	D34RS2	0
340	WORK31	0	341	DBWRK1	0	342	WORK97	0	343	WORK98	0
344	DB019X	0	345	WORK05	0	346	DB021A	53	347	WORK66	0
342	VMRES4	27	343	VMRES5	30	344	TEST03	0	345	D34PR3	0
346	DB0C4X	0	347	D34SY1	0	34A	DB021Y	3254	34B	WORK96	0
34C	D34IN1	0	34D	VMRES8	0	34E	DB016X	0	34F	D34TS2	0
342	DB017Y	0	343	DB018Y	16	344	D34IN2	0	345	WORK95	0
346	D34TP2	0	347	D34P21	3	580		0	581		0
582		0	583		0	584		0	585		0
586		0	587		0						

Abb. 4 Grafik-Monitor (Aktivitäten der virtuellen Maschinen, SIO's auf Platten und Bänder)

```
  DATE     TIME
01/25/79  07:34  UUUUUUUU                              ***IhWWWhW
01/25/79  C7:35  UUUUUUUJUU                           **IWWWhW
01/25/79  C7:36  UUUUUUUU                           **IWWhhWWWhW
01/25/79  07:37  UJUUU                            *IIIIIIhWWWdWWWhWWWdWW
01/25/79  C7:38  UUUJUJUU                           ************II I I
01/25/79  C7:40  UUUJUU                         ******IIIIIIIIIIIIWWhW
01/25/79  C7:41  UJUU                          *IIWhWWWWWWhhhWWhWWWWhhhWWWha
01/25/79  C7:42  UUU                           **IIIIWhhhWWWdWWWhhhWWWWW
01/25/79  C7:43  UUUUUU                            *IIIIIIIIIWWW
01/25/79  C7:44  UUUUUUUJU                           IIIIIIIIII
01/25/79  07:45  UUUJUUUUJUUUU                          IIIIII
01/25/79  07:46  UUUUUUUUUJJUUUU                         *IIIII
01/25/79  C7:47  UUUUJUUU                         ***IIIIIIWWWWWhhW
01/25/79  C7:48  UUUUUU                          ***IhhWWWhhWWWhW
01/25/79  07:49  UUUU                           *IWhWWWWWWWhhhWWWW
01/25/79  C7:50  UUUU                           *IIhWWWWWWWhhWWWWWW
01/25/79  C7:51  UUU                            IIIIIIIhWWWhhhWhW
01/25/79  07:52  UJUU                           IIIIIWWWWWhWWWWWhWW
01/25/79  C7:53  UUUU                           IWWWWWWWhWWWdhW
01/25/79  07:54  UUUUU                         IIWWWWWhWWWWWWWhWWWWWWW
01/25/79  07:56  UUUUU                        *IhhhhhWhWWWWWWhhhWWWWWWWWhWWWWW
01/25/79  C7:57  UUUJUUUJUU                     ***IIIIIIIWWWWWWWWhW
01/25/79  C7:58  UUUJUUUUJJ                    *IIIIhWhWWhhWWWWWWWhhhWWhW
01/25/79  C7:59  UJUUJUUUJU                     **IIIIIIIIIIhWWWW
01/25/79  C8:00  UUUUUUUJUU                      IIIWWWWWWhhWWWhW
01/25/79  C8:01  UUUUUUUJUU                       *IIIIhWWWWWhhWWWWW
01/25/79  C8:02  UUUUUUUJU                     *IIIIIIIWWhhhWWWWWWWWhhWWWWW
01/25/79  08:03  UUUUJUUUU                     *IIIIWWWWWhWhWWWWWWWWhhhWWWW
01/25/79  C8:04  UUUUUUJUU                      **IIIWWWhhhWWWWWWWWhhWWWWW
01/25/79  C8:05  UUUJUUUUJU                       **IIIhWWWhhWWWWhW
```

Abb. 5 Grafik-Monitor (CPU-Auslastung)

PRAKTISCHE ERFAHRUNGEN BEIM EINSATZ DER VIRTUELLEN MASCHINEN
IN DER INFORMATIK-AUSBILDUNG UND -FORSCHUNG

Heinz Seidlitz
Fachbereich Informatik
Technische Universität Berlin

Zusammenfassung:

Es wird über die Erfahrungen berichtet, die in den Jahren von 1970 bis
1978 mit dem Betriebssystem VM/370 (zuerst CP/67) in Berlin in der
Informatik-Ausbildung und -Forschung gesammelt wurden.

1. Einleitung

Im Rahmen des Überregionalen Forschungsprogramms Informatik wurde der
Technischen Universität Berlin im Jahre 1969 eine IBM 360-67 bewilligt.
Mit dieser Anlage sollte das Forschungsprogramm sowie der neu zu gründen-
de Studiengang Informatik mit Rechenkapazität versorgt werden.

Die IBM 360-67 ist eine 360-65, die über die zusätzliche Hardware zur
Adressenumrechnung verfügt. Man leistete sich den damit verbundenen finan-
ziellen Mehraufwand, da das Betriebssystem CP/67 mit dem Konzept der virtuellen Maschinen verwendet werden sollte. Obwohl dieses Betriebssystem
damals noch nicht über die Stabilität und den Komfort des heutigen
VM/370 verfügte, überzeugte das Konzept so, daß es noch heute im Einsatz
ist. Die heutige Konfiguration der Anlage zeigt Abb. 1.

2. Das Konzept der virtuellen Maschine

Während normale Dialogbetriebssysteme für den Teilnehmerbetrieb jedem
Benutzer eine "Benutzerschnittstelle" verfügbar machen, stellt ein Betriebssystem mit dem Konzept der virtuellen Maschine dem Benutzer eine
leere Maschine, d. h. die "Hardwareschnittstelle" zur Verfügung. Das ist
eine sehr wichtige Sache für die Benutzer, die wirklich eine leere Maschine brauchen, weil sie z. B. ein Betriebssystem entwickeln oder
testen wollen.

Ca. 90 % unserer·Benutzer brauchen dieses Werkzeug nicht. Sie erledigen Arbeiten, die man auch an der Benutzerschnittstelle durchführen kann. Ja, sie benötigen sogar diese Benutzerschnittstelle, weil sie nicht auf die Unterstützung eines Betriebssystems verzichten können oder wollen. Sogar derjenige, der das Konzept der virtuellen Maschine benutzt, verwendet für die Vorbereitungen seiner Arbeit die Benutzerschnittstelle.

Die Ausbreitung dieses Betriebssystems erfolgte in den ersten Jahren sehr zögernd, weil die Verwendung dieses aufwendigen Hilfsmittels den Preis der Computerleistung erheblich verteuerte.

Der Mehraufwand liegt im Prinzip der virtuellen Maschine: Das Betriebssystem, welches der Benutzer in der virtuellen Maschine verwendet, ist für eine reale Maschine geschaffen worden. Das bedeutet, daß es z. B. bei einem Startvorgang alle Informationen aufbereitet und geprüft an die Hardware übergibt. Hier gehen diese fertigen Unterlagen an den Steuerteil des VM/370 und werden noch einmal transformiert. Privilegierte Operationen führen, da das Betriebssystem der virtuellen Maschine im Problemstatus läuft, grundsätzlich zu einem Programm-Interrupt. Hinzu kommt der Aufwand, den der virtuelle Speicher erfordert. - Das alles hat einen hohen Preis in Bezug auf die Performance.

VM/370 konnte sich überhaupt nur durchsetzen, weil das CMS nach einigen Jahren grundsätzlich verändert wurde. CMS hörte auf, ein selbständiges Betriebssystem zu sein und war nur noch zusammen mit dem CP-Teil des VM/370 verwendbar. Damit war der Weg frei, CMS so zu gestalten, daß ein großer Teil der oben beschriebenen Doppelarbeit vermieden werden konnte.

Über die Diagnose-Instruktion, die sonst in der virtuellen Maschine keinerlei Bedeutung hat und als "Hypervisor-Call" benutzt wird, kann sich CMS direkt mit dem CP-Teil des VM/370 kurzschließen. Die Diagnose-Instruktion liefert dem CP-Teil einen Code, aus dem entnommen werden kann, welche Unterstützung vom CP gefordert wird.

Durch diese und weitere Maßnahmen wurde die Performance so verbessert, daß VM/370 auch für normale Anwender diskutabel wurde, und sich schneller als zu Anfang verbreitete.

3. Vorteile für den Betrieb

Außer den Benutzern, die wirklich die leere Maschine brauchen, ist die
Betriebsgruppe der Hauptnutznießer dieses Konzeptes. Für Systemarbeiten,
die eine leere Maschine erfordern und an anderen Rechenzentren am Wochen-
ende durchgeführt werden müssen, nimmt man im Falle des VM/370 einfach
eine leere virtuelle Maschine. Fast alle Arbeiten lassen sich so parallel
zum normalen Betrieb ausführen, insbesondere alle Generierungsarbeiten.

Für uns in Berlin ist diese Möglichkeit auch deshalb so wichtig, weil wir
auf Grund unserer bunt gemixten Hardware nicht ohne Änderungen im System
auskommen.

Da wir ungefähr 30 verschiedene Compiler anbieten, muß man immer damit
rechnen, daß in der neuen Version des Betriebssystems der eine oder andere Compiler nicht mehr läuft. Bis die entsprechenden Probleme beseitigt
sind, wird in solchen Fällen außer der neuen CMS-Version die alte weiter
angeboten, außer IPL CMS gibt es dann noch IPL AltCMS.

Es gehört zu den besten Eigenschaften dieses Betriebssystems, daß der
CP-Teil und das CMS konsequent voneinander getrennt sind. Das ist natürlich eine Folge des Konzeptes der virtuellen Maschine. Der Hersteller
war so weise, dieses Prinzip nicht zu verwässern bei der oben beschriebenen Performance-Verbesserung.

Von großem Vorteil für den Betrieb ist es, daß man für viele Zwecke spezielle Maschinen einrichten kann, einer sinnvollen Betriebsgestaltung
eröffnen sich so viele Möglichkeiten. Im nächsten Abschnitt wird über einige solcher Maschinen berichtet.

Man spricht so häufig davon, daß in komplizierten Systemen die Notwendigkeit einer Entkopplung der verschiedenen Teile erforderlich ist. Diese
Forderung erfüllt das Konzept der virtuellen Maschinen in großem Umfang.
Nur ein Beispiel hierfür: Jede virtuelle Maschine hat ihren eigenen Plattenplatz zur permanenten Aufbewahrung von Dateien. Das ist eine Mini-
Disk, die aus einigen Zylindern einer realen Platte besteht. Kommt es
durch Unachtsamkeit oder Fehler dazu, daß dieser Plattenplatz überläuft,
so wird von diesem Mißstand nur diese eine Maschine tangiert. Von anderen
Rechenzentren ist bekannt, daß in solchen Fällen der ganze Betrieb zusam-
menbricht.

Der Preis dieser Sicherheit: man braucht viel Plattenplatz, denn die Ausnutzung privater Bereiche ist nicht sehr gut.

Für den Betrieb sehr günstig ist die Tatsache, daß das System sehr betriebsfreundliche Zuteilungsstrategien (Recource-Management) hat. Insbesondere die mehrstufige Time-Slice-Technik ist in der Lage, sich den verschiedenen Belastungszuständen in weiten Bereichen automatisch anzupassen. Operateureingriffe sind nicht erforderlich.

4. Spezielle virtuelle Maschinen

Eine Aufzählung der wichtigsten virtuellen Maschinen, die neben den ganz normalen CMS-Benutzermaschinen benutzt werden, gibt einen guten Einblick in die Verhältnisse des Rechenzentrums.

4.1 Die VS1-Batchmaschine

Die Einrichtung der ersten Batchmaschine im Jahre 1970 (damals ein OS-MFT) hatte folgenden Grund: Den Technikern der Firma IBM reichten die damals vorhandenen Hardware-Testmöglichkeiten des CP/67 nicht aus. Sie glaubten zunächst, auf die im OS vorhandenen Testunterstützungen nicht verzichten zu können.

Nach kurzer Zeit kamen zwei neue Gesichtspunkte hinzu, die auch heute noch aktuell sind. Es gab einmal immer wieder Interessenten im Hochschulbereich, die das IBM-Batchbetriebssystem benutzen wollten oder sogar mußten, und andererseits erkannten wir bald, daß es im Dialogbetrieb sehr schwache Stunden gibt, in denen man die Anlage gern mit einer Batchlast im Hintergrund ausnutzen würde.

Das OS-System in der virtuellen Maschine wurde laufend der Entwicklung angepaßt: Aus MFT wurde MVT und schließlich VS1.

4.2 Die CMS-Batchmaschine

Das OS-System ist in den Spitzenzeiten des Tagesbetriebs nicht zu verwenden, da es auf Grund seines hohen Speicherbedarfs den Dialogbetrieb sehr stark behindert. Außerdem ist in solchen Zeiten die ohnehin schlechte Performance des Batchsystems noch wesentlich schlechter.

Man braucht jedoch für den Ausbildungsbetrieb mit den vielen kleinen Test-Jobs ein ökonomisches Batchsystem, denn wer hat so viele Datenstationen, um die 200 bis 250 Teilnehmer der Anfängerübungen an Terminals arbeiten lassen zu können? VM/370 bietet für diese Zwecke das CMS-Batchsystem. Obwohl es an diesem System sehr viel auszusetzen gibt, wird es bei uns verwendet.

Es besteht keine Notwendigkeit, sich auf eine Batchmaschine zu beschränken. Wenn es sich als zweckmäßig erweist, richten wir für verschiedene Übungen unterschiedliche Batchmaschinen ein, z. B. eine für PASCAL, eine für FORTRAN usw. Auch der CMS-Batch ist wie das CMS speziell für die Benutzung in einer virtuellen Maschine des VM/370 entwickelt und vermeidet daher den großen Performance-Verlust, wie er z. B. beim Betrieb des VS1 nicht zu vermeiden ist (außer mit V = R).

4.3 Die RSCS-Maschine (Remote Spooling Communications Subsystem)

RSCS kontrolliert die Datenfernübertragungseinrichtungen und -leitungen und ermöglicht den Datentransport zwischen Datenstationen, Batchstationen und Satellitenrechnern. RSCS hat eine eigene Operatorkonsole, an der man erforderliche Wege definieren kann. Mit geeigneten Kommandos lassen sich dann Datensätze im Rahmen der definierten Möglichkeiten wie Pakete verschicken.
Eine Hochschule, die in verschiedenen Gebäuden sitzt, ist auf solche Möglichkeiten geradezu angewiesen. Auch hier ist wieder die Möglichkeit, mehrere RSCS-Maschinen einzurichten, wenn eine Trennung in mehrere Bereiche erwünscht ist oder wenn die Antwortzeiten zu lang werden, sehr nützlich.

4.4 Die STORUS-Maschine

Weiter oben wurde ausgeführt, daß private Speicherbereiche große Vorteile haben. Aber auch wir haben nicht soviel Plattenplatz, allen Studenten, z. B. für die Arbeit an Projekten eine Minidisk zur Speicherung angefangener oder fertiger Programmteile zur Verfügung zu stellen. Von Studentischen Mitarbeitern wurde daher eine spezielle Maschine zur Speicherung solcher Daten eingerichtet.

Diese Maschine bietet eine große Sicherheit, obwohl sie öffentlich ist.
Es ist dafür gesorgt, daß nur der, der befugt ist, auf gespeicherte
Programme (über PASSWORD) zugreifen kann. Der Datentransfer wurde unter
Umgehung des SPOOL-Bereiches mit VMCF organisiert und ist dadurch be-
sonders effektiv.

4.5 Weitere spezielle Maschinen

Es gibt noch weitere virtuelle Maschinen, die hier nicht beschrieben werden.

5. Der Ausbildungsbetrieb

Wie bereits weiter oben angedeutet, wird die Anfängerausbildung im Batch-
betrieb durchgeführt. Es wäre einfach nicht möglich, zusätzlich zum normalen Betrieb 200 bis 250 weitere virtuelle Maschinen für die Übungsteilnehmer einzurichten. Zur Anwendung kommt CMS-Batch in mehreren Batchmaschinen, so daß eine Trennung nach Übungen oder verwendeten Compilern
möglich ist.

Für Übungen von Studenten höherer Semester werden so viele virtuelle Maschinen eingerichtet, wie Datenstationen im Übungsraum vorhanden sind.
Zur Zeit sind das 9 Geräte. Die Teilnehmer jeder Übung bekommen einen
solchen Satz von 9 PASSWORD's. Die Daten, die über längere Zeiten auf-
bewahrt werden müssen, werden der STORUS-Maschine übergeben.

Es kommt vor, daß in einer Übung ein sehr uneffektiver Versuchs-Compiler
verwendet werden soll. Gleichzeitige Compilationen in mehreren virtuellen Maschinen führen zu sehr langen Antwortzeiten. In solchen Fällen dürfen die Übungsteilnehmer in ihren Übungsmaschinen nur die EDIT-Arbeiten
ausführen. Zur Compilation wird das Programm in eine besondere Compi-
lationsmaschine übertragen. Auf diese Weise wird sichergestellt, daß der
uneffektive Compiler gleichzeitig nur in _einer_ virtuellen Maschine betrieben wird.

Eine direkte Anwendung der virtuellen Maschinen waren Projektarbeiten,
die die Entwicklung von   Übungsbetriebssystemen zum Ziel hatten.

Für die Vorbereitung des Übungsbetriebes ist die EXEC-Sprache von besonderer Bedeutung. Mit dieser Sprache lassen sich ganze Sequenzen von System-Kommandos zu einem einzigen Kommando zusammenfassen. Die Übergabe von Parametern, bedingte Sprünge nach vorn und hinten sind möglich.

6. Der Forschungsbetrieb

Es gibt eine Anzahl von Gründen, die die Verbreitung des Systems VM/370 begünstigt haben, ohne daß diese Gründe direkt im Konzept enthalten sind. Gemeint sind z. B. die gute Kommandosprache des VM/370, das sehr handliche File-Management und der sichere Betrieb. Von diesen Eigenschaften hat der Forschungsbetrieb ganz allgemein profitiert.

Auf der anderen Seite muß man auch auf Umstände hinweisen, die es dem Forschenden verleidet haben, die virtuelle Maschine zu verwenden.

Die leere virtuelle Maschine, wie sie VM/370 liefert, ist eine IBM 360 oder 370 mit der diesen Maschinen eigenen Architektur. Die ASSEMBLER-Programmierung mit ihren recht komplizierten und teilweise hinterlistigen Adressierungsverfahren wird von vielen Informatikern als sehr benutzerunfreundlich empfunden und erschwert damit den Leuten den Einstieg.

In unserem Fall in Berlin sah das so aus, daß sich die Forschungsgruppe Betriebssysteme lieber eine PDP 11/40 anschaffte und begann, auf dieser Anlage ein Forschungsbetriebssystem zu entwickeln.

Gewisse Aktivitäten der Betriebsgruppe selbst kann man unter diesem Punkt auflisten. Heute sind Software-Monitoren zur Überwachung des Betriebssystems, die man entweder vom Hersteller selbst oder von Softwarehäusern bekommt, sehr verbreitet. Wir haben bereits vor Jahren erkannt, daß eine virtuelle Maschine für solche Aufgaben sehr geeignet ist. Entsprechende Programme für eine Überwachungsmaschine wurden entwickelt. Auf diese Weise konnten Erkenntnisse gewonnen werden, die es erlaubten, den Nutzen von bestimmten Hardwareerweiterungen recht genau vorherzusagen.

7. Schlußbemerkungen

Wenn man abschließend fragt, ob VM/370 das richtige Betriebssystem für die Informatik-Forschung und -Ausbildung ist, so kann man diese Frage vom Standpunkt der Betriebsgruppe bejahen. Wir sind der Meinung, daß es mit keinem anderen der üblichen Betriebssysteme möglich gewesen wäre, eine so flexible und sichere Versorgung mit Rechnerleistung anzubieten.

Einige Einschränkungen sollte man jedoch machen:

1. Zu Anfang, d. h. von 1970 - 74 war der Hardwarepreis für die gebotenen Möglichkeiten sehr hoch. Heute gilt diese Einschränkung nicht mehr.

2. Die Verwendung der leeren Maschine wird sehr stark erschwert durch die benutzerunfreundliche Architektur, genauer durch die sich daraus ergebende Befehlsstruktur.

3. Auch heute noch ist der CMS-Batch so dürftig, daß er ohne Änderungen kaum verwendbar ist.

Eine interessante Weiterentwicklungsrichtung sei zum Schluß noch erwähnt: Immer mehr Funktionen des CP-Teils des VM/370 werden in die Mikroprogrammebene verlegt. Damit ist es möglich geworden, VM/370 auch auf relativ kleinen Anlagen zu fahren. Größere Anlagen werden entsprechend leistungsfähiger.

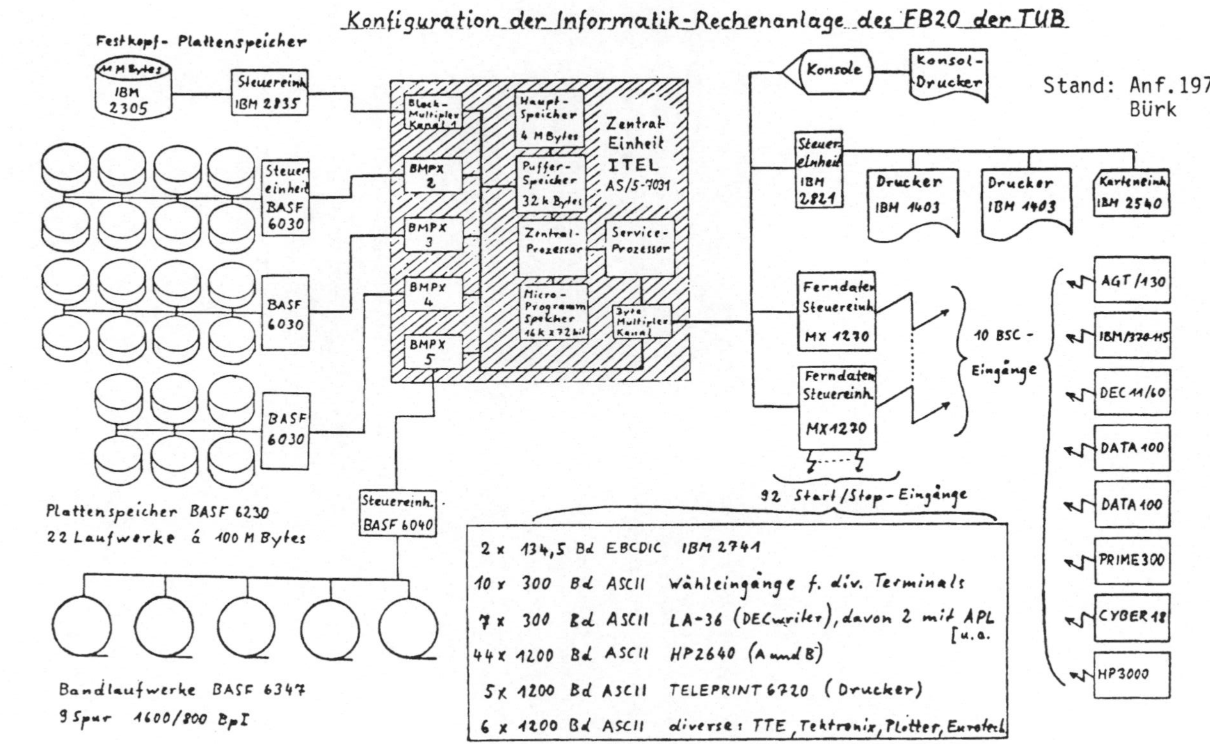

Abbildung 1: Konfiguration der Informatik-Rechenanlage der Techn. Universität Berlin

PERFORMANCE OF A VIRTUAL MACHINE MONITOR

Stanley C. Vestal, Honeywell Inc., Bloomington
Raymond A. Liuzzi, U. S. Air Force, Griffiss Air Force Base
Dr. Harold Schwenk and Allan Levy, BGS Systems Inc., Lincoln

GOALS AND HISTORY

This paper describes the performance of a Virtual Machine Monitor. A
Virtual Machine Monitor (VMM) is an operating system which executes on
the native hardware and allows other (standard) operating systems to
execute in an environment much like the environment an operating system
provides for user programs. These sub-operating systems are called
virtual machines, or VMs. A VM looks to its contained operating system
much like the actual machine looks to the VMM.

While the VMM is aware of the actual hardware complement available, a
VM is aware of only the hardware (or simulated hardware in the case of
some peripherals) provided to it by the VMM. By providing these virtual
environments, a single hardware base can be used by a number of different
standard and nonstandard operating systems.

The values of such an arrangement are many, particularly in an environment which engages in research on operating systems. A standard production service can be provided concurrently with an experimental or low-use
service. Thus, the need for off-hour scheduling of machine time and
interrupted service for boot and re-boot can be reduced.

VMM Research in Honeywell and the industry (particularly by IBM: VM/370)
has a long history [0]. Honeywell's interest in VM's began in the early
1970's as a strategy for porduct line unification and to provide more
flexible internal use of computer equipment.

Interest at Rome Air Development Center (RADC) began in approximately 1974
with an intense look at the security aspects of providing isolated environments for operating systems separated from each other by hardware enforced
boundaries. This led to a study of the GCOS Environment Simulator or
GCOS encapsulation on Multics [1]. This tool, though not as powerful
conceptually as the VMM, is currently in use at RADC.

In 1975, RADC initiated an effort with Harvard University for research in
the area of virtual machines. This led to the developemnt of an experimental virtual machine monitor for a PDP11/40 mini-computer. A technical
report by Gagliardi and Jain [2] describes a virtual system that allows

The research described in this paper was partially supported by the
United States Air Force, Rome Air Development Center (RADC) under contract
number F30602-77-C-0097.

virtual machines executing on the PDP-11 to utilize the I/O devices available on a DEC System-10.

Following this study RADC initiated three additional virtual machine studies. First in 1976, RADC entered into negotiations with Honeywell's Federal Systems Operations to procure a VMM for study at RADC [3]. This led to the installation of the VMM at RADC in 1976.

Second, a further study with Harvard University [4] was initiated in 1977 to examine the effects of virtualization techniques in a debugging environment. This effort has led to debugging specifications, with virtual techniques, that allow a user to obtain extensive snapshots of the state of a complex software system.

RADC initiated a third study in 1977 with MIT University to investigate the development of a software programming environment using virtual machine technology as an integrating tool. This study, under the direction of Madnick and Lam [5], has led to the development of an approach for integrating existing, often incompatible systems by using virtual machines.

The effort described in this paper was initiated when the Honeywell VMM was installed and examined at RADC by Honeywell's Systems and Research Center. This main objective was to study a VMM's performance under typical operating systems loads and to locate bottlenecks known to exist in two primary operating systems GCOS and MULTICS. A further objective was to explore the benefits of virtual machine techniques for Air Force applications. The findings of this task constitute a detailed analysis of the performance of the Honeywell VMM and suggestions for its improvement.

In order to perform this task, a model of the VMM performance was constructed by BGS Systems Inc, using the proprietary modelling package BEST/1$_{TM}$.

The remainder of this paper contains a summary and conclusions of the experiments; description of the means used to collect data; an analysis of the data collected; plans for the evolution of the VMM including recommendations for extending its functionality; and suggestions for further research.

SUMMARY OF RESULTS

Results based on live data experiments and the BEST/1$_{tm}$ analysis show the following:

- o VMM overhead has its greatest effect on work loads exhibiting an intermediate amount of I/O activity (15 to 35 connects per second of processor busy time).

- o For work loads with a small amount of I/O activity, VMM has only a minor effect on performance. With large amounts of I/O, contention at the I/O devices is the limiting factor.

o   In GCOS, the VMM overhead was determined to be in the range of
    15 to 28 percent depending upon the I/O mix. This results in an
    overhead of 3.5 percent of processor busy time and 4.5 msec of
    overhead per connect.

o   In Multics, the VMM overhead was determined to be between 13 and
    60 percent. These higher figures are due to the increased
    dependence of Multics on I/O activity to process page faults.

Based on these figures and the insufficiency of data (particularly in the
Multics case), it can be observed that VMM overhead is directly related
to I/O activity. Thus, any further work on the performance of this VMM
should concentrate on I/O monitoring and speedup.

CONCLUSIONS

Study of the results shows that

1. The VMM was not designed for high performance (commercial) use
    and thus the level of performance was low.

2. The performance analysis methodology was valid and cost effec-
    tive. That is, the use of benchmarks, regression analysis, and
    analytic modelling provided valid data.

3. Input-output is the highest leverage performance factor
    (probably since other critical aspects had been considered first
    during VMM design).

4. Multics suffers worse performance under VMM than GCOS due to its
    high degree of paging (I/O) activity.

5. Even though performance suffered, the VMM was still a useful
    development tool.

6. GCOS CPU-bound applications were impacted relatively little by
    VMM and thus the VMM may have significant utility as a multi-
    GCOS environment.

CONFIGURATION

The Virtual Machine Monitor consisted of a modified 6180 processor, IOM,
and Datanet 355. The experiments were conducted using a memory configuration of 512 K words and a single processor. When executing a native
mode experiment, an operating system was allowed to use 256 K words of
memory. During VMM execution analysis, the VMM occupied 256 K and the
virtual machine used the second 256 K. In this way the memory utilization for a given operating system was held constant for comparison
between native and virtual mode. Dual operating system performance
(GCOS/GCOS, Multics/GCOS, and Multics/Multics) under the VMM was not
monitored due to the time constraints of the project.

GCOS MONITORING TOOLS

A set of measuring tools were chosen to measure the performance of GCOS
under VMM. In surveying available tools, one called Peripheral Resource
Monitor (PRM) was thought to be the best of those available, particularly
in regard to graphical displays. The key measurements centered around
processor time both for GCOS and VMM. After some investigation, the
"virtual time slippage" problem was investigated in some detail. The
essence of the problem is as follows. In GCOS all time is derived from
the processor interval timers. These are saved and restored by VMM each
time control of the processor is taken from and returned to GCOS. As a
result, GCOS maintains accurate virtual processor time, but its real wall
clock time will become inaccurate when running under VMM. The effect of
"virtual time slippage" on a program like PRM (which measure processor
idle directly and processor busy by subtracting idle from elapsed wall
time) is that the processor is measured under VMM to be 100 percent busy
whether it is 10 percent busy or 100 percent busy.

In an effort to correctly capture GCOS virtual processor time and also
provide such VMM data as VMM processor and idle time, a special monitor
program was written called VMMON. The key design feature of the program
was that VMMON read the system controller clock which is accurate independent of software. This real elapsed time was compared with GCOS
time every 15 seconds which under VMM showed a distinct and increasing
discrepancy as time continued. Using this technique, VMMON can accurately
measure virtual GCOS processor and idle time and, also, VMM processor overhead in an environment which is relatively processor bound with only one
GCOS under VMM. The various tests have proved out this technique for the
environment as described.

In an attempt to measure processor utilization for an environment of VMM,
GCOS, and Multics, the following steps were taken. Changes to VMM were
designed which would record in GCOS memory: VMM processor time, real
system idle time, and Multics processor time. VMMON was designed to read
this data from GCOS memory and display how this data changed at each
sample period.

WORKLOADS

GCOS: Two fabricated work loads were generated for the GCOS VMM benchmark tests and were designed to produce an average-type load and an I/O
bound load. These loads tested the VMM performance under a range of work
load types which represent those typical of a data processing site.

MULTICS: The means by which the Multics operating system is driven in
order to collect performance data is somewhat different than that of GCOS.
Since Multics is primarily an interactive system, a simulation of interactive work loads was used in conjunction with the absentee facility of
Multics.

ANALYSIS RESULTS

There are demonstrable penalties in running a job stream in a virtual
machine rather than in a real machine environment. Such penalties
include the consumption of extra system resources (e.g., processor
cycles) as well as potential degradation to various measures of overall
performance (e.g., response time and throughput).

BENCHMARK ANALYSIS

A variety of benchmark experiments in both a native GCOS environment
(i.e., in a non-virtual machine mode) and in a VMM/GCOS environment (i.e.,
under VMM control) were performed. These experiments were performed in
a completely isolated environment; no system activity other than that
defined in the benchmark was present.

Three test series were run on both native GCOS (on a Multics system with
VMM processor) and GCOS under VMM. The test series spanned the spectrum
of processor bound to channel bound, thus reflecting how VMM performs
under a variety of loads. The three separate benchmarks consisted of:

    1.   Compute-Bound Activity--heavily CPU demanding tasks.
    2.   Channel-Bound Activity--heavily I/O demanding tasks.
    3.   Average-Load Activity--average CPU and I/O demanding tasks.

Two software monitors were used during each benchmark experiment. The
System Resource Monitor (SRM), an updated version of a previous monitor
(CSMON), was available from Honeywell Information Systems. The Virtual
Machine Monitor (VMMON) was developed specifically for the benchmark anal-
ysis effort.

In the native GCOS environment, both monitors provided substantially the
same results. Under the VMM environment, however, SRM was completely
inadequate. This was largely due to <u>virtual time slippage</u>. The SRM, in
its attempts to obtain timing information in the virtual machine environment, unknowingly accesses GCOS's software clock. VMMON on the other
hand compensates for the situation by accessing the system controller
clock, a microsecond clock which remains accurate under both the native/
GCOS and the VMM/GCOS environments. In addition, VMMON reports both the
value of the GCOS time and the actual time, thereby permitting the virtual
time slippage to be deduced.

In the VMM/GCOS environment, the virtual time slippage is caused only by
VMM overhead activity and system idle activity. The virtual time
slippage, therefore, provides a convenient mechanism for establishing
overhead attributable to the VMM. One need only concentrate on periods
in the native system where the processor is known to be 100 percent busy.
Virtual time slippage will, in this case, accurately represent VMM overhead only.

Two of the benchmark test series run in the native/GCOS environment--the
processor bound and the average load activities--managed to consume 100
percent of the processor. In the channel bound tests, however, the

native/GCOS was approximately 66 percent idle and so the VMM overhead could not be deduced without additional data. Attempts to obtain this data through applications of various patches to the VMM were not successful.

The data below shows a summary of the average workload experiment only, due to space constraints. Data for time intervals T1 through T6 in both the native/GCOS and VMM/GCOS environments is shown. The following summarizes the information presented:

GCOS Time: time interval captured by GCOS
Real Time: time interval captured by the system controller clock
GCOS Ovhd: percentage of GCOS overhead time
VMM Ovhd: percentage of VMM overhead time
Idle: percentage of processor idle time
Connects: number of connects per second of GCOS time

	Interval Statistic	T1	T2	T3	T4	T5	T6
Native GCOS Environment	GCOS Time (sec)	124.2	216.5	339.6	274.5	216.1	340.1
	Real Time (sec)	124.1	216.4	339.4	274.3	216.0	339.9
	% GCOS Ovhd	10.2	10.0	10.0	9.5	8.7	9.8
	% VMM Ovhd	0.0	0.0	0.0	0.0	0.0	0.0
	% Idle	0.16	0.14	0.09	0.09	0.12	0.0
	Number of Connects/sec	38.3	38.0	38.0	35.9	32.3	37.4
VMM/GCOS Environment	GCOS Time (sec)	154.1	278.4	461.0	186.1	306.9	400.2
	Real Time (sec)	184.8	334.1	548.9	223.3	364.1	479.8
	% GCOS Ovhd	9.9	9.9	9.3	9.9	9.1	9.1
	% VMM Ovhd	19.9	20.0	19.1	20.0	18.6	19.9
	% Idle	0.0	0.0	0.0	0.0	0.0	0.0
	Number of Connects/sec	36.7	36.8	34.7	36.9	33.7	36.6

GCOS-VMM OVERHEAD REGRESSION ANALYSIS

The quantity of interest for the analyses that follow is the VMM overhead. This quantity represents the processor time consumed by the VMM in servicing users' requests for system resources. The approach to be used to compute VMM overhead is described below.

The various time periods for which measurements are available are denoted by T_i ($i = 1,2,\ldots,n$). The measured VMM overhead time (i.e., the virtual time slippage in the ith time period) is denoted by t_i. Suppose there are M different types of requests which the VMM must service. If

n_{ij} (j-1,...m) is the measured quantity of requests of type j during the ith interval and θ_j is the VMM overhead incurred in servicing the type j request, then the total VMM overhead time spent in the ith time interval may be approximated by:

$$t_i = \sum_{j=1}^{m} \theta_j\, N_{ij} \tag{1}$$

The coefficients $\theta_1, \theta_2, \ldots, \theta_m$ can be determined by the method of least squares so as to minimize the sum of the squares of the residuals, i.e.,

$$\min S(\theta_1, \theta_2, \ldots, \theta_m) = \sum_{i=1}^{n} r_i^2$$

where residual r is defined as

$$r_i = t_i - \sum_{j=1}^{m} \theta_j\, N_{ij}$$

If the r_i turn out to be relatively small, then Equation (1) is considered to yield a suitable fit to the data. The goodness of fit criteria incorporated below is the multiple correlation coefficient obtained by comparing the sum of the residual squares to the sum of the squares of the deviation of the measurements from their mean value $(\bar{t})$, i.e.,

$$R^2 = 1 - \sum_{i=1}^{n} r_i^2 \Big/ \sum_{i=1}^{n} (t_i - \bar{t})^2$$

Based upon the information obtained from the benchmark analyses, two resource quantities were selected as being major contributions to VMM overhead. For the ith time interval, T_i, these were

- o n_{i1} --the CPU busy time during T_i
- o n_{i2} --the number of channel connects requested during T_i

Equation (1) in this case reduces to

$$t_i = \theta_1\, n_{i1} + \theta_2\, n_{i2}$$

Using the benchmark experiment data previously shown, the method of least squares was applied to the equations represented below.

Work Load	T_i	VMM Overhead Time (t_i) in T_i (sec)	GCOS Busy Time (n_{i1}) in T_i (sec)	Total Number of Connects (n_{i2}) in T_i
Average Load	1	30.7	154.1	5661.6
	2	55.7	278.4	10242.3
	3	87.9	461.0	16010.5
	4	37.2	186.1	6876.4
	5	57.2	306.9	10351.7
	6	79.6	400.2	14647.3

The results of the regression analysis of the data yielded the following:

$$\theta1 = 0.0351, \quad \theta2 = 0.0045, \quad R^2 = 0.98$$

These results indicate that the processor overhead incurred through usage of the VMM is approximately 0.0045 seconds overhead for each channel connect and an additional 3.5 percent of non-idle processor time. The extremely high correlation coefficient indicates that these results represented a suitable fit to the data.

It should be pointed out that, although an extremely high correlation coefficient has been achieved, the results may not be statistically precise. The method on which the coefficient values are based depends on the assumption that the coefficients are constant--not variable. This assumption is not valid for the data above. Clearly different user requests place significantly different demands on the system, for example. The true accuracy of these coefficients, therefore, has not been established. It is possible, however, with additional measurements, to construct more statistically accurate results. This remains a source for future investigations.

BEST/1$_{tm}$-GCOS ANALYSIS

Based on the values of θ_1 and θ_2 derived in the previous section, it was possible to hypothesize several configuration and work load alternatives and determine their respective performance degradation when executing GCOS in a virtual machine rather than in a native machine environment. This was done with the help of BGS Systems' proprietary modeling package BEST/1$_{tm}$. First, the performance of each of the hypothesized alternatives running in a native/GCOS environment was analyzed. Next the previously determined coefficients, θ_1 and θ_2, were used to determine the VMM overhead degradation of the hypothesized work loads in the VMM/GCOS environment. Finally, the performance impact of executing that same configuration and work load, under GCOS, in the virtual machine environment was determined.

The configuration and work load models constructed consisted of a canonical job stream executing on a single processor system, in one case including and in one case excluding the effects of I/O device contention. Individual tasks in the job stream were assumed to consume approximately 1 second of CPU time and to perform a varying number of I/O operations (0 to 50) at approximately 35 μsec per connect. The analyses were performed for the job stream under several distinct levels of system load, ranging from a single thread environment to a level of threading equal to 15.

The models chosen and analyzed were directed toward determining the VMM overhead impact on two important measures of system performance: response time and system throughput. A sample of the data produced by BEST/1$_{tm}$ is shown on the graph which follows.

MULTICS BENCHMARKS AND OVERHEAD ANAYLSIS

The benchmark experiments run for Multics differ significantly from their GCOS counterparts. Rather than defining several distinct work load types and performing a series of benchmarks for each, as was done with GCOS, only a single work load type was defined for the Multics case. This work load consisted of a single PL/1 program which itself issued primarily processor consuming requests through a large iterative loop (the effect of flush was also considered). The work load was run in both the native/Multics and VMM/Multics environments with three distinct levels of threading (multiprogramming levels 1, 15, and 20).

Statistics were gathered for this benchmark series through the use of the Multics System Metering tools. These tools, however, were not applied solely to the intervals of interest (i.e., the intervals in which the PL/1 work load was active). Therefore, the data that was collected and reported turned out to be insignificant.

Fortunately, another source of information was available: a PL/1 source program referred to as LOAD-CONTROL. This program was used to monitor the work load and report the number of iterations per minute that it achieved. This provided a single data point in each environment   which was somewhat useful in determining the VMM overhead degradation.

There are several factors which affected the usefulness of the LOAD-CONTROL data. Foremost was the fact that configurations for the native/ Multics and VMM/Multics were not identical. The PL/1 work load was run under native/Multics without the use of a high-speed cache memory and under VMM/Multics with use of the cache. Since the cache memory has a significant effect on such factors as instruction fetch rates, performance analyses using this data would clearly be affected.

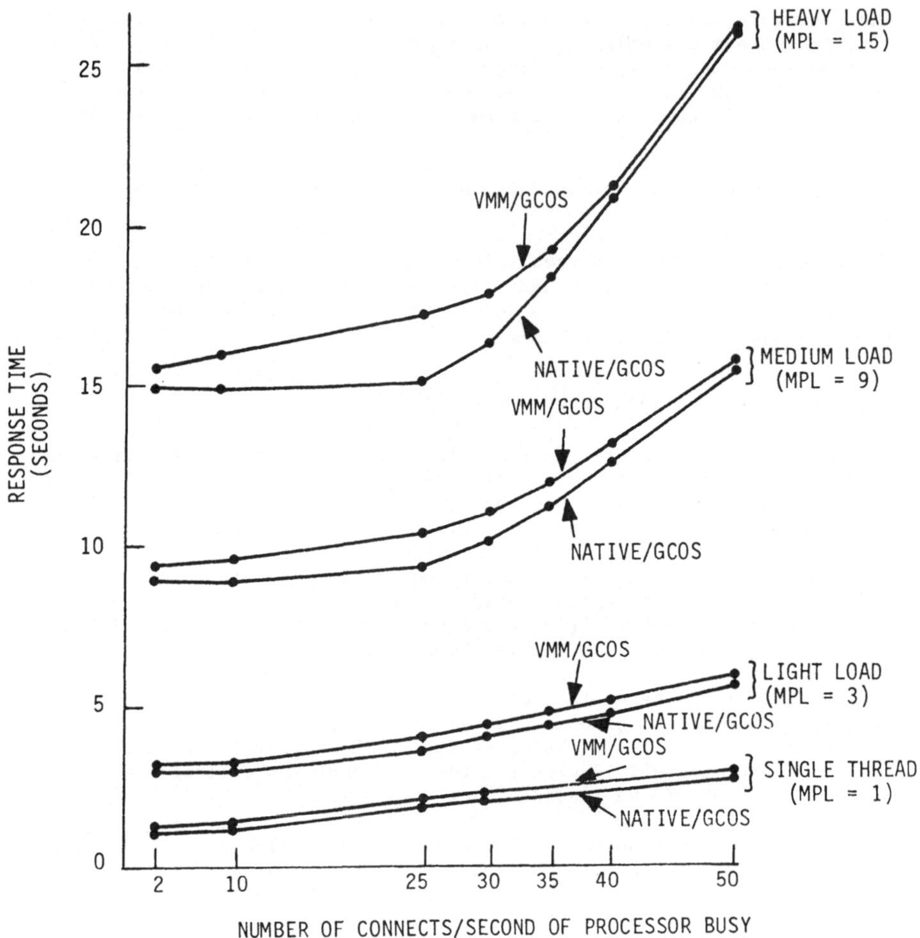

Effect of VMM vs. Native GCOS on Response Time
as a Function of I/O Activity (I/O Contention)

	Native/Multics[**]	VMM/Multics[*]
Number of Iterations/min Single Thread	3.58	3.15

*With high-speed memory cache.
**Without high-speed memory cache.

Even so, a first-order analysis of the data was attempted. Based on the
above data, it was deduced that under the native/Multics environment
16.76 seconds were required per iteration while under VMM/Multics this
number increased to 19.05 seconds per iteration; this implied an observed VMM overhead degradation of 13.7 percent.[*]

Since in the benchmark experiment for the VMM/Multics case the cache
memory was incorporated, this figure represents a lower bound on the VMM
overhead degradation.

The actual degradation would clearly be more significant for larger
effective iteration speedups contributed by use of the cache. Since typical speedup factors introduced by the use of a high-speed cache may range
from 5 to 30 percent for processor bound work loads, this leads to the
ranges of VMM overhead degradation depicted below.

---

*This represents an increase factor of 4 over the degradation for the pro-
cessor busy contribution in the GCOS use. These numbers are <u>not</u> intended to
to be compared, however. Paging activity, for example, which <u>is</u> not present in the GCOS environment, causes a significant performance impact in
the Multics environment. The effect of Multics paging activity has in
effect been aggregated into the Multics processor busy contribution. Ex-
plicitly determining the degradation contributed by paging would require
additional benchmark experiments and substantial further investigation.

ESTIMATED VMM OVERHEAD DEGRADATION
AS A FUNCTION OF CACHE CONTRIBUTION

Effective Cache Contribution %	Estimated VMM/Multics (Second/iteration without cache)	Percent Degradation VMM: Native
0	19.05	13.7
5	20.05	19.6
10	21.17	26.3
15	22.41	33.7
20	23.81	42.1
25	25.4	51.6
30	27.2	62.3

BEST/1$_{tm}$-MULTICS ANALYSIS

Even with the minimal amount of data provided by the benchmark experiments in the Multics case, examination of the performance impact of the VMM degradation for a variety of hypothesized configuration and work load alternatives was attempted.

For purposes of this analysis, the θ_2 factor in the VMM/Multics case was assumed to be the same as that in the VMM/GCOS case (0.0045 seconds/connect). The θ_1 factor was varied over the end points of the range of effective cache contributions described previously. Next the coefficients θ_1 and θ_2 were used to determine the VMM overhead degradation of the hypothesized systems under Multics in the virtual machine mode. BEST/1$_{tm}$ was then used to determine the performance impact of executing the hypothesized systems under VMM/Multics.

As in the BEST/1$_{tm}$-GCOS analysis, the configuration and work load models consisted of a canonical job stream executing on a single processor system. Two hardware configurations were modeled: one including the effects of I/O device contention, and one excluding these effects. Individual tasks in the job stream were assumed to consume approximately 1 second of processor time and to perform a varying number of I/O operations (0 to 50) consuming approximately 35 msec per connect. The analyses were performed for the job stream under several distinct levels of system load, ranging from a single load to a load level of 15.

The models chosen were directed toward determining the VMM overhead impact on two important measures of system performance: response time and system throughput. A sample of the analysis results follows.

SOFTWARE EXTENSIONS: THE SERVICE MACHINE

The VMM under evaluation represents an implementation of functionality which was known to be a partial fulfillment of the goals of a long-term project. Therefore, there are several areas of functional extension which are known to be desirable from several points of view. Among these are extensions for sharing peripheral equipment, including front end processors, enhanced system console functionality to permit dynamic

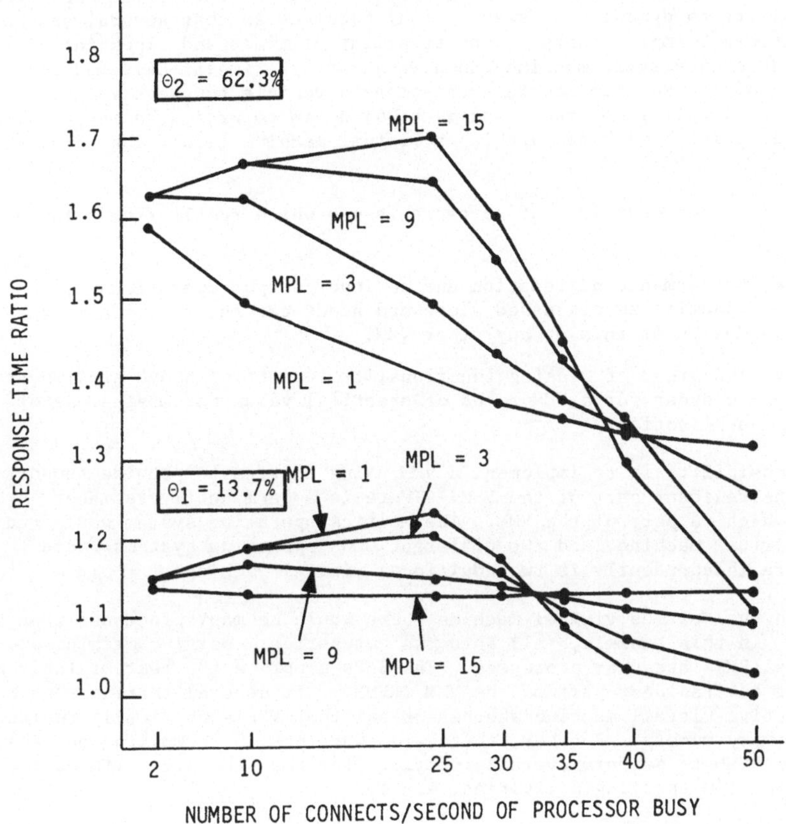

Ratio of VMM: Native Response Time for Multics as
a Function of I/O Activity (I/O Contention Included)

changes in virtual machines being run and their real resource assignments, an ability to dynamically swap virtual machines so that several can be multiplexed, improvements to the treatment of timer and clock information so that each virtual machine can have a correct time-of-day, and implementation of the service machine concept as a vehicle to greatly enhance the VMM functionality for those services which can tolerate the internal delays associated with dispatching a virtual machine (i.e., the service machine).

The main recommendations of software issues which result from this analysis are that:

- Performance degradation due to input/output operations is substantial as discussed above and needs careful analysis in the design of this or any other VMM.

- The areas of missing functionality identified above are important in order for a VMM to be of practical value for most areas of application.

One possibility is to implement a VMM using Multics to provide support for the resident part of the VMM. There is a permanently resident area which is part of the VMM. The Multics operating system would run in one virtual machine, and two different GCOS operating systems would operate independently in two additional virtual machines.

Within the Multics virtual machine there would be many processes running which, in this example, fall into two categories: service machine processes (SMP) and user processes. The SMPs comprise the rest of the VMM beyond the resident part of the VMM (RVMM). In general there is one SMP per active virtual machine whether or not that VM is physically resident in primary memory. Further, there are additional SMPs working on behalf of the RVMM to perform overall functions for the VMM (e.g., VMM operator console, I/O spooling activities, etc.).

The virtual machine which is running the operating system supporting the resident part of the VMM is called the service virtual machine or service machine (SM) for short. This virtual machine has some constraints placed upon it by RVMM due to the special nature of the SM. For example, RVMM knows how to bootstrap the SM into operation at system initialization and will not allow the SM to be halted.

HARDWARE EXTENSIONS

The main hardware issues in the design of any VMM relate to the question of how much of the system's overall resources are used in supporting virtual machines. Each real resource of a computer system (processor, memory, devices, channels, switches) needs to be replicated for each virtual machine. To do this, the hardware must either directly perform the mapping between virtual and real resources, or it must have some mechanism of intercepting references to virtual resources, capturing the complete state of the virtual machine, and passing control to some other agent (e.g., a software or firmware VMM). This agent then simulates the correct behavior of the virtual resource and returns control to the

virtual machine for further execution under direct hardware control. The
agent consumes real resources in performing this simulation and this
effect can be substantiated.

In the VMM under study it was shown that the amount of real system resources consumed by the VMM in processing input/output operations is a
significant level for normal computer system work loads. The percent of
the central processor needed for this purpose ranged from 10 to 30 for
normal GCOS work loads and somewhat higher for Multics.

Direct hardware support for input/output operations is the single most
important potential for decreased VMM overhead. Such support would not
be required for all I/O devices. A study of the device usage shows that
disk and tape units have the most potential for reducing VMM overhead
since I/O operations occur most frequently on these units.

Further investigation into the architectural approaches to communications
front end processor support is necessary before the question of appropriate
hardware support for virtualization can be answered. The importance of
such support is, of course, dependent on the types of work loads that
might be processed.

Another area in which hardware support is of great importance is that of
main memory mapping. The present VMM statically allocates the full
real memory required by a virtual machine. For several classes of use
of virtual machines, it would be desirable to have more dynamic control
of the mapping between virtual and real memory resources. In particular,
a block assignment or paging mechanism could be investigated for its effect on VMM overhead for different classes of work loads.

SUMMARY

This paper has described a detailed analysis of a virtual machine monitor.
Several performance tradeoffs for utilizing a VMM in an operational
environment have been identified. In the VMM studied the most fruitful
area for further research appears to be in the design of a VMM which is
more tolerant of I/O activity.

Decreasing hardware costs indicate that in the future VMM's will either
be integrated within the hardware or firmware supported. The results of
this performance analysis can be utilized to design a more efficient
hardware oriented virtual machine monitor.

BIBLIOGRAPHY

0. IBM Virtual Machine Facility/370: Introduction, Release 3, IBM Corp.
    Publication No. GC 20-1800-5, 1976.

1. Kalynycz I., "Handbook for Conversion of GCOS III Application
    Programs to the GCOS Simulator of MULTICS," RADC-TR-77-241,
    Sept. 1977.

2. Gagliardi, U. O. and Jain, R. I., "Research on Virtual Machines,"
    RADC-TR-77-57, May 1977.

3. Vestal S., Krocak, T. K., Schwenk H. S., Levy A., "H6180 Virtual
    Machine Monitor Performance Analysis," RADC-TR-XXXX, Sept. 1978.

4. Gagliardi, U. O. and Jain, R. K., "Software Tool Development,"
    Contract F30602-77-C-0058, Oct. 1978, to be published.

5. Madnick, S. E. and Lam, C. L., "Strategies for Intrafacing Virtual
    Machines," Contract F30602-77-C-0058, March 1978, to be published.

6. Madnick, S. E. and Lam, C. L., "Composite Information Systems-- A New
    Concept in Information Systems," RADC Contract F30602-77-C-0205,
    May 1978, to be published.

ZUGRIFFSFUNKTIONEN ZUR UNTERSTÜTZUNG
DER SPEICHERVERWALTUNG BEIM VIRTUELLEN
MASCHINENBETRIEB

H. Gümbel
Siemens AG, München

When designing virtual machine systems memory management
becomes a problem because the virtual machines must be kept
from handling physical addresses. A method is proposed
that neither needs much   hardware nor does it produce
software overhead. This method consists in a set of access
functions that are implemented as privileged machine
instructions. These instructions are described and their
usage is demonstrated using a characteristic example.
The implications of the access functions on real machine
operation and reconfiguration are outlined and the
possible limitations of this approach are discussed.

1. Einleitung

Die Lösung des Speicherverwaltungsproblems beim Betrieb
virtueller Maschinen besteht in der Aufteilung der Ver-
waltungsbefugnisse über den physikalischen Speicher;
dabei obliegt

o   die Gesamtaufteilung des Speichers zwischen den
    virtuellen Maschinensystemen einer zentralen In-
    stanz, dem Virtual Machine Monitor (VMM), während

o   das Speichermanagement innerhalb der virtuellen Ma-
    schinensysteme (VMS) durch das jeweilige Betriebs-
    system der VMS erfolgt.

Üblicherweise macht die Speicherverwaltung - auch innerhalb der VMS - das Hantieren mit physikalischen
Adressen erforderlich. So entsteht die Gefahr, daß die
VMS auf fremde Datenbestände zugreifen können, was aus
Gründen des Schutzes und der Ablaufsicherheit uner-
wünscht ist. Diese Gefahr wird dadurch beseitigt, daß
man aus jenen physikalischen Adressen, die den VMS bekannt sind, "pseudo-physikalische" Adressen macht. Dies
geschieht durch Zwischenschalten eines Abbildungs-
schrittes - z.B. durch das Führen von Schattentabellen
wie bei VM/370 [5] und in gewissem Sinne auch bei
SIM BS1000 [10] oder einer zusätzlichen Stufe bei der

Adressenübersetzung wie bei VM 7.700 [1]. Eine weitere
Lösungsmöglichkeit besteht darin, die problematischen
physikalischen Adressen aus dem Hardware/Software-
Interface der VMS in jeder Form zu eliminieren und zu
versuchen, die Speicherverwaltung innerhalb der VMS
ausschließlich auf der Basis virtueller Adressen
durchzuführen.

2. Randbedingungen

Die Zugriffsfunktionen für die Speicherverwaltung wurden im Zuge der Arbeiten für eine neue Rechnerarchi-
tektur erarbeitet [1], die sich in vielen Punkten an
die bekannte Architektur des Siemens-Systems 7.700 an-
lehnt [9]. Hauptmerkmal dieses Architekturmodells ist
eine Anhebung der Hardware/Software-Schnittstelle, um
einige häufig ablaufende Betriebssystemfunktionen aus
der Software herauszulösen und mittels Hardware oder
Firmware zu realisieren. Im Zusammenhang mit der
Speicherverwaltung ist hier insbesondere als eine
dieser Funktionen die Zuteilung des Prozessors zu den
einzelnen Prozessen (Tasks) zu nennen, da hierbei auch
die Möglichkeit eines Adressraumwechsels impliziert
werden muß. Jede Task im System wird dabei durch einen
Task Control Block (T.CB) beschrieben, der von der Software erstellt wird und von der Hardware/Firmware unmittelbar ausgewertet werden kann. Sobald eine Task
einen Prozessor zugeteilt bekommt, werden aus dem zugehörigen T.CB sowie anhängenden Tabellen Informationen in
maschineninterne Register übertragen - z.B. die sicher-
gestellten Mehrzweckregister und auch der Zeiger auf das
Adressenübersetzungstafelwerk der betreffenden Task.

Die Task-beschreibenden Datenstrukturen (also etwa der
T.CB) sind aus Sicherheitsgründen in einem normalen,
nichtprivilegierten Tasks nicht zugänglichen Adreßraum
untergebracht. Die Tasks lassen sich zu Gruppen zusammenfassen; jede solche Gruppe kann als ein VMS aufgefaßt
werden.

Eine weitere wesentliche Randbedingung ist die Möglichkeit, Ein-/Ausgaben unter der Verwendung virtueller
Adressen durchzuführen [2]. Da die Ein-/Ausgabe-Hard-
ware virtuelle Adressen "versteht", wird es möglich,
physikalische Hauptspeicheradressen gänzlich aus dem
Hardware/Software Interface der VMS zu eliminieren.
Hierzu muß man allerdings auch die Adreßübersetzungstafeln dem direkten Zugriff der VMS entziehen, denn
diese Tafeln enthalten ja physikalische Adressen. Um
dennoch die nötigen Manipulationen dieser Tafeln seitens
der VMS vornehmen zu können, werden geeignete Zugriffsfunktionen eingeführt.

---

1) Die diesem Vortrag zugrundeliegenden Arbeiten werden
   mit Mitteln des Bundesministeriums für Forschung und
   Technologie im Rahmen des Datenverarbeitungs-För-
   derungsprogramms gefördert. Die Verantwortung für den
   Inhalt liegt jedoch allein beim Autor.

2) Im Prinzip ist die Verwendung virtueller Adressen bei
   der Ein-/Ausgabe schon bei einigen Systemen üblich
   [8] , [11].

3. Zugriffsfunktionen

Man kann nun folgende eingeschränkte Definition eines
VMS in diesem Architekturmodell aufstellen:

Ein VMS ist eine Gruppe von Tasks, die einen bestimmten Anteil des physikalischen Hauptspeichers
besitzt. Dieser Hauptspeicheranteil wird dem VMS
bei seiner Erzeugung zugewiesen; er braucht nicht
zusammenhängend zu sein. Der einem VMS gehörende
physikalische Speicher zerfällt dabei in zwei
Kategorien:

1) Speicher, der Task-beschreibende Datenstrukturen
   beinhaltet (d.h. T.CBs, Adreßübersetzungstafeln
   etc.). Diese Datenstrukturen sind während der
   Existenz eines VMS immer resident.
   Dieser Speicher soll hier Klasse I-Speicher genannt werden. Er fungiert gewissermaßen als eine
   Art "Schattenspeicher" der VMS.

2) Speicher, in welchem sich jene Teile der virtuellen
   Speicher des VMS befinden, die nicht gerade auf
   einen Hintergrundspeicher ausgelagert sind. Dies
   ist der eigentliche physikalische "Nutzspeicher"
   der VMS und soll hier als Klasse II-Speicher bezeichnet werden.

Das VMS hat in jedem Falle eine Vorstellung von seinem
Klasse II-Speicher; er stellt den "working-set" des
VMS dar. Innerhalb der Grenzen dieses Klasse II-
Speichers kann das VMS die Verwaltung seines working-
sets autonom und ohne jegliche Kontakte und dem VMM
durchführen. Die Vorgabe eines festen Klasse I-
Speichers beschränkt das virtuelle Adressierungsvolumen
(d.h. die Summe der virtuellen Seiten und Segmente
aller VMS-Tasks) des VMS auf analoge Weise, wie dies
heute durch den für Paging verwendbaren Hintergrund-
speicherplatz bei bekannten Betriebssystemen der
Fall ist (z.B. bei dem Siemens Betriebssystem BS2000
[12]).

Innerhalb der durch die jeweilige Größe des Klasse I-
und des Klasse II-Speichers gegebenen Grenzen kann
das VMS

- die Struktur seiner virtuellen Adreßräume verändern
  (etwa durch Verringern des Adreßraumes einer Task
  beim gleichzeitigen Vergrößern des Adreßraumes einer
  anderen oder durch gemeinschaftliche Benutzung von
  Segmenten, die zuvor individuell belegt waren) und
  auch

- die Abbildung dieser Adreßräume auf den working-set
  des VMS etwa durch das Paging von Seiten oder Segmenten variieren.

Ferner gestattet das Vorhandensein eines virtuellen
Speicherschutzes die Veränderung von Zugriffs-
befugnissen der VMS-Tasks durch das VMS selbst.

Die zu diesem Zwecke vorgesehenen Zugriffsfunktionen
sind privilegierte Maschinenbefehle, d.h. sie sind
ausführbar, wenn sich das betreffende VMS im privilegierten Zustand befindet.

Innerhalb der Zugriffsfunktionen sind folgende Funktions-
komplexe zu unterscheiden:

o Display-Funktionen -
   sie teilen dem Aufrufer die Status-Anzeigen der
   betreffenden Adreßübersetzungstafel-Einträge
   mit

o Transitions-Funktionen -
   mit ihnen läßt sich der Status der angesprochenen
   Adreßübersetzungstafel-Einträge verändern

o Zuweisungs-Funktionen -
   mit ihnen ist eine Veränderung der Zuordnung einer
   virtuellen Adresse auf die zugehörige physikalische
   Adresse möglich.

Generell sind diese Funktionen für jede Stufe des
Adreßübersetzungssystems vorgesehen; bei einem zweistufigen System also auf Segment- und Seitenniveau.

In der Folge soll von einem zweistufigen System, wie
es bei dem Siemens System 7.700 vorhanden ist, ausgegangen werden [9].

3.1 Display-Funktionen
Die Display-Funktionen stellen dem Aufrufer (d.h. dem
Betriebssystem des VMS) Status-Informationen von Segment-
oder Seitentafeleinträgen einer Task in dem betreffenden
VMS zur Verfügung. Damit erübrigt sich für den Aufrufer
die Buchführung über die von ihm gesetzten Status-
Informationen; außerdem sind manche Indikatoren gar
nicht auf dem Wege einer solchen Buchführung zu ver-
walten, da sie von der Hardware beim Zugriff auf die
entsprechende Seite erst gesetzt werden.

3.1.1 Display Segment Indicators
Die Display-Funktion stellt auf Segment-Ebene
folgende Informationen zur Verfügung: [1]

o SD-Bit ("segment defined")
  Dieses Bit zeigt die Gültigkeit des Segmenttafel-
  Eintrages an (SD≠1: Eintrag ist gültig)

o SP-Bit ("segment present")
  Dieses Bit zeigt an, ob das Segment im Hauptspeicher steht (SP=1) oder nicht (SP=0) [2]

o NX-Bit ("no execute")
  Dieser Indikator regelt den Zugriff zu Befehlen
  in diesem Segment (NX=0: Befehlszugriff erlaubt;
  NX=1: Zugriff zu Befehlen ist verboten)

o RNR-Angabe ("ring number for read access")
  Hier wird die Ring-Nummer für Lesezugriffe
  für das betreffende Segment angegeben. Im
  Zusammenhang mit der im Interrupt Status
  Register ("ISR") [9] eingetragenen, maschinen-
  zustandsspezifischen Ringzustandsanzeige RSI
  wird ein Speicherschutz auf virtueller Ebene,
  nämlich auf Segmentniveau bewirkt. Dabei gelten
  folgende Festlegungen:

  RSI ≤ RNR   Lesezugriff zu Daten in diesem
                Segment erlaubt

  RSI > RNR   Lesezugriffe zu Daten in diesem
                Segment sind verboten

o RNW-Angabe ("ring number for write access")
  Dies ist die Ring-Nummer für Schreibzugriffe
  auf dieses Segment. Die oben gemachten Aussagen für RNR gelten sinngemäß auch für RNW.

---

1) Die Bezeichnungen und Bedeutungen sind identisch mit
    den entsprechenden Termini im Siemens System 7.700
    [9].

2) Bei dem System 7.700 kann das SP-Bit auch bedeuten,
    daß die zugehörige Seitentafel nicht im Hauptspeicher
    steht. Da die VMS aber nicht eine Auslagerung der
    Seitentafeln durchführen können, entfällt hier diese
    zweite Bedeutung des SP-Bits.

Der Befehl "Display Segment Indicators (DSI)"
wird wie folgt aufgerufen:

DSI   <task-id> , <pointer to parameter-area>

wobei die Argumente des Befehls folgende Bedeutung
haben.

<task-id>   bezeichnet die Task innerhalb des
                              VMS, deren Tafelwerk gemeint ist.
                              Die Hardware kann man aus dem TCB
                              dieser Task die Adresse des zuge-
                              hörigen Adressübersetzungstafel-
                              werkes entnehmen

<pointer to
parameter-area>   ist ein Zeiger auf einen Bereich,
                              der folgende Felder enthält: 1)

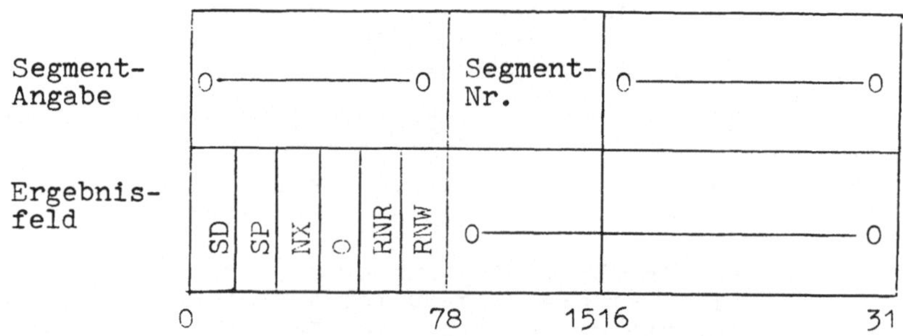

Der Befehlsablauf läßt sich aus Bild 1 ersehen; nachdem mit Hilfe der Angaben <task-id> und der Segment-
Nummer der betreffende Segment-Tafel-Eintrag ermittelt
ist, wird er unter Abstreifen des Verweises auf die entsprechende Seitentafel in das Ergebnisfeld übertragen.
Das Ergebnisfeld wird nach rechts mit binären Nullen
aufgefüllt. (Die Einführung eines speziellen Parameter-
feldes erfolgte, um den Befehl in das SS-Format der
Serie 7.700 einreihen zu können.)

---

1)   In diesem wie in folgenden Parameterfeldern wird die
     ursprüngliche Ausrichtung der entsprechenden Felder
     in den Adreßübersetzungstafeln beibehalten. Dies ge-
     schieht mit Rücksicht auf die Effizienz der Imple-
     mentierung der Funktion.

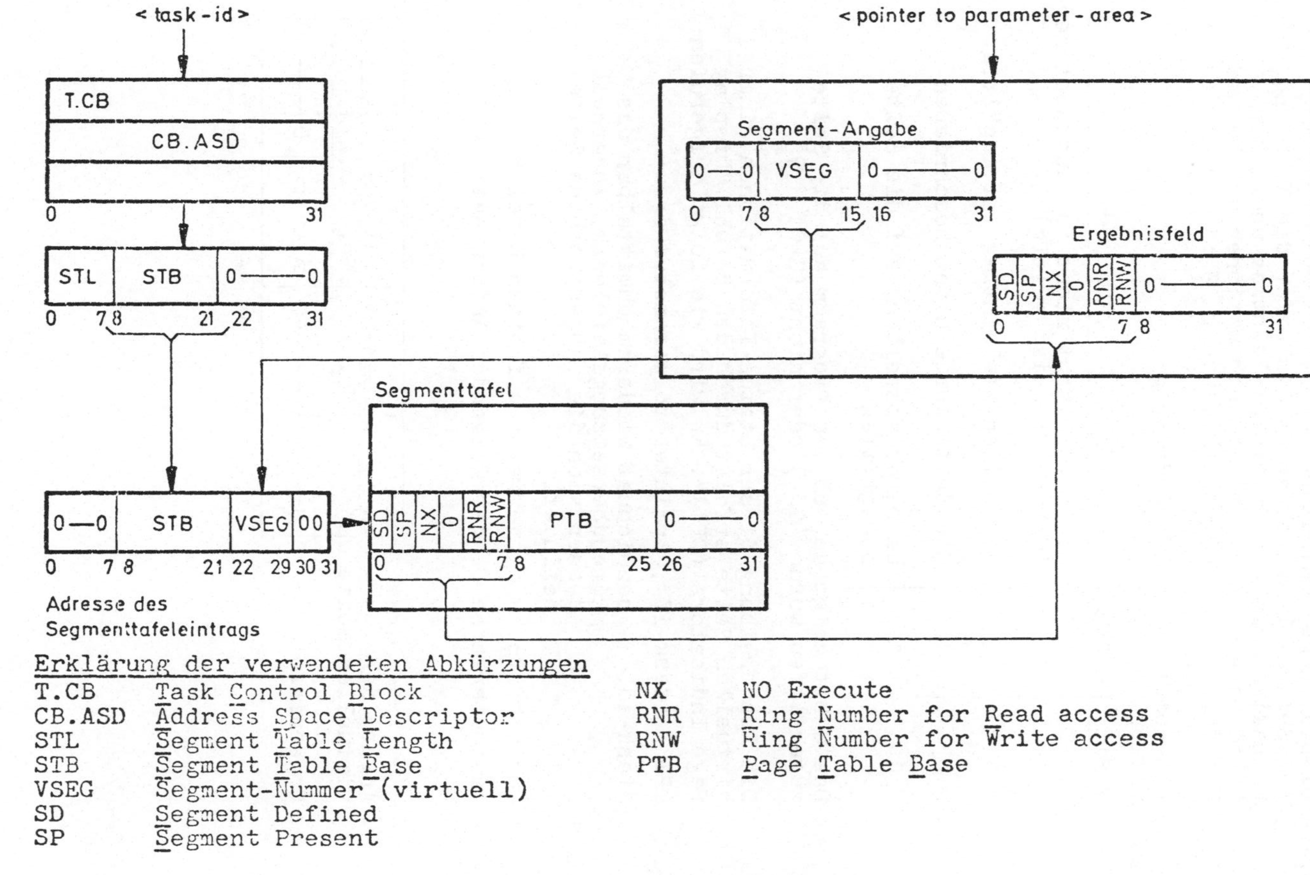

Erklärung der verwendeten Abkürzungen

T.CB	Task Control Block	NX	NO Execute
CB.ASD	Address Space Descriptor	RNR	Ring Number for Read access
STL	Segment Table Length	RNW	Ring Number for Write access
STB	Segment Table Base	PTB	Page Table Base
VSEG	Segment-Nummer (virtuell)		
SD	Segment Defined		
SP	Segment Present		

Abb. 1 Ablauf des Befehls "DISPLAY SEGMENT INDICATORS (DSI)"

3.1.2 Display Page Indicators

Auf Seiten-Ebene werden dem Aufrufer die W, G und
U-Anzeigen aus dem Seitentafeleintrag übergeben.
Dabei haben die einzelnen Kombinationen der W- und
U-Anzeige-Bits folgende Bedeutung [9]:

Bit-Kombination		Bedeutung
W-Bit	U-Bit	
0	0	die Seite steht nicht im Hauptspeicher (der Eintrag ist gültig)
1	0	der Seitentafeleintrag ist ungültig
0	1	die Seite wurde nicht beschrieben
1	1	es wurde schreibend auf die Seite zugegriffen

Das G-Bit zeigt an, ob vom Programm auf die Seite
zugegriffen wurde (G=1) oder nicht (G=0) [9].

Die Beschreibung dieser Status-Informationen einer
virtuellen Seite erfolgt durch den Befehl "Display
Page Indicators (DPI)". Er wird wie folgt aufgerufen:

DPI   <task-id>, <pointer to parameter-area>

<task-id>   bezeichnet wiederum unmittelbar das
                Adreßübersetzungstafelwerk, innerhalb
                dessen sich die angesprochene Seite
                befindet.

<pointer to   verweist auf einen Bereich,
parameter-area>   der folgenden Aufbau hat:

	0 — 7	8 — 15	16			19 20	21 — 31
Angabe der virtuellen Seite	0——0	Segment-Nr.	Seiten-Nr.				0——0
Ergebnisfeld	0————0		W	G	U	0	0——0

Den Befehlsablauf kann man aus Bild 2 entnehmen.
Mit Hilfe der Angabe < task-id > wird zunächst wieder
der T.CB ermittelt; in ihm ist ein Verweis auf die
zugehörige Segmenttafel. Segment- und Seiten-Nummer
der angegebenen virtuellen Seite dienen dazu, den
gewünschten Eintrag aufzufinden. Der Eintrag wird
an das Ergenisfeld übertragen; die im Eintrag vorhandene physikalische Seitennummer wird dabei jedoch abgeschnitten.

3.2 Transitions-Funktionen
Bei den Transitions-Funktionen handelt es sich um die
Gegenstücke zu den Display-Funktionen. Formal ist der
Aufbau genau wie derjenige der Display-Funktionen;
der Aufrufer kann alle Indikatoren setzen, die ihm
durch die Display-Funktionen aufgezeigt werden können.
Der Aufruf sowie der Ablauf der Befehle "Set Segment
Indicators (SSI)" und "Set Page Indicators (SPI)"
wird in der nachfolgenden Übersicht (Bild 3) sowie
den Bildern 4 (für SSI) und 5 (Für SPI) dargestellt.

3.3 Zuweisungs-Funktionen
Um die Aufteilung des VMS-working-sets auf die Tasks
eines VMS zu ermöglichen, benötigt man Funktionen,
welche physikalischen Speicher, der zuvor von Task
"T1" benutzt wurde, an Task "T2" geben. Es handelt
sich also hierbei um eine Umverteilung des einem
VMS zugewiesenen physikalischen Speichers. Da die
Zuweisungsfunktionen die Segment- oder Seitentafel-
einträge von einem Adreßübersetzungstafelwerk
in ein anderes kopieren, läßt sich auf diese Weise
auch die gemeinsame Benutzung virtuellen Speichers
durch mehrere Tasks ("sharing") bewerkstelligen.
Sind Ursprungs- und Zieltabellenwerk identisch,
so liegt eine Umordnung innerhalb des working-sets
einer VMS-Task vor.

Die Zuweisungsfunktionen sind wieder für 2 Ebenen
definiert: Segment- und Seitenebene. Der Aufruf der
zugehörigen Befehle lautet dabei wie folgt:

<function-id>   <pointer to parameter-area 1>,
                       <pointer to parameter-area 2>

<function-id>   TFS / TFP

   TFS   Funktion "Transfer Segment"
                       Dieser Befehl überträgt den
                       Segment-Tafeleintrag E1 der
                       Task T1 auf den Platz des
                       Segment-Tafeleintrages E2
                       der Task T2.

TFP

Funktion "Transfer Page"
Dieser Befehl überträgt den
Seiten-Tafeleintrag E1 der
Task T1 auf den Platz des Seg-
ment-Tafeleintrages E2 der
Task T2.

<parameter-area 1>

Dieser Parameter-Bereich enthält die Task-Identifier der
Tasks T1 und T2.

<parameter-area 2>

Dieser Parameter-Bereich ent-
hält die Verweise auf E1 und E2.
Bei dem Befehl "Transfer Segment
(TFS)" hat er folgenden Aufbau:

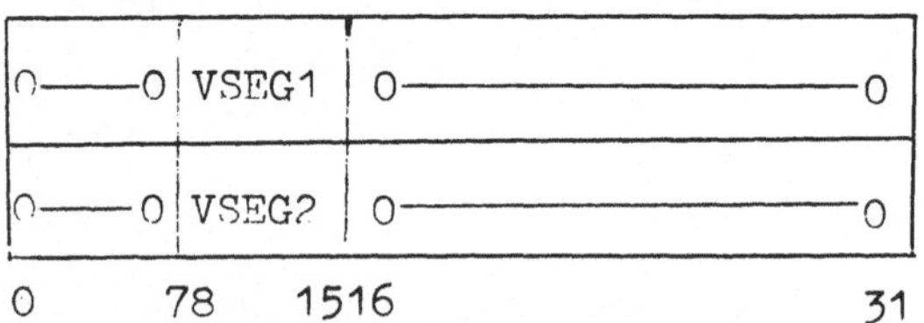

VSEG1: Segment-Nummer des Eintrages E1
VSEG2: Segment-Nummer des Eintrages E2

Der Aufbau des Parameter-Bereiches
beim Befehl "Transfer Page (TFP)"
ist:

VSEG1, VPAG1: Segment- und Seiten-
nummer des Eintrages
E1

VSEG2, VPAG2: Segment- und Seiten-
nummer des Eintrages
E2

Der Ablauf der Zuweisungsfunktionen läßt sich anhand
von Bild 6 für TFS und Bild 7 für TFP verfolgen. Aus
dem Parameterbereich 1 werden die Task-Identifier entnommen; über die jeweiligen Task Control Blocks können
die Adreßübersetzungstafeln der betroffenen Tasks auf-
gefunden werden.

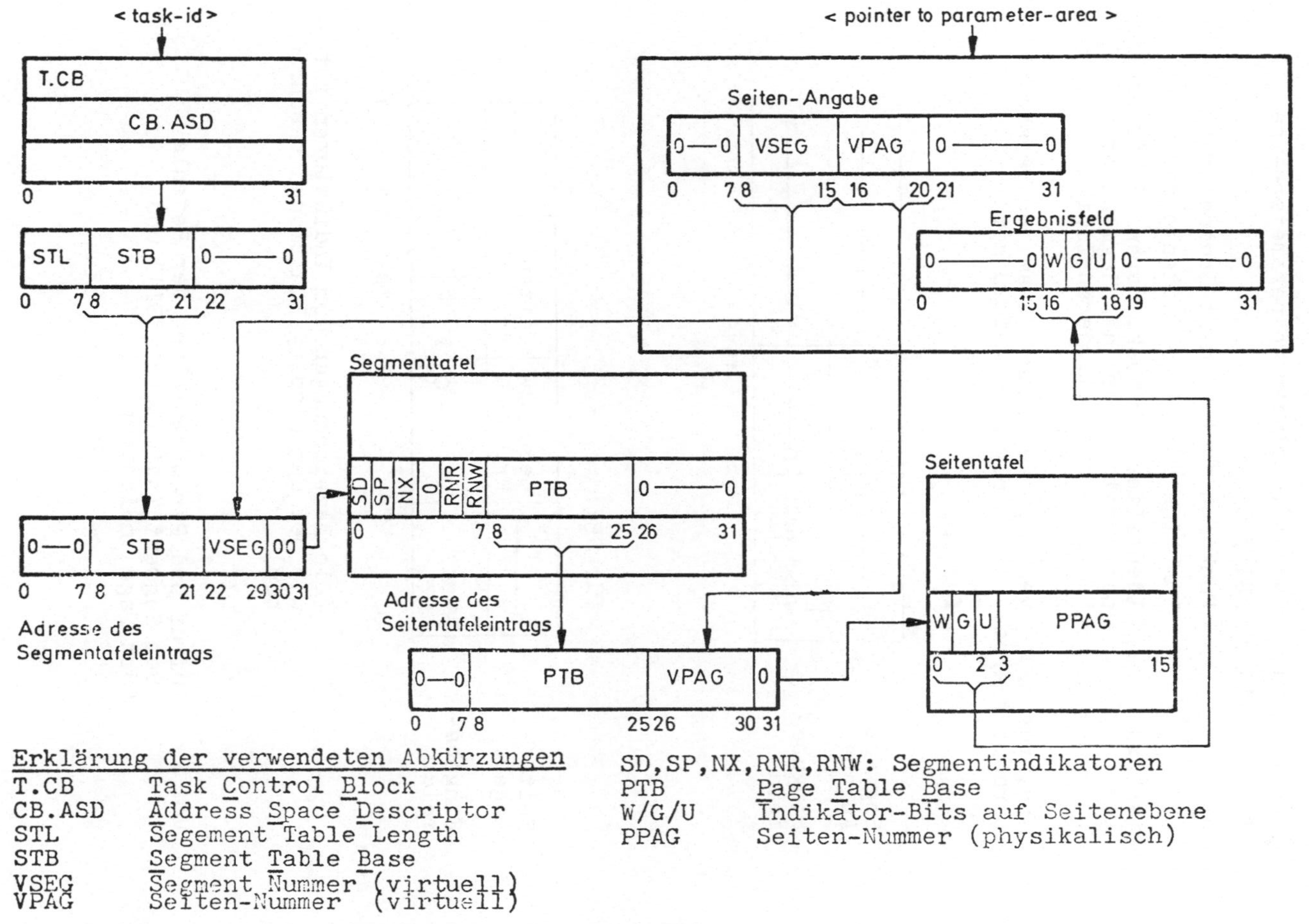

Erklärung der verwendeten Abkürzungen

T.CB	Task Control Block	SD,SP,NX,RNR,RNW:	Segmentindikatoren
CB.ASD	Address Space Descriptor	PTB	Page Table Base
STL	Segement Table Length	W/G/U	Indikator-Bits auf Seitenebene
STB	Segment Table Base	PPAG	Seiten-Nummer (physikalisch)
VSEG	Segment Nummer (virtuell)		
VPAG	Seiten-Nummer (virtuell)		

Abb. 2 Ablauf des Befehls "DISPLAY PAGE INDICATORS (DPI)"

< function-id > < task-id> <pointer to parameter-area >

< function-id >:   SSI / SPI

SSI   Funktion "Set Segment Indicators"

SPI   Funktion "Set Page Indicators"

< task-id >: Identifier der Task, deren Adreßüber-
setzungstafelwerk das Segment oder die
Seite beinhaltet, deren Indikatoren
zu setzen sind

< pointer to verweist auf einen Parameter-Bereich,
parameter area > der folgenden Aufbau hat

für SSI:

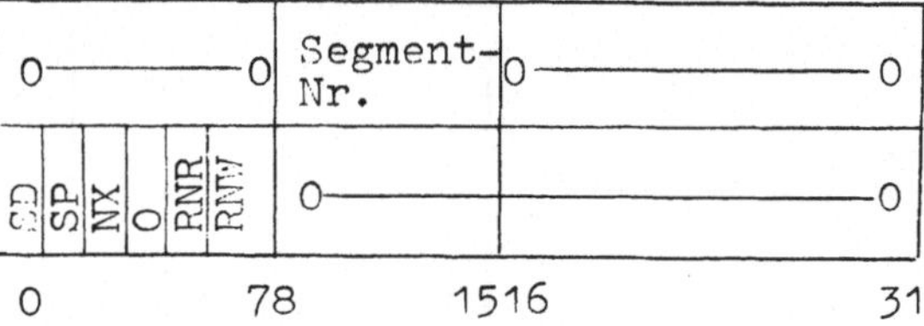

für SPI:

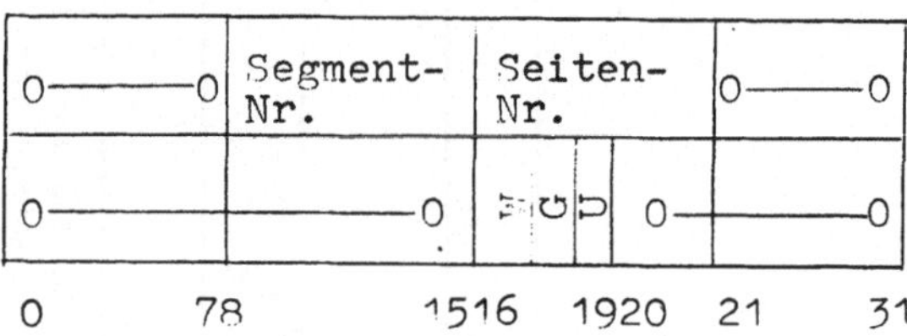

(Die Bezeichnungen der Indikatoren ist
wie bei den Display-Funktionen beschrieben)

Abb. 3 Aufruf und Parameterfelder der Befehle
"Set Segment Indicators (SSI)" und
"Set Page Indicators (SPI)"

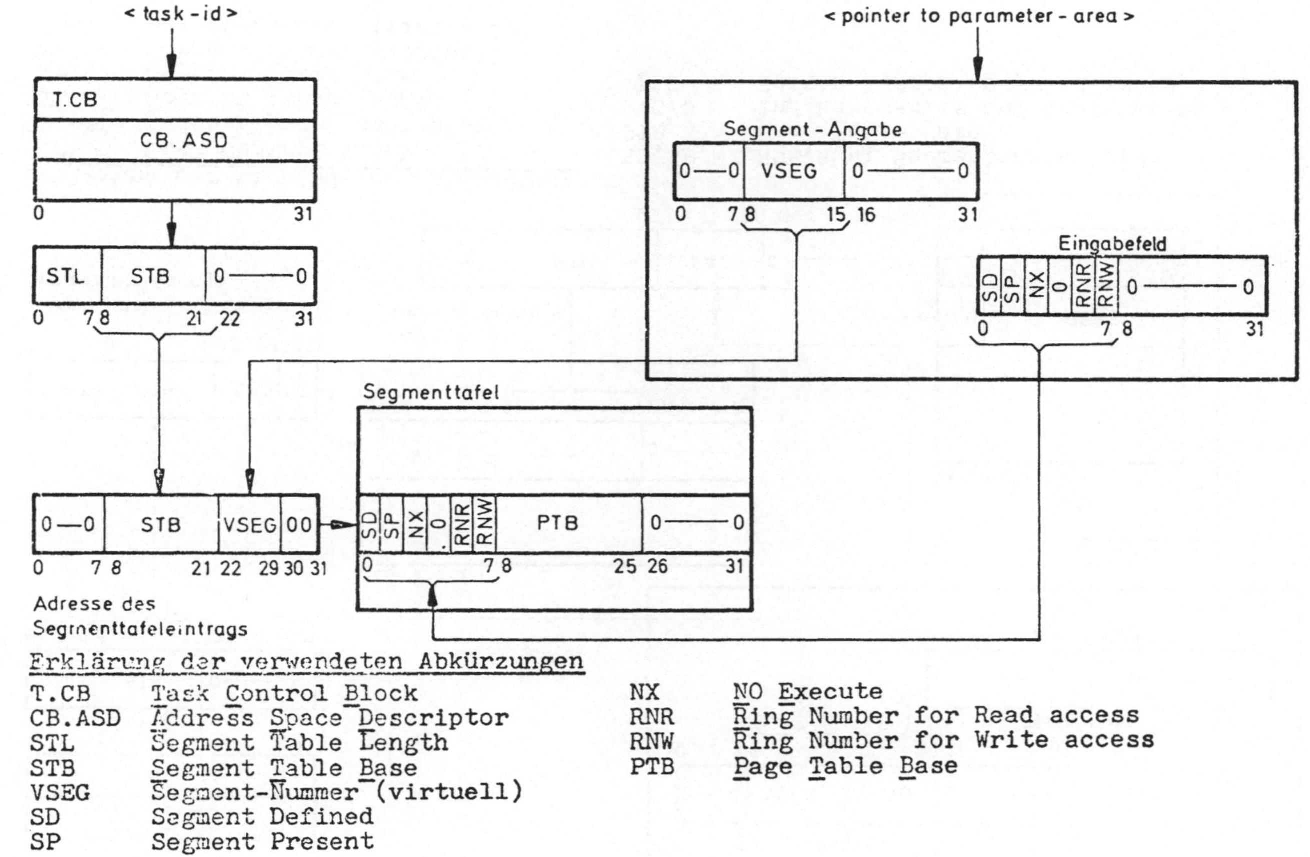

Erklärung der verwendeten Abkürzungen

T.CB	Task Control Block	NX	NO Execute
CB.ASD	Address Space Descriptor	RNR	Ring Number for Read access
STL	Segment Table Length	RNW	Ring Number for Write access
STB	Segment Table Base	PTB	Page Table Base
VSEG	Segment-Nummer (virtuell)		
SD	Segment Defined		
SP	Segment Present		

Abb. 4   Ablauf des Befehls "SET SEGMENT INDICATORS (SSI)"

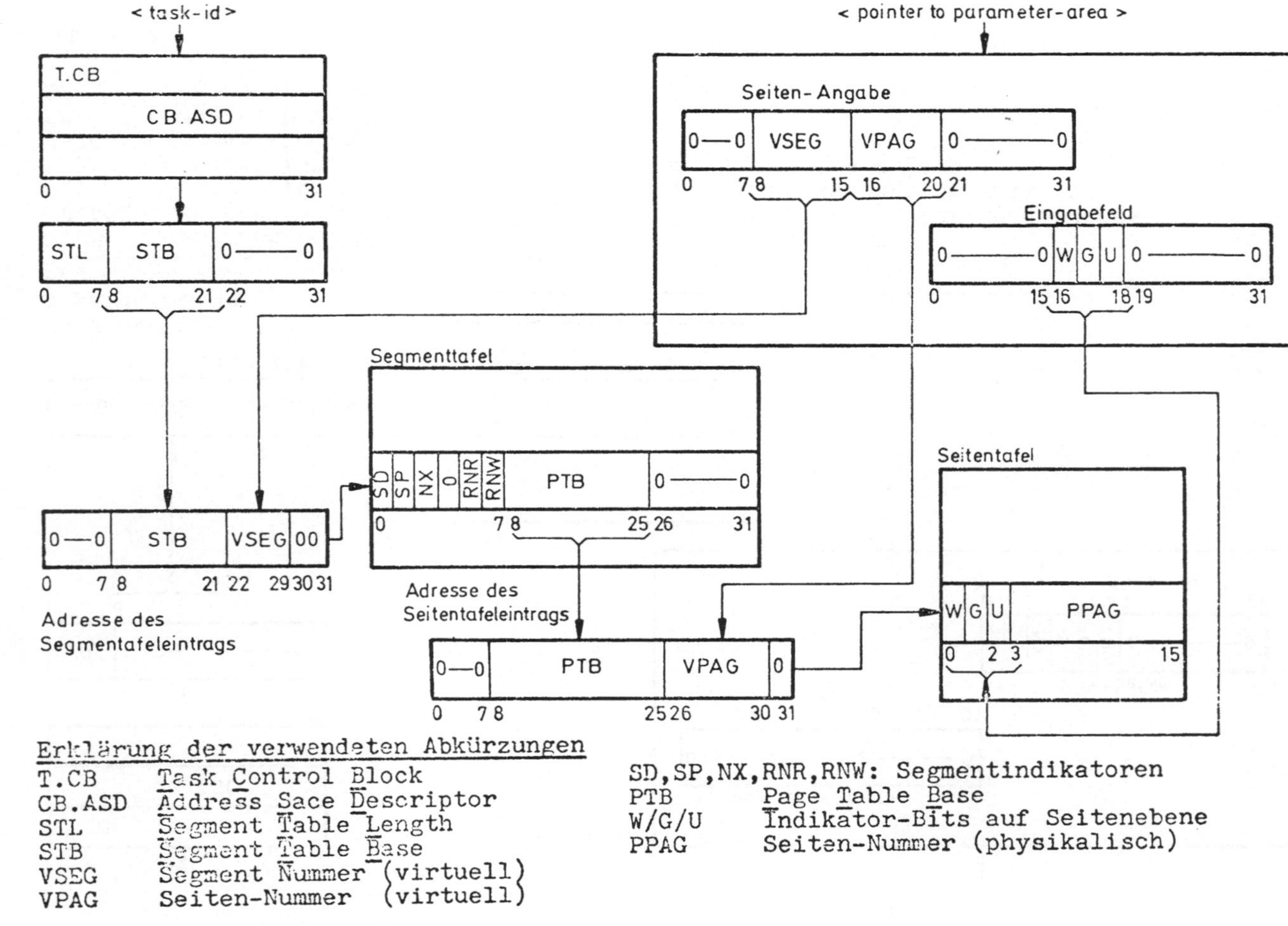

Erklärung der verwendeten Abkürzungen

T.CB	Task Control Block
CB.ASD	Address Sace Descriptor
STL	Segment Table Length
STB	Segment Table Base
VSEG	Segment Nummer (virtuell)
VPAG	Seiten-Nummer (virtuell)

SD,SP,NX,RNR,RNW:	Segmentindikatoren
PTB	Page Table Base
W/G/U	Indikator-Bits auf Seitenebene
PPAG	Seiten-Nummer (physikalisch)

Abb. 5 Ablauf des Befehls "SET PAGE INDICATORS (SPI)"

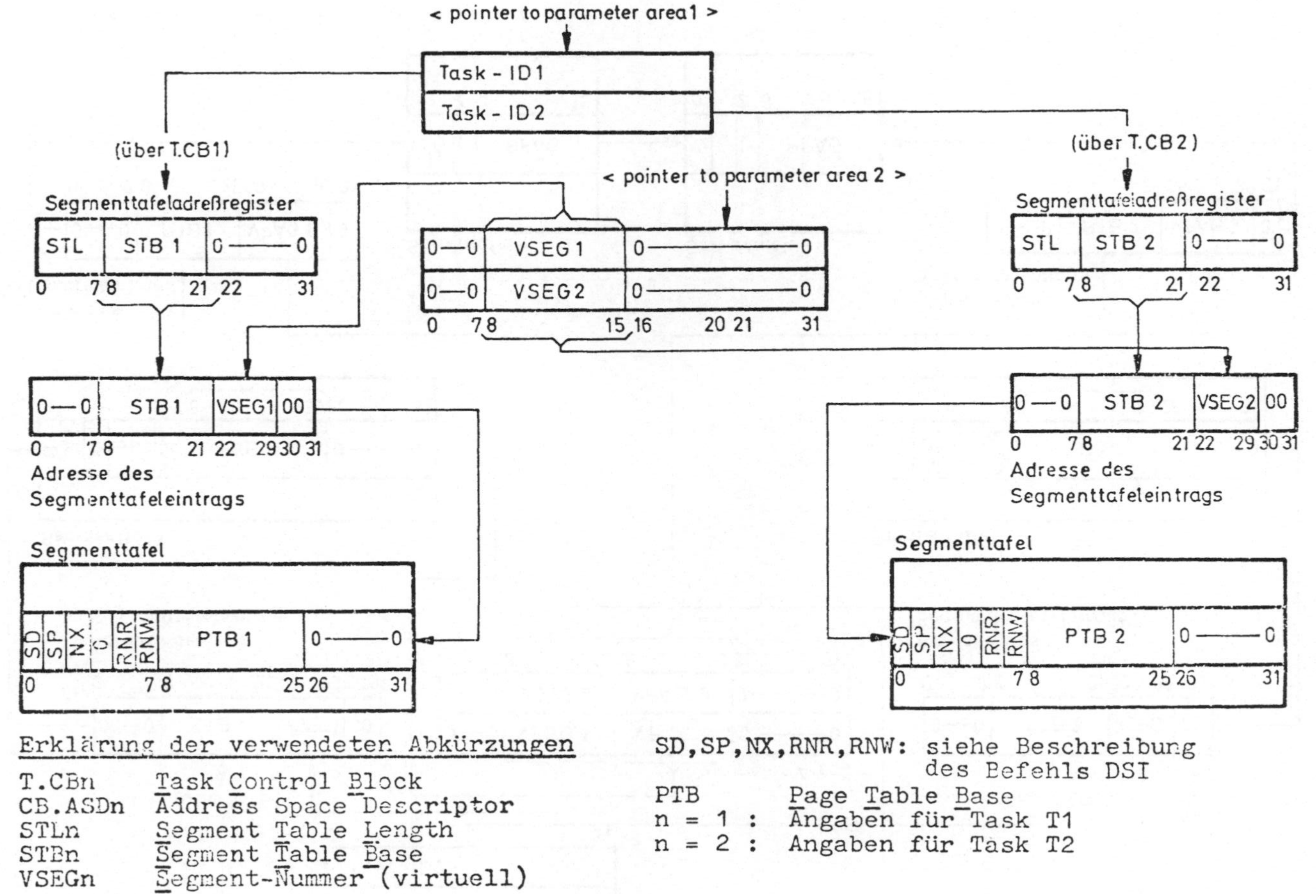

Erklärung der verwendeten Abkürzungen

T.CBn	Task Control Block
CB.ASDn	Address Space Descriptor
STLn	Segment Table Length
STBn	Segment Table Base
VSEGn	Segment-Nummer (virtuell)

SD,SP,NX,RNR,RNW: siehe Beschreibung des Befehls DSI

PTB	Page Table Base
n = 1 :	Angaben für Task T1
n = 2 :	Angaben für Task T2

Abb. 6   Ablauf des Befehls "TRANSFER SEGMENT (TFS)"

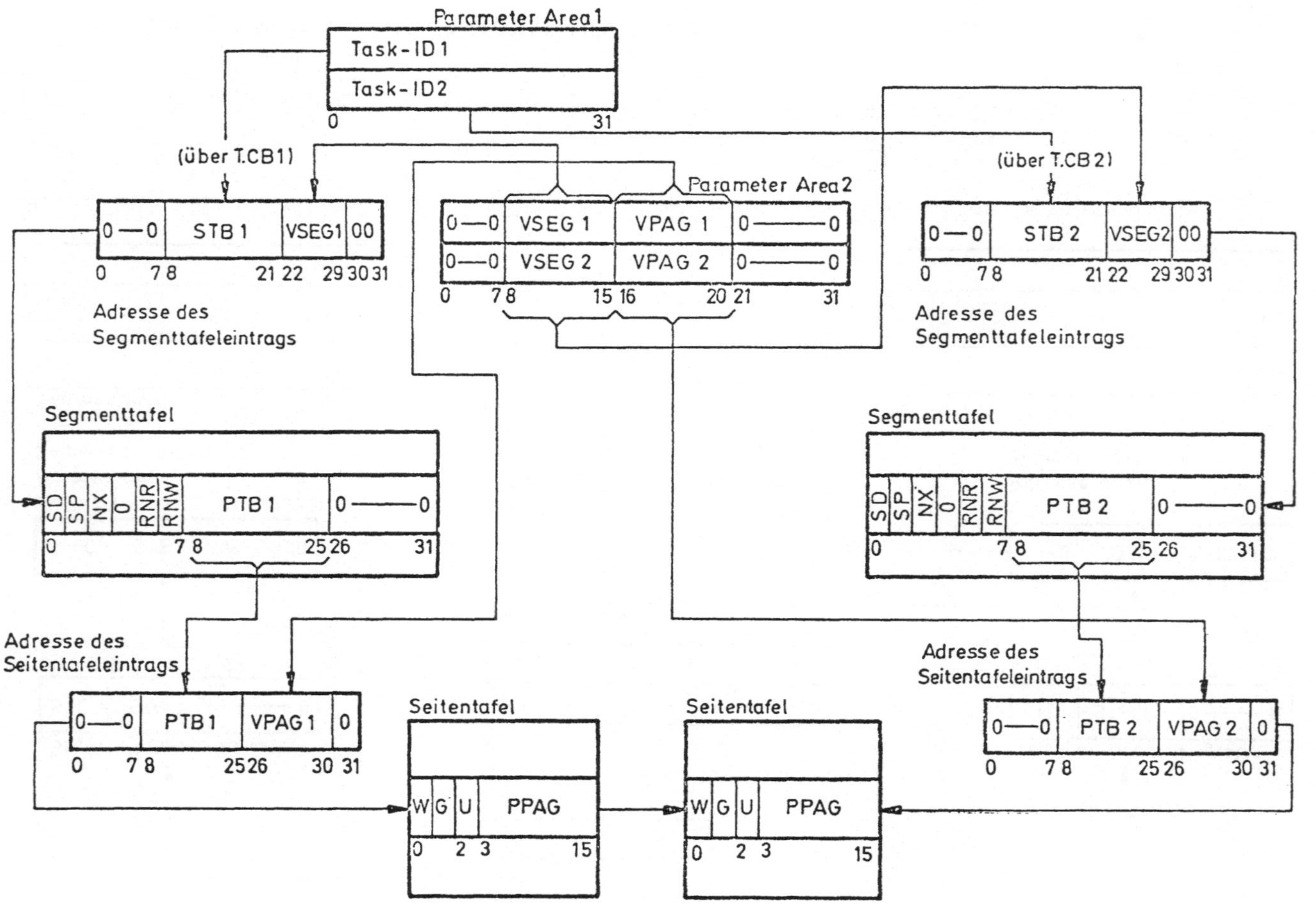

Abb. 7 Ablauf des Befehls "TRANSFER PAGE (TFP)"

<u>Erklärung der verwendeten Abkürzungen</u>

T.CBn	Task Control Block
CB.ASDn	Address Space Descriptor
STLn	Segment Table Length
STBn	Segment Table Base
VSEGn·	Segment-Nummer (virtuell)
VPAGn	Seiten-Nummer (virtuell)
SD,SP,NX,RNR,RNW:	siehe Beschreibung
	des Befehls DSI
PTBn	Page Table Base
W,G,U	Indikator Bits auf Seiten-Ebene
PPAG	Seitennummer (physikalisch)
n = 1 :	Angaben für Task T1
n = 2 :	Angaben für Task T2

Bei dem Befehl "TFS" (siehe Bild 6) wird nun mit
Hilfe des ersten Wortes im Parameterbereich 2
der gewünschte Eintrag in der Segmenttafel der Task
T1 adressiert. Es wird auf den durch das 2. Wort des
Parameter-Bereiches gegebenen Platz in der Segment-
tafel von T2 kopiert. Die dort zuvor vorhandene
Information wird überschrieben.

Der Ablauf für den Befehl "TFP" ist analog; es werden hier lediglich statt der Segmenttafeleinträge
Seitentafeleinträge übertragen (siehe Bild 7).

4. <u>Anwendungsfall</u>

Die Anwendungen der geschilderten Zugriffsfunktionen
soll anhand eines Beispiels der Behandlung eines
Page-Faults demonstriert werden (vgl. Bild 8). Die
folgende Schilderung ist als eine vereinfachte Prin-
zipskizze anzusehen.

Nachdem als Unterbrechungsursache das Fehlen der Seite
mit dem Seitentafeleintrag E1 der Task T1 erkannt wurde, muß durch die Algorithmen der Speicherverwaltung
des VMS festgestellt werden, ob die Fehlseitenbedingung
durch eien Seitenrahmen innerhalb des working-set von
T1 oder durch einen Rahmen einer anderen Task T2 des
VMS befriedigt werden soll. Anschließend wird durch
einen LRU-("least recently used") Algorithmus der
Rahmen einer Seite ermittelt, der zur Befriedigung
des Page-Faults herangezogen wird. Da für den LRU
Algorithmus die Indikatoren der Seitentafel-Einträge
herangezogen werden, werden sie mit dem Befehl "Display Page Indicators (DPI)" Eintrag für Eintrag ge-
lesen und ausgewertet. Falls die diesen Seitenrahmen
belegende Seite kein gültiges Abbild auf dem Hintergrundspeicher besitzt, muß sie herausgeschrieben werden. Anschließend wird Platz im Hauptspeicher für die
fehlende Seite zugewiesen: Mit Hilfe des Befehls
"Transfer Page (TFP)" wird der Eintrag E2 der ausgewählten, im Hauptspeicher befindlichen Seite auf den
Platz des Eintrages E1 der fehlenden Seite kopiert.
W- und U-Bit von E2 werden mit Hilfe des Befehls
"Set Page Indicators (SPI)" auf "o" gesetzt; hierdurch wird die entsprechende Seite als nicht im
Hauptspeicher befindlich markiert [9].
Die Indikatoren des Eintrages E1 werden ebenfalls
durch einen SPI-Befehl gesetzt: Das W-Bit erhält den
Wert "o" und das U-Bit wird auf "1" gesetzt.

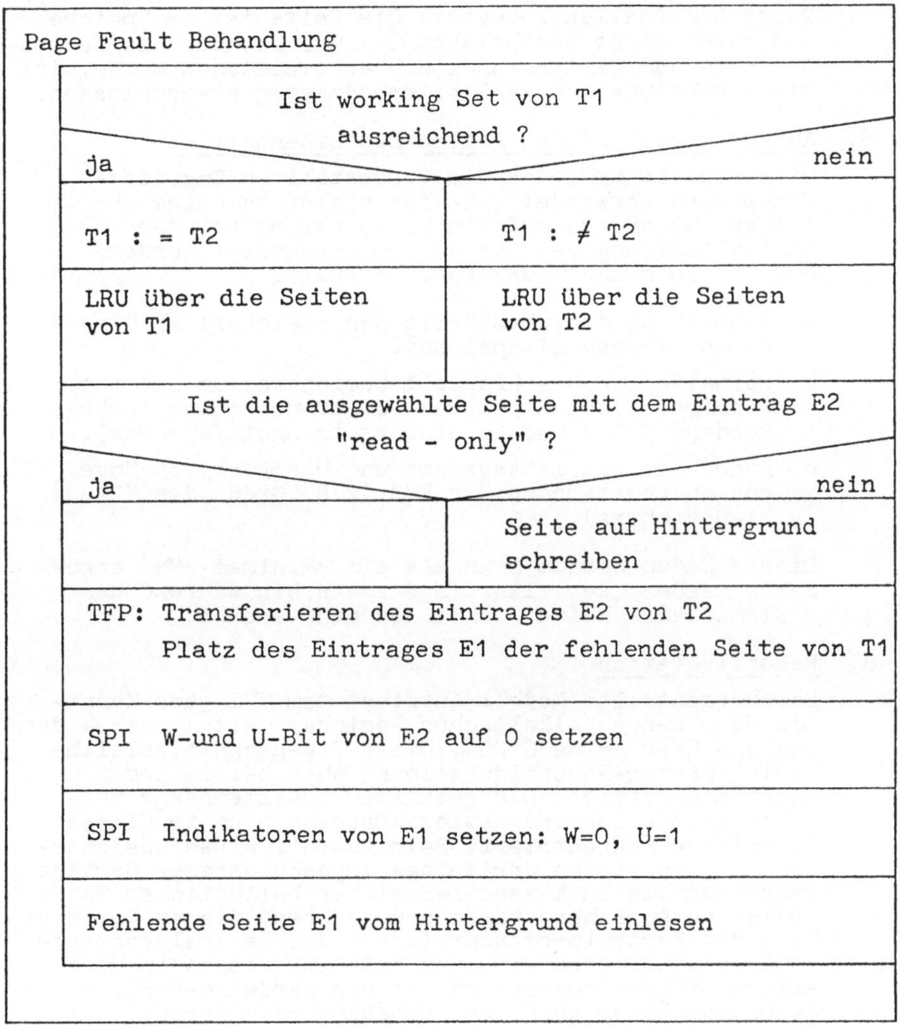

Page Fault Behandlung

Ist working Set von T1
ausreichend ?

ja   nein

| T1 : = T2 | T1 : ≠ T2 |
| LRU über die Seiten von T1 | LRU über die Seiten von T2 |

Ist die ausgewählte Seite mit dem Eintrag E2
"read - only" ?

ja   nein

| | Seite auf Hintergrund schreiben |

TFP: Transferieren des Eintrages E2 von T2
Platz des Eintrages E1 der fehlenden Seite von T1

SPI   W-und U-Bit von E2 auf 0 setzen

SPI   Indikatoren von E1 setzen: W=0, U=1

Fehlende Seite E1 vom Hintergrund einlesen

Abb. 8   Ablauf der Behandlung eines "Page Fault"

Diese Kombination bedeutet: Die Seite ist im Speicher und wurde nicht beschrieben 1) [9]. Nachdem die fehlende Seite vom Hintergrundspeicher eingelesen wurde, ist die Behandlung der Fehlseitenbedingung abgeschlossen.

5. Auswirkungen auf den realen Maschinenbetrieb

Will man ein VMS, das die vorgestellten Zugriffsfunktionen verwendet, auf der realen Maschine ablaufen lassen, so muß ein Ladeprogramm bei der Initialisierung des Systems vorgeschaltet werden, daß die folgenden Funktionen erfüllt:

o Einteilung des physikalischen Speichers in Klasse I- und Klasse II-Speicher.

o Formatierung des Klasse I-Speichers, um die notwendigen Datenstrukturen aufzubauen (hier insbesondere T.CBs und Adreßübersetzungstafelwerke).

o Laden des Betriebssystems und Übergabe von Umgebungsparametern an das VMS (z.B. Größe des Klasse II-Speichers).

Dieses Ladeprogramm kann als ein "Minimal-VMM" angesehen werden, der allerdings späterhin während des Systemablaufs keine Funktionen mehr ausübt.

6. Rekonfiguration

Das vorgestellte Modell entzieht dem VMS jede Kenntnis über den physikalischen Speicher, mit Ausnahme des Wissens über seine Größe. Diese Eigenschaft erleichtert Speicher-Rekonfigurationen auch bei realem Maschinen-Betrieb. Die gesammten Zusammenhänge zwischen virtuellen und realen Adressen sind im Klasse I-Speicher konzentriert. Beim Ausfall eines Speichermoduls kann ein an der Anlage angeschlossener Service-Prozessor die im Klasse I-Speicher befindlichen Tabellen entsprechend verändern. Während dieses Vorgangs ruht der Zentralprozessor (oder: die Zentralprozessoren); anschließend wird dem VMS-Betriebssystem über seinen Eingang zur Behandlung von Hardware-Fehlern die Reduktion (oder auch, bei Behebung der Störung, die Vermehrung) der Menge des zugewiesenen physikalischen Speichers mitgeteilt.

---

1) Der nachfolgende Ein-Ausgabevorgang verändert die Indikatoren nicht.

7. Leistungsfähigkeit und Grenzen der Anwendung

Die vorgestellten Zugriffsfunktionen gestatten eine
weitgehend autonome Verwirklichung der Speicherverwaltung der VMS; d.h. zu keinem Zeitpunkt des Ablaufes
nach Initialisierung der VMS muß der VMM in das Geschehen eingreifen. Dabei müssen allerdings einige
Beschränkungen hingenommen werden.

Die erste Beschränkung betrifft die feste Aufteilung
von Klasse I-und Klasse II-Speicher. Diese Aufteilung
wird vom VMM bei Initialisierung des VMS festgelegt;
danach ist eine Verschiebung dieser Grenzen nur unter
"Mitwirkung" des VMS möglich. Sie wirkt gewissermaßen
als Rekonfiguration. Allerdings ist bei normalem Produktionsbetrieb nicht anzunehmen, daß diese Beschränkung von großer Bedeutung ist: VM-Systeme werden auf
einen bestimmten Arbeitsanfall und eine vermutete
Lastverteilung hin generiert; während einer Produktions-
schicht ändert sich das Lastprofil nicht wesentlich [1].
Man kann dies zusammenfassend mit "Performance ist
wichtiger als Dynamik" bezeichnen.

Die zweite Beschränkung ist eng mit der ersten ver-
wandt und betrifft das Paging von Speicher, der aus
der Sicht eines VMS im Hauptspeicher ist. Dies ist
beim vorgesehenen Konzept nicht möglich, läßt sich
allerdings mit einer Erweiterung realisieren. Man
kann nämlich Seiten- und Segmenttafeleinträge mit
einem zusätzlichen Indikator versehen, der in Verbindung mit dem SP-Bit (bei Segmenttafeleinträgen)
und dem W- und U-Bit (bei Seitentafeleinträgen) das
"wirkliche" Vorhandensein im Hauptspeicher anzeigt.
Man darf diesen Indikator den VMS nicht zugänglich
machen - weder lesend nich schreibend. Ist dieser
Zusatzindikator nicht gesetzt, so wird der VMM von
der Hardware verständigt, der dieses Ereignis behandelt [2]. Durch diese Erweiterung ließe sich auch
die erste Beschränkung eliminieren.

---

1) Diese Annahme liegt auch im wesentlichen den
   Arbeiten von Dedié und Zabel zugrunde [1].

2) Bei dem dargestellten Entwurf der Adreßübersetzungstafeln ist eine Unterbringung dieses
   Indikators nicht möglich, da der Platz bei den
   Seitentafeleinträgen fehlt. Hier müßte ein
   neues Format festgelegt werden.

Die dritte Beschränkung betrifft die Eigenschaft der
Rekursivität. Hier handelt es sich bekanntlich darum,
unter einem VMS eine Kopie des VMM so ablaufen zu
lassen, daß der VMM alle Eigenschaften eines VMM
beibehält [7]. Dies bedeutet eine Schachtelung von
Task-Familien und Klasse I-Speichern in unserem Modell,
die mit den vorgeschlagenen Mitteln nicht zu ver-
wirklichen ist. (Man könnte sich hier eine Stack-
Einrichtung vorstellen, die zur Verwirklichung dieser
Schachtelung heranzuziehen wäre. Der Aufwand ist
sicher nicht gering.) Der einzige Ausweg hier ist,
auf eine Hardware-Unterstützung zu verzichten und
die unter einem VMS ablaufende VMM-Kopie mit einer
Software-Komponente auszustatten, welche die Rolle
der Zugriffsfunktionen wahrnimmt. Dies ist möglich,
da die Zugriffsfunktionen als privilegierte Instruktionen ausgebildet sind, die abgefangen und
vom VMM abgehandelt werden können. Insofern ist
auch zu erkennen, daß die Zugriffsfunktionen
praktische ein Teil des VMM sind, der bei jener
Kopie des VMM, der auf der realen Maschine abläuft,
von der Hardware/Firmware dargestellt wird [1].

8. Schluß

Dies führt uns auf die eigentliche Zielsetzung zurück, die bei dem Entwurf der Zugriffsfunktionen
galt: Maßnahmen zu finden, die den "Normalfall"
begünstigen. Dies bedeutete im vorliegenden Fall,
Kompromisse zugunsten von Geschwindigkeit und Sicherheit und, falls tragbar, zu Lasten der Flexibilität
einzugeben. Hierbei sollte der Hardware-Aufwand
in vertretbaren Grenzen gehalten werden; die Neu-
entwicklung der Betriebssystem-Software war eine
akzeptierte Randbedingung, welche erst die skizzierte
Vorgehensweise möglich machte.

Die Verwendung von Zugriffsfunktionen innerhalb der
Siemens-Universalrechner ist dabei nicht eigentlich
neu; bisher wurden sie im wesentlichen benutzt,
um Hardware-Eigenschaften wie etwa die Ablage von
Kontrollinformationen, die abhängig von den Modellen
der einzelnen Zentraleinheiten einer Familie sind,
zu virtualisieren [8]. Neu am geschilderten Vorgehen
ist demgegenüber, daß die Zugriffsfunktionen auch
dazu verwendet werden, einen Schutz zwischen 2 Soft-
warekomplexen (nämlich VMM und VMS) zu konstruieren.

---

1) Vgl. auch die Diskussion über "impure virtual
machines" [2].

9. Literatur

1   Dedié G., Zabel D.: Ein leistungsfähiges VM-Konzept
    für das Siemens System 7.700. Im selben Band

2   Goldberg R.P.: Survey of virtual machine research.
    Computer 7:6, p. 34-45 (1974)

3   Goldberg R.P., Schwenk H.S.: Benefits of virtual
    machine rechniques for input/output. In: Infotech
    (ed.): State of the art report 22. Maidenhead/Berks.:
    Infotech 1975, p. 318-337

4   IBM (ed.): IBM Virtual machine facility/370:
    introduction, Release 3.Publ. No. GC-20-1800-5.
    Burlington/Mass.: IBM 1976

5   IBM (ed.): IBM Virtual machine facility/370:
    control program (CP) program logic, Release 2PLC4.
    Publ. No. SY-20-0880-3. Burlington/Mass.: IBM 1974

6   Parmelee R.P. et al.: Virtual storage and virtual
    machine concepts. IBM Systems Journal, 11:2,
    p. 99-129 (1972)

7   Popek G.J., Goldberg R.P.: Formal requirements
    for virtualizable third generation hardware.
    Comm. 17, p. 412-421 (1974)

8   Tang T., O'Flaherty K.: Virtual machines and the
    NCR Criterion. Datamtion 24:4, p. 129-134 (1978)

9   Siemens A.G. (Hrsg.): Siemens-System 7.000, Be-
    schreibung und Befehlsliste. Bestell-Nr. D 15/
    D 15/5104-03. München: Siemens A.G. 1978

10 Siemens A.G. (Hrsg.): Siemens-System 7.000/4004,
    Betriebssystem BS2000, SIM-BS1000, Beschreibung.
    Bestell-Nr. D 15/5383-01. München: Siemens A.G. 1976

11 Siemens A.G. (Hrsg.): Siemens-System 7.800, Modelle
    7.870, 7.872. Allgemeine Beschreibung. Bestell-Nr.
    D 16/6000-01. München: Siemens A.G. 1978

12 Siemens A.G. (Hrsg.): Siemens-System 7.000/4004,
    Betriebssystem BS2000, Systemgenerierung, Be-
    schreibung. Bestell-Nr. D 15/5140-03

SIMULATION NEUER SYSTEM-ARCHITEKTUREN

MITTELS VIRTUELLER MASCHINEN

A. Schaten *)
IBM Deutschland
Bereich Entwicklung und Forschung
Boeblingen

*)   Das Projekt wurde realisiert im IBM Laboratorium Boeblingen
unter Mitarbeit von

Hans Boettiger, Karl Klenk, Bobby Lie, Richard Pohl, Alfred Schaten

Abstract

The 4300-Maschine Simulation facility is an enhancement
package for the control program (CP) of VM/370. It allows the
function of a virtual 4300-Maschine in addition to the already
available IBM/360 and IBM/370 virtual machines. 4300-Maschine
simulation provides all functions to simulate all new
4300-Maschine instructions, the 4300-Maschine storage and I/O
instructions.

The project was realized to allow the development of the
operating system and hardware test programs for a new
computing system.

1.0 EINFUEHRUNG

4300-Maschinen Simulation ist eine experimentelle Erweiterung fuer VM/370, um Benutzern virtuelle Maschinen mit der 4300-Architektur zur Verfuegung zu stellen. Es handelt sich um ein Entwicklungswerkzeug, das die Entwicklung und das Testen eines Betriebssystems fuer diese Architektur ermoeglicht.

Alle bereits vorhandenen Funktionen des VM/370 sind weiterhin verfuegbar und nicht veraendert. Es ist daher moeglich, Betriebssysteme wie CMS, DOS/VS, VS1, MVS gleichzeitig auf einer realen Maschine zu betreiben. Der Benutzer muss lediglich mit Hilfe eines Kontrollprogramm-Befehls die richtige Architektur definieren.

2.0 ZWECK DER ENTWICKLUNG

Die Entwicklungszeit eines neuen Rechnersystems ist in den letzten Jahren immer kuerzer geworden. Ausserdem ist festzustellen, dass Entwicklungszeit und -kosten fuer die Software einen immer groesser werdenden Anteil im Verhaeltnis zu dem Gesamtaufwand fuer sich beansprucht. Bei Fertigstellung der Hardware und Auslieferung an Kunden muss auch das Betriebssystem zur Verfuegung stehen. Daraus ergibt sich, dass die Entwicklung von neuer Hardware und Software fuer ein Rechnersystem zeitlich parallel erfolgen muss. Es muss daher eine Moeglichkeit fuer die Entwicklung und das Testen der Software bestehen zu einer Zeit, da die vorgesehene Hardware noch nicht verfuegbar ist.

In diesem Fall soll unter 'Software' das neue Betriebssystem (evtl. mit Anwendungsprogrammen) und Hardware-Test-Programm (z.B. fuer Testabteilungen und Technischer Aussendienst) zu verstehen sein.

Zwei Loesungen bieten sich an:

    1. Entwicklung eines Hardware-Simulators

    2. Software-Simulatoren

2.1 HARDWARE-SIMULATOREN

Als Hardware-Simulatoren koennen vorhandene Maschinen verwendet werden,

    1. deren Architektur der neuen moeglichst aehnlich ist,

    2. die moeglichst mit einem Microprogramm gesteuert werden,

    3. die in genuegender Anzahl und zu annehmbaren Kosten verfuegbar sind.

Eine durch logische Schaltungen und Microcode veraenderte Maschine verhaelt sich genau wie die zu entwickelnde Maschine, lediglich ein anderes Leistungsverhalten ist gegeben.

Ausser dem geaenderten Rechner ist es oft notwendig auch neue Eingabe/Ausgabe zu simulieren. Fuer die Steuerung dieser Einheiten ist es in der Regel von Vorteil, wenn die Simulation in Steuereinheiten mit Hilfe von Microcode-Modifikationen oder mit programmierbaren Einheiten vorgenommen werden kann.

Ist fuer die Simulation eine Aenderung von logischen Schaltkreisen notwendig, so bedeutet dies normalerweise eine laengere Entwicklungszeit, groessere Probleme bei Aenderungen, hoehere Kosten.

2.2 SOFTWARE-SIMULATOREN

Software-Simulatoren sind zu unterscheiden nach solchen, die

    a) Anwendungsprogramme und Teile eines Betriebssystems und

    b) ein Betriebssystem als Ganzes

simulieren.

In den folgenden Ausfuehrungen soll lediglich der Punkt b) (Simulator fuer den Betrieb eines Betriebssystems) behandelt werden.

An einen solchen Simulator sind folgende Forderungen zu stellen:

1. Moeglichst vollstaendige Simulation der fuer das Betriebssystem vorgesehenen Architektur.

2. Verfuegbarkeit fuer alle Programmierer waehrend normaler Arbeitszeit.

3. Uebertragbar in weitere Entwicklungslabors.

4. Akzeptables Leistungsverhalten.

5. Gute Testeinrichtungen fuer den Programmierer.

6. Leicht anpassungsfaehig fuer Aenderungen der Architektur waehrend der Entwicklungsphase.

Virtuelle Maschinen sind besonders geeignet diese Erfordernisse zu erfuellen. Da VM/370 bereits virtuelle Maschinen mit IBM/360 und IBM/370 Architektur enthaelt, wurde dieses System gewaehlt, um auch die 4300-Architektur zu simulieren.

2.3 VORTEILE VON VIRTUELLEN MASCHINEN GEGENUEBER HARDWARE-SIMULATOREN

Neben der Erfuellung der im vorigen Abschnitt beschriebenen Erfordernisse, bieten virtuelle Maschinen einige weitere Vorteile gegenueber Hardware-Simulatoren:

1. Sie sind in beliebiger Anzahl verfuegbar

2. Weniger Platzbedarf

3. Bessere Testmoeglichkeiten fuer das Betriebssystem (Adressen-Vergleich, Anzeige und Aenderung von Speicherstellen und Registern, Verfolgung des Instruktionsablaufs, etc.)

4. Kein Ausfall durch defekt werdende Komponenten

5. Weniger Wartungsaufwand

6. Geringere spezielle Kenntnisse fuer die Wartung

7. Bessere Ausbeutung des verfuegbaren Rechners

8. Bedienung der (virtuellen) Maschine vom normalen Arbeitsplatz.

3.0 ARCHITEKTUR KOMPONENTEN

Bei der Simulation einer neuen Architektur sind folgende
Rechnerkomponenten von besonderer Bedeutung:

Daten- und Programmspeicher

Basis- und Kontrollregister

Program Status Word

Speicherschluessel

Instruktionsformat und -umfang

Systemunterbrechungen

Steuerung der Eingabe/Ausgabe Einheiten

Im folgenden sind einige Erlaeuterungen ueber die in dem
durchgefuehrten Projekt simulierte Architektur aufgefuehrt, im
besonderen die Aenderungen gegenueber der vorhandenen
(IBM/370) Architektur.

3.1 DATENSPEICHER

Der vorhandene Speicher ist ein Ein-Adress-Bereich Speicher
mit einer maximalen Kapazitaet von 16.777.216 Bytes. Dieser
Speicher ist immer ein virtueller Speicher, der vorhandene
reale Speicher kann mit Hilfe von Instruktionen nicht
adressiert werden. Wird vom Programm eine Speicherstelle
adressiert, so findet immer eine Adressumformung statt.

Der virtuelle Speicher wird aufgeteilt in 'Pages', jede 'Page'
enthaelt 2048 Bytes.

Der reale Speicher wird aufgeteilt in 'Page Frames'.
Kontrollinformationen, die jeder 'Page' zugeordnet sind, und

verschiedene Zaehler geben Auskunft ueber den Status einer 'Page Frame' und ob eine 'Page' einer 'Page Frame' zugeordnet ist.

3.2 BASIS- UND KONTROLLREGISTER

Anzahl und Verwendung der Basisregister ist unveraendert. Die Bits in den Kontrollregistern haben zum Teil eine etwas veraenderte Bedeutung als in IBM/370.

3.3 SPEICHERSCHLUESSEL

Ein 5-Bit-Speicherschluessel ist jeder 'Page' zugeordnet.

3.4 INSTRUKTIONSFORMAT UND -UMFANG

Da das Instruktionsformat gegenueber IBM/370 keine Unterschiede aufweist, musste bei der Simulierung nur auf den Instruktionsumfang Ruecksicht genommen werden. Dabei ist von Bedeutung, dass nur privilegierte Instruktionen (d. h. solche, die nur im Supervisormodus arbeiten) geaendert, geloescht und neue hinzugefuegt wurden. Es handelt sich im wesentlichen um solche Instruktionen, die mit der geaenderten Kontrolle des Datenspeichers zusammenhaengen.

3.5 SYSTEMUNTERBRECHUNGEN

Bei den Systemunterbrechungen sind, ebenso wie bei dem Instruktionsumfang, solche geaendert bzw. neu hinzugefuegt, die mit der Adressierung des Speichers zusammenhaengen.

3.6 STEUERUNG DER EINGABE/AUSGABE-EINHEITEN

Die Steuerung der Eingabe/Ausgabe-Einheiten geschieht bei der IBM/370 mit sogenannten 'Channel Command Words', 'Channel Address Words' und 'Channel Status Words'. Dieses Prinzip ist in der neuen Architektur beibehalten. Fuer neue Einheiten sind lediglich neue Kanal-Befehle hinzugefuegt worden.

_4._0 IMPLEMENTIERUNG DER 4300-MASCHINEN ARCHITEKTUR IN VM/370

4.1 DEFINIEREN EINER VIRTUELLEN 4300-MASCHINE

Jeder Benutzer, der unter VM/370 mit einer virtuellen Maschine arbeiten moechte, muss zunaechst definieren, mit welcher Architektur er arbeiten moechte. Das kann er tun mit Hilfe eines Befehls im Kontrollprogramm Modus, oder es geschieht automatisch, wenn ein Eintrag in dem fuer jeden Benutzer vorhandenen Benutzerverzeichnis eingefuegt ist.

Bei der Definierung der 4300-Maschinen Architektur im VM/370 laufen folgende Funktionen ab:

Erweiterung des Benutzer-Kontrollblocks (VMBLOK, ECBLOK)

Aufbau der Kontrollblocks, die den virtuellen Speicher der 4300-Maschine beschreiben

Aufbau von Kontrollblocks (Page- und Segmenttable), die den status der 'Pages' der 4300-Maschine beschreiben.

Nach dieser Initialisierung ist es moeglich, 4300-Maschinen Instruktionen ausfuehren, bzw. ein IPL (Initial Program Load) durchzufuehren. Das folgende Diagramm zeigt vereinfacht die Relationen der Kontrollblocks. Im naechsten Abschnitt ist eine naehere Erlaeuterung der Tabellen enthalten.

```
          VMBLOK                      SEGTABLE                    PAGETABLE
    *---------------*        *----->*----------*        *----------*
       I             I    I    I        --I---------->I          I
       I        -----I----*    I        I             I          I
*---I--            I         I        I             I          I
I  I              I         I        I             I          I
I  I              I         *----------*           I          I
I  I--------------I                                 *----------*
I  I virtuelle    I
I  I Basisregister I
I  I--------------I
I  I              I
I  *--------------*
I
I          ECBLOK                     ESEGTABLE                  EPAGETABLE
*-->*--------------*        *----------*        *----------*
    I        -----I---------->I        --I---------->I          I
    I              I         I        I             I          I
    I--------------I         I        I             I          I
    I virtuelle    I         I        I             I          I
    I Kontrollreg. I         I        --I--*        I          I
    I--------------I         *----------*  I        I          I
    I              I                        I        I          I
    *--------------*                        I        I          I
                                            I        I          I
                                            I        *----------*
                                            I
                                            I        EPAGE DESCRIPTION
                                            *-------->*----------*
                                                      I          I
                                                      ISpeicher- I
                                                      IschluesselI
                                                      I          I
                                                      *----------*
```

4.2 BETRIEB DES SPEICHERS EINER VIRTUELLEN 4300-MASCHINE

Wird eine 4300-Maschine unter VM/370 betrieben, so muss ein Speichersystem mit drei Ebenen betrachtet werden.

Die erste Ebene ist der reale Speicher der IBM/370, auf der VM/370 laeuft. Diese Ebene wird von VM/370 kontrolliert.

Die zweite Ebene ist der reale Speicher von der virtuellen Maschine aus betrachtet, in Wirklichkeit (vom VM/370 betrachtet), jedoch ein virtueller Speicher.

Nun hat die 4300-Maschine selbst einen virtuellen Speicher. Dies ist die dritte Ebene und wird als virtuell - virtuell - Speicher bezeichnet.

```
    Speicher der           Speicher der virt. Maschine
       IBM/370                 'real'            'virtuell'

    *-----------*          *-----------*        *-----------*
    I           I          I           I        I           I
    I           I          I           I        I           I
    I  VM/370   I          I           I        I           I
    I           I          I           I        I           I
    I           I          *-----------*        I           I
    I           I                               I           I
    *-----------*                               I           I
                                                I           I
                                                *-----------*

    1. Ebene              2. Ebene               3. Ebene

    realer               virtueller             virt.-virt.
    ----------------------------------------------------------
               Speicher fuer VM/370
```

Virtuelle Speicher in der IBM/370 Architektur werden beschrieben mit sogenannten 'Segment'- und 'Page'-Tabellen.

Ein solcher Satz von Tabellen beschreibt die jeweils naechste Ebene eines Speichers, z. B. die Segment- und Page-Tabellen im VM/370 beschreiben die 2. Speicherebene. Wenn eine Maschine mit einem virtuellen Speicher unter VM/370 betrieben wird, so ist ausserdem ein Satz Tabellen notwendig, der die 3. Ebene in Relation zur 1. Ebene beschreibt, das sind die E-Segment- und Page-Tabellen. Wenn VM/370 die Kontrolle an die virtuelle 4300-Maschine uebergibt, so werden die E-Segment- und E-Page-Tabellen fuer die Kontrolle des Speichers benutzt.

4.2 SIMULATION DER KONTROLLREGISTER

Waehrend die Basisregister bei der Uebergabe der Kontrolle an die virtuelle Maschine unveraendert in die reale Maschine uebernommen werden koennen, muessen die virtuellen Kontrollregister der virtuellen 4300-Maschine bei der Uebergabe in die reale Maschine den Bedingungen der IBM/370-Architektur angepasst werden.

4.3 BEHANDLUNG DES SPEICHERSCHLUESSELS

Bei der 4300-Maschine kann jeder 'Page' ein Speicherschluessel zugeordnet werden. Dieser Schluessel (er befindet sich in einer Tabelle, die ueber die ESEGTABLE zugreifbar ist) wird beim Laden einer 'Page' in den realen Speicher in die reale Maschine uebertragen.

4.4 SIMULATION DER 4300-MASCHINEN INSTRUKTIONEN

Fuehrt im VM/370 eine virtuelle Maschine eine privilegierte Instruktion oder aber eine Instruktion aus, die in der IBM/370-Architektur unbekannt ist, so fuehrt dies zu einer Programmunterbrechung und VM/370 bekommt die Kontrolle. Es

kann jetzt analysieren, welcher Art die Instruktion war, die
die Unterbrechung hervorgerufen hat. Falls es eine virtuelle
4300-Maschine war, so wird ueber eine Decodiertabelle
festgestellt, ob es sich um eine neue oder geaenderte
Instruktion handelt. In diesem Fall simuliert das
Kontrollprogramm diese Instruktion. Im folgenden Bild ist der
Ablauf dieses Vorganges dargestellt.

Simulation neuer Instruktionen

```
                                      I
                                      I
                          *-----------*-----------*
                          I    Programmunter-     I
                          I      brechung         I
                          *-----------*-----------*
                                      I
                                      I
                  nein  *-----------*-----------*
      *---------------*       Ist es eine       I
      I               I virt. 4300-Masch.?      I
      I               *-----------*-----------*
      I                           I ja
      I                           I
      I         nein  *-----------*-----------*
      +---------------*       Ist es eine      I
      I               I gueltige InstruktionI
      I               *-----------*-----------*
      I                           I ja
      I                           I
      I               *-----------*-----------*
      I               I    Simulation der     I
      I               I      Instruktion      I
      I               *-----------*-----------*
      I                           I
   *---------+---------*          I
   I Uebergabe der   I   *-----------*-----------*
   IUnterbrechung an I   I Erneute Uebergabe    I
   Idie virt. Masch. I   I an die virt. Masch. I
   *-----------------*   *-----------*-----------*
```

4.5 BEHANDLUNG DER SYSTEMUNTERBRECHUNGEN

Bei Systemunterbrechungen (Programmunterbrechungen oder solche, die mit der Adressierung des Speichers zu tun haben) bekommt VM Kontrolle und kann daher die Unterbrechung behandeln. Unterbrechungen, die nur im Modus der neuen Architektur vorhanden sind, koennen nicht waehrend des Laufs der virtuellen Maschine festgestellt werden, sondern dies geschieht in der Regel waehrend der Simulation neuer Instruktionen, d. h. wenn VM/370 die Kontrolle hat. Es ist daher moeglich, die Unterbrechung an die virtuelle Maschine weiterzugeben.

4.6 BETRIEB NEUER EINGABE/AUSGABE-EINHEITEN

Der Anschluss neuer Eingabe/Ausgabe-Einheiten ist unter VM/370 ohne groessere Probleme, - solange fuer die Ansteuerung IBM/370 Kanal-Architektur benutzt wird. Im VM/370 wird in der Regel keine Kontrolle ueber die Gueltigkeit eines Kanalwortes durchgefuehrt, sondern dies ist Aufgabe der entsprechenden Steuereinheit.

5.0 SIMULATION DER RECHNER-KONTROLLFUNKTIONEN

Hier handelt es sich im wesentlichen um die Simulation des 'Initial Program Load' (IPL). Diese Funktion muss vom Kontrollprogramm durchgefuehrt werden, oder es wird eine Routine in den Speicher der virtuellen Maschine geladen. Diese Routinen laden dann die ersten Informationen von dem Medium, auf dem das Programm gespeichert ist.

6.0 BEREITSTELLUNG VON TESTHILFEN

Fuer das Entwickeln und Testen eines neuen Betriebssystems unter VM/370 sind Testhilfen erforderlich. Da diese Funktionen im Kontrollprogramm ablaufen, ist die Steuerung verhaeltnismaessig einfach. Es handelt sich im wesentlichen um

Stoppen des Programmablaufs an einer vorher bestimmten Stelle

Anzeige der ausgefuehrten Instruktionen bzw. Verzweigungen (evtl. Stoppen nach jeder Instruktion)

Anzeige der ausgefuehrten Eingabe/Ausgabe-Operation, Programmunterbrechungen, Supervisor-Aufrufe, etc.

Anzeige und Veraendern von Daten im Speicher und in den Registern.

7. ZUSAMMENFASSUNG

Es hat sich bei dem durchgefuehrten Projekt gezeigt, dass es moeglich ist, im VM/370 virtuelle Maschinen mit neuer Architektur zu implementieren. Der groesste Aufwand ist, abhaengig von der Architektur, die Behandlung des Speichers, der neuen Instruktionen und evtl. der Eingabe/Ausgabe-Geraete.

Einschraenkungen bei der Implementierung der Architektur muessten u. a. gemacht werden, wenn

vorhandene nicht privilegierte Instruktionen geaendert waeren

der Adressbereich ueber 16 MByte hinausgehen wuerde

der Speicherschluessel erhoeht wurde

prinzipielle Aenderungen gegenueber der IBM/370 Architektur vorhanden waeren (anderes System der Unterbrechungen, andere Eingabe/Ausgabe Kanalsteuerung).

VIRTUAL MACHINES AND DISTRIBUTED PROCESSING*

Robert P. Goldberg
Peter S. Mager

BGS Systems, Inc.
Lincoln, Mass., U.S.A.

John G. Perry, Jr.

Naval Surface Weapons Center
Dahlgren, Virginia, U.S.A.

Abstract:

This paper proposes a taxonomy for classifying networks of virtual
machines in terms of the complexity of the communication mechanisms and
the layering of communication functions. It shows how four currently
implemented networks using (1) the virtual service machine approach, (2)
embedding of communication functions in the control program, (3) a
packet switching communication subnetwork and (4) a multiprocessor
system fit into this framework. Implications for future developments
are then discussed.

1. Introduction

For the last decade computer centers have been using Virtual Machine
based systems such as VM/370 as an effective mechanism to achieve
isolation among users and to allow multiplexing of several logical
machines on a single physical machine. This has been particularly
useful for the testing of new versions of operating systems and for the
provision of interactive time sharing (time slicing based) services. It
has also had the effect of encouraging modular programming by dividing
operating system functions between a small highly stable kernel -
virtual machine monitor or VMM (e.g. the CP or control program of

----
* This paper does not necessarily express the official views or judgment
of the Naval Surface Weapons Center.

VM/370) and a higher level operating system containing the user
interface (e.g. CMS).

Because allocation of real resources and multiplexing between users can
be handled by the VMM, the operating system in a virtual machine can be
made relatively simple and can concentrate on providing a user friendly
interface to application programs and people. This tends to increase
the reliability and usefulness of the total system [GOLDBERG 74].

In recent years the advent of cheaper small computers and an increased
awareness of the advantages of dispersing data processing functions
among geographically remote sites has created a need to combine
conventional techniques for supporting multiple users in a computer
system with communication mechanisms that allow the computational load
to be shared among multiple processors. This is partially to allow data
files to be stored and accessed at multiple locations convenient to
users and more commonly to allow data centers to acquire additional
resources (processors) over time and to integrate them into their
computer systems in a smooth and reliable manner.

In this paper we will explore the technologies useful for doing this,
develop a classification methodology to help analyze how existing
systems relate to these techniques and analyze 4 systems that approach
the integration of virtual machine technology and distributed processing
in different ways. We will then speculate on future directions these
technologies may take.

2. Principles of VM Networks

One of the most appealing properties of the VM approach has been
isolation. Each VM is guaranteed to be an efficient isolated duplicate
of a real machine. Software runs in the virtual machine and is free of
contamination or side effects from other virtual machines. Most of the
early and current applications of virtual machines make extensive use of
the isolation property.

As VM technology and applications evolved, inter-VM (intra-host)
communications facilities were developed. The most prevalent early
mechanisms in VM/370 utilized the pair-wise association of virtual card
punches and virtual card readers for communications. Subsequent
developments (both research and product line) included a number of new
mechanisms and implementation techniques. However, some of these
approaches compromised the "purity" of the VM. They included the page
swap and data move methods, segment storing, channel to channel
adaptors, and various SPY/VMCF facilities that use the DIAGNOSE
instruction. Donovan and Jacoby [DONOVAN 77] provide examples and
references for some of these approaches.

The complete isolation of individual virtual machines has given way to
formalized controlled sharing and communications between them.
Analogously, the isolation of individual host machines is evolving into
networks. These networks include both geographically dispersed and
local configurations, systems containing simple nodes (single
processors) and complex ones (multiprocessors), and differing levels of
interconnection between host processors.

In order to view this maturing field of system activity, it is helpful
to have a conceptualized framework with which to characterize current
and future VM network systems. In the section which follows, we
introduce two unifying frameworks. One addresses topological issues and
the other addresses architectural levels of abstraction.

2.1 Characteristics for Classifying VM Networks

Virtual machine networks can be classified in terms of the techniques
used for inter-host communications and in terms of the services the
networks provide.

Two considerations that affect the choice of techniques and the types of
services that can be provided are the extent of separation between
communicating virtual machines and the complexity of each node of the
network. The separation can be characterized by the topology,
geographical distances and number of hosts (cardinality) supported by

the network. The node complexity is determined by whether each node consists of a single host, multiple processors, a local subnetwork or some combination of the above.

The extent of separation between virtual machines is often the dominant consideration in current VM networks. This separation or dispersion can be illustrated in a hierarchical fashion. See Figure 2-1.

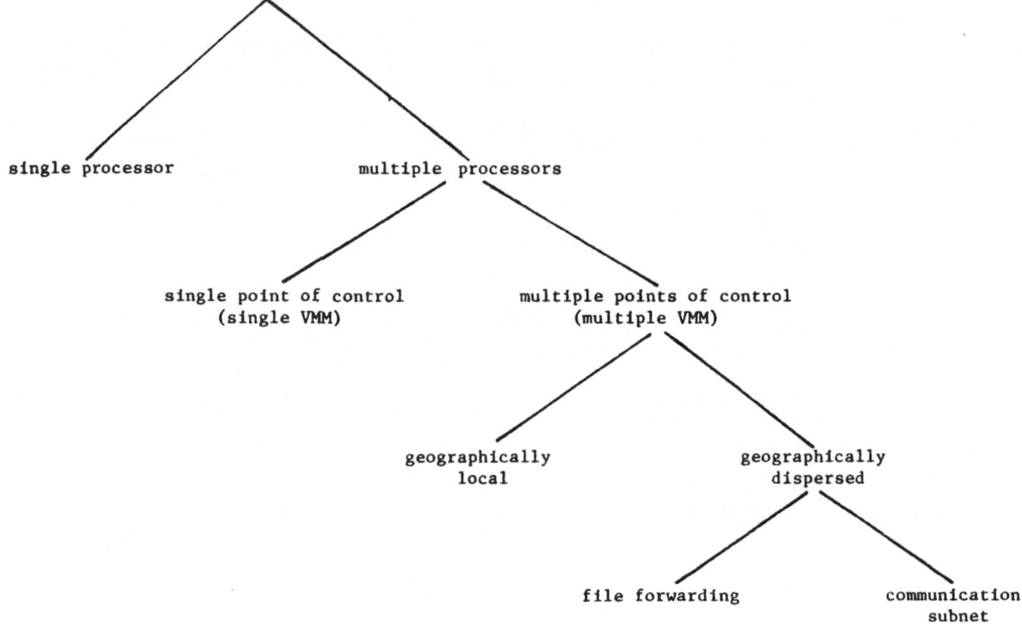

Figure 2-1 Levels of Complexity in a VM Network

The uniprocessor leaf of the tree is a degenerate case, and is not discussed separately in this paper.

The multiple processor single host (single VMM) configuration potentially allows load sharing and process (VM) migration. This type of configuration is illustrated by the MICS system described below. More conventional examples include the VM/370 asymmetric multiprocessing system described by Holley et al [HOLLEY 79] and the experimental Honeywell L68 VMM system described by Goldberg et al [GOLDBERG 76].

Multiple VMM systems usually involve an additional level of protocol
(that between hosts) beyond the VM to VM communication of single VMM
systems. The type of communication used is often determined by
technology and is thus dependent on the bandwidth of the connection
between hosts. The overriding factor is usually whether the hosts are
geographically local allowing some shared memory or shared DASD
interface or geographically remote forcing reliance on more standard
(and slower) communication mechanisms. A geographically local system
developed by the Interactive Data Corporation to share workloads between
2 IBM 370/168's each running VM/370 is discussed below and contrasted
with 2 approaches toward communication in geographically dispersed
systems: a store and forward file spooling system developed by IBM and a
packet switching communication subnetwork approach used by National CSS.

2.2 VM Network Layers

A VM network can be thought of as consisting of three main layers each
of which may be divided into one or more sublayers or levels [GASPAR 78,
THURBER 78]. As illustrated in Figure 2-2, these layers are:

* application
* VM network or function management
* communications subnetwork or transmission

The lowest layer (communication subnetwork) conveys information from one
host machine to another, from a terminal to a host machine or between 2
terminals. It may append whatever control information it deems
appropriate on top of the information to be transferred or may exchange
information between nodes in separate units or packets. The information
is treated as data by the subnetwork. It may be broken up into packets
(several packets per information unit or message) or combined into
transmission units (several information units or pieces of information
unit per transmission unit or packet). When the packets get to their
final destination they are reassembled into messages and presented to
the host (or next level of protocol) as a single coherent message. The
fact that the message may have been broken up and the pieces transmitted
separately is transparent to the host and higher levels.

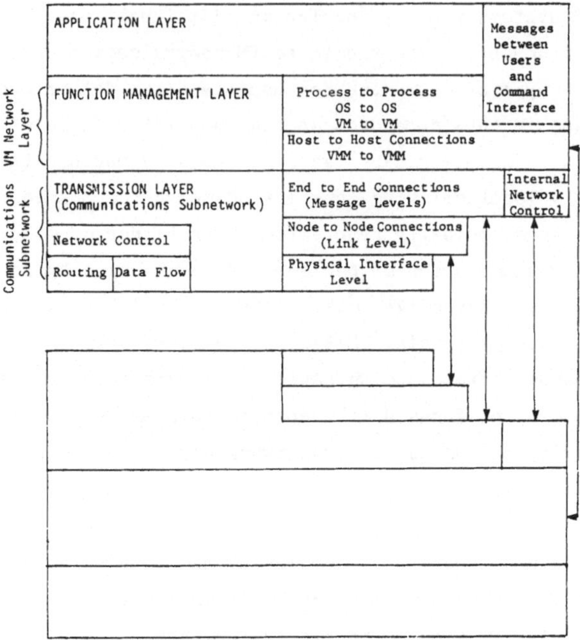

Figure 2-2   VM Network Layers

The intermediate (function management layer) contains the control
information needed to get data from one virtual machine (or supporting
operating system on the VM) to another VM that may reside on a different
host processor in the network.   It does this by using the underlying
communications layer.

The function management layer is usually divided into two sublayers:

* the host to host sublayer responsible for transporting data
  between host processors and

* the process to process (or VM to VM) or inter-process
  communication (IPC) sublayer

These layers perform such functions as session and connection
establishment, synchronization, and data flow control [SCHWARTZ 77].

The top layer (Application Layer) is a flexible group of sublayers under
the control of application programs running in a particular environment
(in this case a virtual machine with supporting operating system). The
communication mechanism at the highest layer is usually in the form of
user visible commands. For example, it may be the command level of an
electronic mail system, a command level interpreter of an operating
system, the command interface of an interactive language system or just
input data and commands to a program. The commands may be presented in
a linear stream or in an interactive manner.

A principal advantage of this layered approach is that the inter-process
communication mechanisms of the VM network (function management) layer
can be made independent of the actual communication mechanisms used.
Thus these higher layers can be made transportable (with relation to the
underlying communication network implementations) and somewhat more
universally applicable.

The layered description above provides a model useful for discussing VM
networks. However, in practice the layering can be somewhat blurred in
implementation. Indeed, historically, systems and networks evolved in
an ad hoc fashion in response to specific user needs that were
recognized gradually over a period of time.

3. <u>Survey</u> <u>of</u> <u>Existing</u> <u>Approaches</u>

We will here survey 4 basic approaches, 3 of which are in current use,
the other employed in an experimental system designed to test the
viability of the VM approach in a multi-processor environment:

> (1)   The virtual service machine approach exemplified by
> VNET (and associated networking systems, NJI and
> HASP/NJE), RASP, and RSCS.
>
> (2)   The direct connection approach, exemplified by IPC.
>
> (3)   The communications subnetwork/packet switching
> approach exemplified by NCSS.
>
> (4)   The multiprocessor approach exemplified by MICS/2.

3.1 The RSCS/RASP/VNET Virtual Service Machine Approach

The generally available VM networking products for VM/370 use virtual
service machines to support networking [IBM, MARSHALL 78, MACKINNON 78].
Programs in user virtual machines (application programs and operating
systems) communicate with the communication virtual service machine
(VSM) via standard IPC calls, handled, for example, by VMCF (in VNET) or
spool files (in RSCS). The IPC calls (typically implemented using a
privileged instruction such as DIAGNOSE) are intercepted by the VMM,
which then transfers the information to the service machine. See Figure
3-1.

A service machine is treated like any other virtual machine by the VMM.
The chief difference is that its function is to support users and
processes running on (one or more) other virtual machines in a semi-
transparent way rather than running a user level program or operating
system. It provides a way to offload a function from the control
program (CP) and in this case isolates inter-machine communication
functions in a modular way.

A communication VSM handles line interfaces, spooling, routing, and
other control functions related to inter-machine communication task
management.

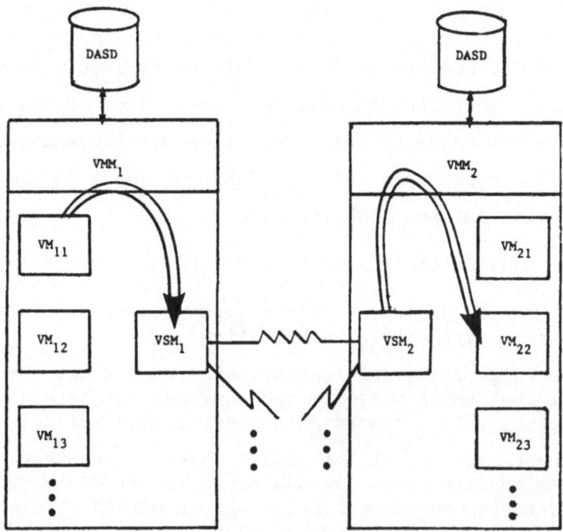

Figure 3-1   Inter-host Communication via Virtual Service Machines

3.1.1 RSCS

The Remote Spooling Communication System (RSCS) predated RASP and VNET
and provides the ability to spool files between machines. Each file is
transferred as an entity from the source processor to the next link on
the route from source to destination. An intermediate link stores the
entire file on disk and, when the entire file has been received, may
begin transmission to the next processor (link) on the route. Only very
primitive facilities are provided for error recovery if a processor or
line goes down during transmission. RSCS has been used mainly as a
remote job entry type of facility and for spooling output data sets and
input data streams between users at remote work stations or hosts and
the host that processes a job.

3.1.2 RASP

RASP and VNET are extensions of RSCS developed by groups at SHARE and
IBM respectively. They are intended to correct some of the limitations
encountered by early users of this type of networking and provide some
facilities for the relatively rapid exchange of short messages and
control information between host processors.

RASP alleviates many of the limitations of RSCS by providing:

* reentrant line drivers that can support more than one line
  of the same type without duplicating code,

* multileaving of several logical paths on a single physical
  line so that short messages and commands can be sent in
  parallel with file transmission over a single line,

* host error recovery at the driver level so that garbled
  messages or files lost because of an intermediate node
  going down can be automatically retransmitted (timeouts,
  etc.),

* a dynamic logon capability so that remote users can be
  connected to any available port rather than to one that is
  prededicated,

* an automatic dial capability so that connections to remote
  sites can be established as needed, eliminating the cost of
  dedicated telephone lines to sites to which communication
  is sparse,

* the ability to send short messages and commands without
  spooling them at each intermediate node,

* a set of commands (ORDER, PURGE, QUERY, CHANGE, SUSPEND,
  START, STOP) for querying, controlling, and checkpointing
  the flow of files through the network.

RASP keeps a list of the ROUTE'S (intermachine connections) available in
CP (VMM) tables. This list is checked whenever a user requests a spool
file to be sent ("routed") to a remote location so that the legitimacy
of the ROUTE can be verified. The checking is done at the CP level
because a single host can have multiple RASP machines with spooling
ROUTES partitioned among them.

A typical RASP network is shown in Figure 3-2. Short messages are
transmitted directly without spooling. Files are spooled before
forwarding, i.e. Host 2 must receive all of a file from Host 1 before

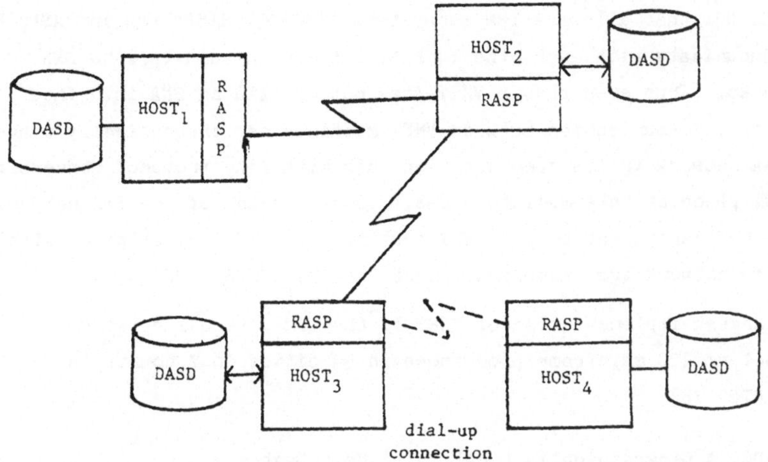

Figure 3-2   File and Message Spooling with RASP

beginning transmission of that file to Host 3.   Short messages are not
delayed by transmission of large files because multi-leaving allows
several logical paths to be available on a single physical communication
line.

3.1.3 VNET

VNET evolved from RSCS in parallel with and independently of RASP and
has similar features.   The development and initial use was internal to
IBM and geared to the need to communicate with a large number of HASP
(MVS/JES2) and ASP (JES3) installations as well as other VM/370
installations.

Extensions to RSCS include store and forward message switching and
alternate path facility, symmetric line protocols, VNET operator
control, an exec facility and accounting record provisions.
Communication is via bisynchronous (BSC) line protocols or channel to
channel adapter (CTCA).

Formally, VNET is one component of a general network interface facility
called NJI that allows 3 IBM subsystems (VM/370, HASP/JES2 and ASP/JES3)
to communicate with each other. HASP/RJE can in turn talk to SNA
networks. Thus even though VNET does not contain an SNA interface
directly, communication between VNET machines can theoretically traverse
an SNA network in its communication path with line protocol conversions
taking place at intermediate nodes. The traversal of the SNA network
would be transparent to the VNET routing (even if several nodes within
the SNA network are traversed) [CRABTREE 77, SIMPSON 78].

The largest implementation of VNET is the IBM internal network
connecting 220 mainframe processors in 53 cities in 7 countries
[COMPUTER 78].

3.2 IDC: A Geographically Local Multi-Host System

The Interactive Data Corporation (IDC) installation in Waltham,
Massachusetts consists of 2 Host computers (IBM 370/168's) connected
together by a channel to channel adapter (CTCA) and shared files on
disks. Users access these processors through a communication subnetwork
that handles terminal support and routes user terminal sessions to a
particular host (i.e. establishes a virtual circuit from a terminal to
the host on which its programs will run). Both host computers have read
only access to the user directory and read/write access to the other
disks. Lockout between machines for the R/W disks can be on a minidisk
level. Alternatively, an enqueue/dequeue type mechanism to allow
minidisk sharing can be used. [BARKALOW 78]

In practice the R/W disks belong to either Host A or Host B. If B wants
to send a file to Host A, it writes the file to its disk and transfers
ownership to A by a control message across the CTCA. A then copies the
file from B's disk to its disk and informs B via a control message so
that the copy on B's disk can be deleted.

Although there are only 2 host processors in the current IDC
installation, the protocols were designed to support an arbitrary number
of processors in both local and geographically remote locations. To

ease sharing of files on direct access devices, users are assigned to a user group which always runs on a given machine. The choice of machine is transparent to the user. Users are transferred between machines offline (by reconfiguring system tables) in order to achieve load balancing.

In the IPC approach network communication is broken up into 3 layers that handle processing of messages: host communication, interprocess (i.e. inter-virtual machine) communication, and user level communication.

The host communication protocol handles hardware dependent functions and data transfer across the communication link or CTCA. Its basic function is to transfer data between hosts. In practice it is broken up into 2 levels: a link level (supporting CTCA protocols) and a session level providing communication across the path provided by the link level.

The next level (the VM to VM or IPC level) is used by system processes (the supervisory functions of the operating system that perform operations desired by the user). These correspond to virtual machine functions such as spooling, console functions, and virtual I/O.

The highest protocol level is for user level communication.

Message traffic is processed by communication handlers buried within CP (the VMM). The associated software provides flow control and error handling.

The IPC host communication protocol (VMM to VMM) performs the following sequence of functions:

* Initiates the connection between hosts (VMMs).
* Identifies the source and destination hosts.
* Transmits or receives one or more messages to/from the connected host.
* Terminates the connection.

The connection initialization consists of a hand-shaking and identification sequence between the source and destination hosts. Upon completion of the dialogue, messages can be transmitted between hosts.

The headers of these messages contain the identities of the source and destination hosts, the symbolic names of the data handlers for the sending and receiving system processes, and a bit identifying the message type as control or data.

The system process-to-process (VM to VM) protocol is implemented by a set of procedures that utilize the host-to-host communication level to transfer control information and data from the source virtual machine to a pseudo-virtual machine on the destination host. The pseudo-virtual machine is an image of the source virtual machine. When this transfer is complete the IPC procedures initiate execution of a system process that transfers information between the pseudo and destination virtual machines. They then transmit any messages and completion codes directed to the source virtual machine back to the source host.

The IPC layer provides a mechanism transparent to the user in which system processes can be executed regardless of the location of the source and destination virtual machines. Typical processes that use this facility are VMCOM and console functions.

The concept of a pseudo-virtual machine simplifies distributing system processes between hosts. See Figure 3-3.

For example, User 1 on VM1 running on Host 1 generates a message (M1) to be sent to User 2 on VM2 running on a different host machine. The I/O request generated by VM1 is intercepted by the VMM that controls Host 1 and given to the communication monitor to execute. CM1 (the communication monitor for Host 1) takes the message and sends it to CM2 on Host 2, the location where it has determined User 2 is running, by looking in its user directory.

CM2 running on Host 2 receives the message and generates an interrupt to VMM2, then creates a pseudo-user (pseudo-user 1) in a special directory and forwards the message to User 2 on VM2 in such a way that the fact that User 1 is running on a different machine is transparent to the user process.

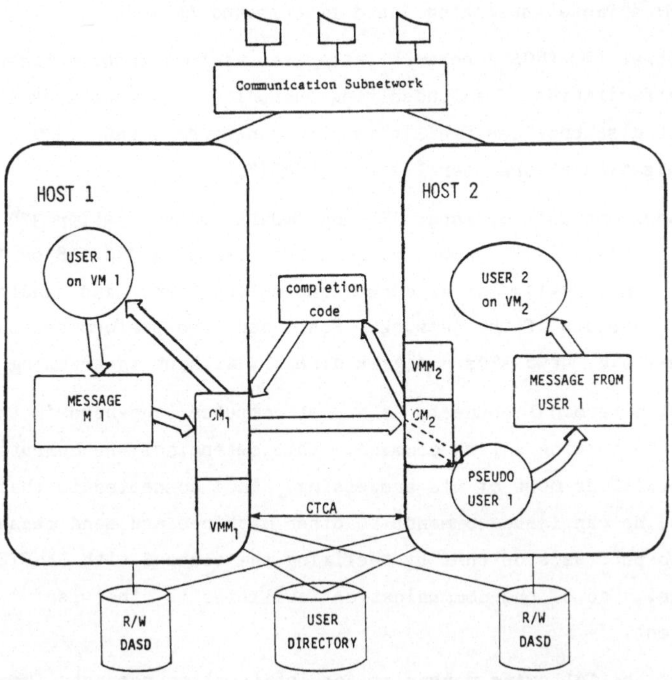

Figure 3-3 Message Transmission Between Different Host Machines

VMM2 then returns a completion code to User 1 via CM2, CM1, and VMM1.
The completion code acts as an acknowledgment of the message or an
indicator of some error condition.

3.3 NCSS: a Packet-switching Based Distributed Network

The National CSS (NCSS) network integrates virtual machine technology
with the facilities of an underlying communication subnetwork (Figure
3-4). It also provides facilities for transparency and
synchronization at the user level. [NCSS 78]

The network consists of large IBM and Amdahl hosts, smaller 370
compatible hosts (NCSS 3200s, roughly the size of a 370/138 or 148) and
PDP-11s. The PDP-11s act as communication front ends and handle packet
switching aspects of the network. Hosts can also perform switching
functions, e.g. two 370s can talk directly without intervening PDP-11s.

A user at a terminal connects to a host computer (anywhere in the
network) by issuing a link command. This determines the computer on
which he will do most of his processing. Once connected to that
computer, he can issue commands to other machines and send messages to
users and processes on them by prefixing the command with REMOTE and the
host name. Use of the communication facilities is otherwise
transparent.

NCSS uses the following mechanism for interpreting requests from virtual
machines for network services. A user issues a command, subroutine
call, or I/O to a file that has been defined to the system as a network
connection (using a FILDEF or file description command). The run time
package for the user's machine (part of the CSS operating system)
interprets the request and decomposes the user's message (which
generally looks to the user like a sequential file) into system level
messages of less than 390 bytes. The VM then requests the data to be
written by issuing a series of Start IO (SIO) instructions to a virtual
device that corresponds to an INTERCOMM (inter machine communication)
device.

The VMM control program (VP) traps the SIO since it is a privileged
operation and transforms it into a call to the network service routines
within VP. The network routines then break up the system level messages
into network sized packets that are transferred through the
communication subnetwork to the remote host.

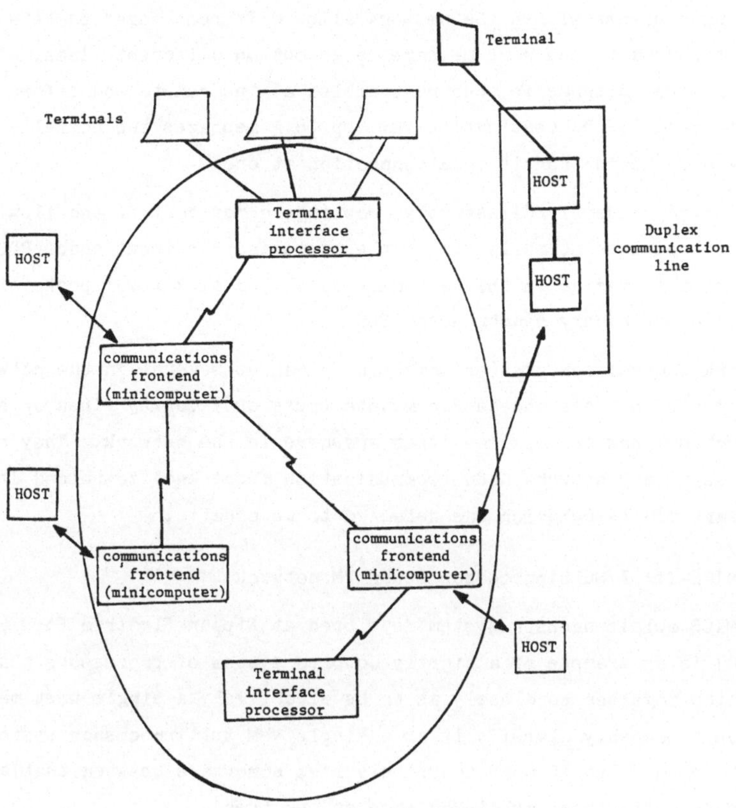

Figure 3-4 NCSS Hosts with Communication Subnetwork

Routing routines within the network allow different sized packets
corresponding to the same message to go out on different lines. The
system level message is then reassembled at the remote end before being
transferred to the destination VM. Up to 2 messages are normally
allowed to be in transit on a connection at once.

The network assembly/disassembly, routing, error control and flow
control routines normally run in the communication front ends (PDP-11s),
but may also reside in the host machines. The link level protocol is a
variation of binary synchronous (BSC).

Network control centers (of which there can be several in the network)
log errors on lines and can terminate (busy out) faulty lines or bring
up (unbusy) new or repaired lines anywhere in the network. They can
also cause any network node (communication front end) to reload its
software if its behavior was detected to be erratic.

3.4 MICS-II: A Multiprocessor based VM network

The MICS multiprocessor system developed at Nippon Electric Co. [OHMORI
78,79] is an example of a tightly coupled system of processors that
function together so closely as to be effectively a single host machine.
We would probably classify it as a single VMM multiprocessor system in
our taxonomy, but it more accurately lies somewhere between that and the
geographically local multi-VMM node on our tree.

The MICS machine (Figure 3-5) is a group of computational modules tied
together by 3 busses into a tightly coupled network. Each module
consists of 2 processors:

* a control processor that runs a communication and control
  interface incorporating many features of the VMM and
* a user processor that supports one or more virtual machines
  running user programs.

The VMM functions are divided between Processing Module Managers (PMMs)
running in each control processor and a single System Manager that runs
as a user virtual machine in a user processor. Each PMM is responsible
for event and communication handling (including detection of system

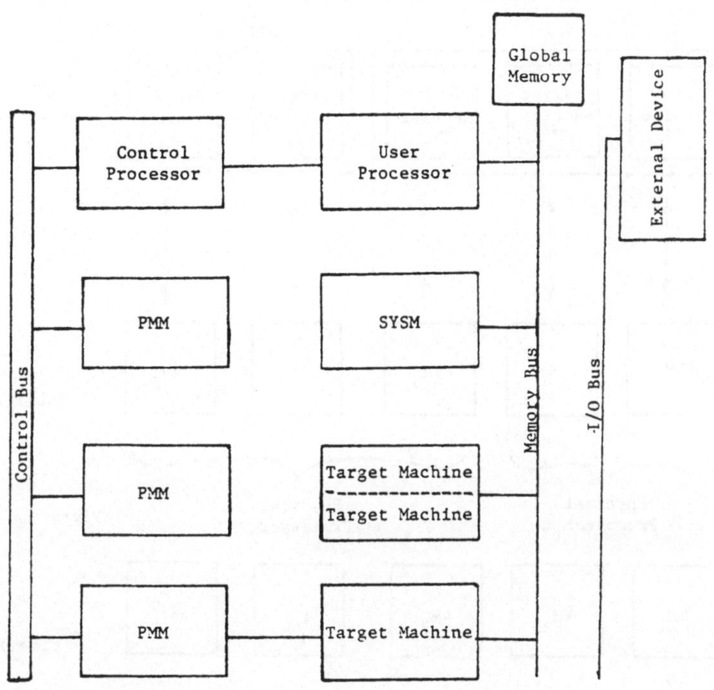

Figure 3-5   The MICS-II Configuration

calls and exceptional events and page fault handling) for its associated
user processor. It also serves as an execution monitor for the user
processor and maintains status information it uses to help control
process (virtual machine) migration between its own and other user
processors.

The System Manager (SYSM) serves as a global resource manager for the
network controlling such things as allocation of processing modules to
jobs and virtual machines at job startup, job initiation/deletion, page
unload/load from/to global memory, and a status reporter/operator
interface for the entire network. The SYSM can, at least in principle,
be recreated on a different user processor if the processor it is
running on crashes.

Mapping of user jobs onto real processors incorporates 2 levels of
abstraction beyond the VM to real processor mapping found in
conventional VM systems (See Figure 3-6). First a user conceptual
system (a job) is mapped into one or more target machines - job

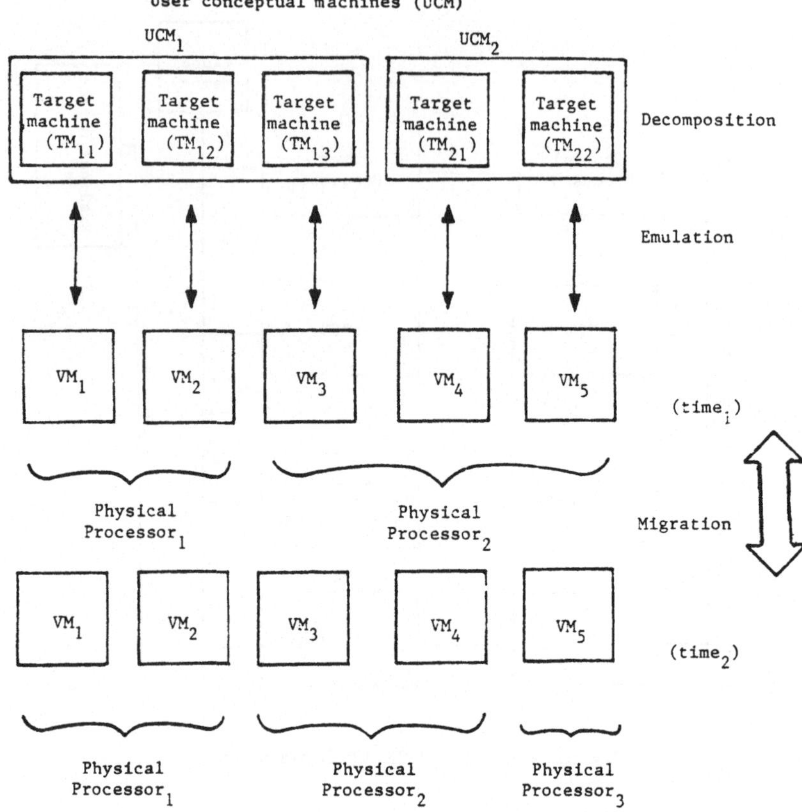

Figure 3-6 Logical to Physical Mapping on User Processors

processes that can be run asynchronously using the resources of separate
logical machines. These logical machines may or may not be identical in
performance and functionality. This mapping might be described as job
decomposition into semi-autonomous processes. Semi-autonomous processes
are processes that can be run independently and which communicate with
each other only via a well defined set of interfaces. The temporal
relationship between the processes may be synchronous or asynchronous.
Next the target machines are mapped one to one onto virtual machines in
a process corresponding to emulation. The virtual machines are then
multiplexed onto real processors using fairly ordinary VM technology.

One aspect of the MICS system that is particularly unusual is that
processes (VMs) can be imported and exported between user modules
(physical processors) to achieve load balancing. This virtual machine

migration is controlled by the PMMs using performance monitoring data
that they constantly acquire and exchange.

The migration algorithm works as follows:

* When a PMM senses that the utilization rate on its user
  processor is below a predefined threshold level throughout
  a monitoring period it signals the other PMM's of an
  "immigration condition" on its machine.

* When a PMM senses that the utilization rate on its user
  processor is above a predefined threshold level and there
  exists at least one other PMM that has signalled an
  immigration condition it sends out an indication of an
  "emigration condition" on the control bus.

* This notice of an emigration condition (migration request)
  is circulated among the PMMs until it reaches one which is
  in an immigration condition. A coupling is then
  established between the PMMs and an appropriate virtual
  machine is transferred between them.

This type of migration is facilitated by global data areas, which tend
to reduce the amount of actual data transfer needed in migration. This
effect is balanced by the memory bus contention caused by sharing global
areas among multiple processors during processing.

The MICS system is noteworthy for the manner it handles load sharing and
logical mapping of heterogeneous target machines. However, there are
significant performance problems in the implementation of this type of
system and perhaps a need to combine some of the other more
communication oriented technologies to make its approach effective in
real production environments.

3.5 Comparison of the Different Approaches

Although the VM networks just described were designed with different
goals, they tend to face similar issues. The table in Figure 3-7
shows how the systems compare as to functionality and usage. Some of
the distinctions and features evolved in an ad hoc fashion as network
usage expanded and user needs became evident. It seems likely that the
alternative approaches shown here can serve as a useful starting point
for the choices involved in the design of future virtual machine
networks.

	VNET/RASP	NCSS	IDC	MICS/II
EXTENT OF USE	Generally available. VNET from IBM. RASP through SHARE.	Dedicated proprietary system.	Dedicated proprietary system.	Experimental system.
PRIMARY USAGE	File spooling. Messages and commands can also be sent.	Packetized message and file transmission through logical connections between users on geographically remote hosts. One logical connection per direction of information flow. Terminal-host and host-host parts of the network are integrated via communications subnetwork.	Message transfer uses a CTCA or shared DASD. Terminal to host communication goes through front end processors in the communications subnetwork. User assignment to a host is determined by host communication subnetwork handshaking.	Programs and data can be relocated via a high speed bus. Control processors sense the relative utilization of different user processors via a separate control bus.
IPC & COMMUNICATION LEVEL ARCHITECTURE	Virtual Service Machine approach. The spooler/network interface runs in a separate VM communicating with other VMs on the same processor via standard IPC calls (VMCF or DICOM) and shared spool files.	The IPC interfaces are embedded in the VMM (VP). The communication interfaces are handled by front end processors (minicomputers) that constitute a communication subnetwork. This subnetwork performs IMP and TIP-like functions.	Communication functions are embedded in the VMM (CP). Shared DASD communication is also possible because of the local nature of the network. IPC calls use a package similar to VMCF.	Communication functions are handled by special front end processors (microcomputers). The network interface is via a highspeed bus. This obviates the need for complex communication protocols.

Figure 3-7   Comparison of VM Networking approaches

	VNET/RASP	NCSS	IDC	MICS/II
NETWORK TOPOLOGY	Supports a geographically distributed network with message and file forwarding. Files are spooled at each node. Complete files must be received before forwarding can commence. VNET has an interface to HASP/JES2 and ASP/JES3 through NJI and an indirect interface to SNA via HASP/JES2/NJE. There is no direct interface to SNA.	Uses a geographically distributed packet switching subnetwork. Host machines are located at data centers in the U.S. and Europe.	Contains only two hosts, both at the same location. An interface for remote hosts is being added.	Contains an arbitrary number of nodes (hosts) each consisting of two processors (a communication and control frontend and a user processor that runs application programs). The nodes, which must be at the same location, are connected by three high speed buses, one each for control, shared memory access and I/O.
ROUTING	Handled using routing tables based on the connectivity of the network and operator assignment. Tables are dynamically updated by the system when a line or node goes down using information on alternate routes previously supplied by an operator.	Handled transparently by the subnetwork. Each packet is routed separately. Packets within the same message can take different routes.	A virtual circuit is established between a terminal and the appropriate host by the communications subnetwork. A direct link is used for inter-host communication.	Broadcast network. Each processor examines each message and takes those destined to it.
SYNCHRONIZATION MECHANISMS	No real synchronization, but there is the ability to query how far a file transfer has progressed.	There are three types of user level synchronization: (1) Serial approach: send message/wait for response.		

Figure 3-7 Comparison of VM Networking approaches (continued)

	VNET/RASP	NCSS	IDC	MICS/II
SYNCHRONIZATION MECHANISMS		(2) Serially reusable approach: send message, continue processing. When processing complete wait for interrupt indicating response. (3) Reentrant approach: overlapped processing supporting multiple communication connections within a single program. When responses are received, they are handled by I/O completion routines asynchronously from program processing. This approach is useful for TP monitors and DBMSs supporting multiple remote users.	Only the serial approach (send message/wait for response) is supported at the user level. Four degrees of IO/CPU overlap are supported at the real machine level. A mechanism to allow a single program to support multiple terminals is also provided.	Complete transparency at the user level. Communication times are similar to ordinary memory access times so no special synchronization at the user level is required.
LOAD SHARING/BALANCING	No load sharing. Some remote command facilities are available	No load sharing. Load balancing can be achieved by assigning users to other hosts in a non-transparent manner. Extensive remote processing and command facilities are available using ROUTE and FILEDEF commands.	Load sharing/balancing is static (done offline by reassigning users to a different machine), but the machine a program runs on is transparent to users. Users are grouped so that those tending to access the same resources are assigned to the same machine, but all disk storage is accessible by both machines.	Load sharing/balancing is handled transparently by an operating system running on a separate processor. Both user virtual machines and the operating system can migrate between processors during processing.

Figure 3-7 Comparison of VM Networking approaches (continued)

4. Future Directions

Combining virtual machine and networking technology potentially extends the traditional benefits of the virtual machine approach

* evolvability
* modularity
* machine independence

to a multi-machine geographically dispersed environment. Scarce resources available at only one location in a network can be incorporated into composite systems accessible from anywhere on the network. Thus VM networking can be viewed as a further step in reducing the dependence between hardware and software.

The traditional VM approach extended to include emulation allows user programs to be

* developed in a VM that simulates hardware under development,
* run in a well protected partition of that hardware once it is developed, and
* continue to be run in virtual machines emulating old hardware after the original hardware is obsolete.

Traditional VM systems allow the expansion of hardware resources without affecting software subsystems by using larger processors. VM networking extends this to allow expansion by adding processors at one or several dispersed geographical locations.

In order to do this effectively networks can usefully incorporate new software techniques and hardware technologies that currently are being investigated as part of experimental systems.

The techniques that appear particularly promising include:

* Increased use of the extended machine and service machine concepts to separate logical and physical processors and provide increased machine independence.
* Use of virtual=real mappings to allow a virtual operating system to run effectively under a VM monitor or to guarantee a response in real time. The use of inexpensive microprocessors or small minicomputers to support this in a networking context may be cost effective.

* Breaking up of user jobs into multiple processes which run
  on separate virtual machines and potentially on separate
  physical processors. This approach was tried in the MICS
  system.

* Use of emulation machines as a generalization of virtual
  machines.

* Increased layering of the communications functions of the
  network to provide mutual independence between layers and
  allow functions at a given layer to be interchanged
  transparently to other layers.

* Increased use of "vertical" and "outboard" migration to
  improve efficiency, throughput, and response.

Certain hardware trends also reduce the overhead of using multiple
processors. These trends include higher bandwidth communications, the
increasing cost effectiveness of microprocessors and small computer
technology, and the development of hardware and software mechanisms for
efficient coordination of parallel processors and processes. This makes
the reliability, cost effectiveness and general usability of distributed
systems increasingly attractive. The rapid development of the
technologies and techniques in this area could make them highly
desirable for inherently distributed applications in the near future.

Some of these issues are being addressed by researchers at a number of
locations [ANDERSON 75, FLINK 77, HARTUNG 78]. For example, the Naval
Surface Weapons Center Dahlgren Laboratory has undertaken a coherent
research program to improve the evolutionary characteristics of complex,
long life-cycle systems. These Naval systems can be viewed as a very
large collection of virtual processors cooperating in a virtual machine
network. Virtual processors are bound to available real processors;
virtual communications is mapped onto real communications. As hardware
evolves over time (number of processors, processor architecture, etc.)
bindings are altered and existing software may be "captured". This
network architecture also encourages software evolution since the
virtual machine isolation property guarantees that changes will be free
of unpredictable side effects. An introductory view of the network
architecture is discussed by Goldberg et al [GOLDBERG 78]. The
extension of virtual machine concepts to include emulation and the

corresponding VMM design is described in [FLINK 77]. Issues relating to
virtualization of computer communications interfaces is described in
[HARTUNG 78].

ACKNOWLEDGEMENTS

We would like to thank Ellen Wax and Harit Nanavati of IDC, Allan Kirby
of NCSS and various people from IBM and SHARE for supplying information
about their systems and reviewing portions of this manuscript. We also
thank Mr. K. Ohmori of NEC for his hospitality and technical
assistance during an on-site discussion about MICS.

Andy Langer and Allan Levy of BGS Systems were very helpful in
critiqueing various revisions of this paper and, in general, for
providing useful insights into many computer related areas.

Sandy Cramm deserves high praise for her patience in editing and
formatting this manuscript and in dealing with computer editors and
document processors.

We particularly want to thank Mr. R.A. Niemann of the U.S. Naval
Surface Weapons Center Dahlgren Laboratory for his encouragement and
support.

REFERENCES

Anderson, D.R.: The EPIC-DPS - A Distributed Network Experiment.
    EASCON. September, 1975.

Anderson, G. and Jensen, E. D.: Computer Interconnection Structures:
    Taxonomy, Characteristics and Examples. Computer Surveys, 7, 4,
    December, 1975.

Barkalow, T.J., Cristoforo, A.J. and Wax, E.J.: Loosely-Coupled VM/370
    Systems at Interactive Data Corporation. Presentation at SHARE 51,
    Boston, August, 1978.

Computer magazine news item: IBM Internal Networks Match Needs.
    Computer. November, 1978, p. 66.

Crabtree, R.P.: Job Networking. IBM Systems Journal, 17, 3, 1978.

Donovan, J.J. and Jacoby, H.D.: Virtual Machine Communication for the
    Implementation of Decision Support Systems. IEEE Transactions on
    Software Engineering, SE-3, 5, September, 1977.

Flink II, C.W.: EASY - an Operating System for the QM-1. MICRO-10.
    1977.

Gaspar, A. and Lamm, P.: A Simulated Data Communication Network. ACM Computer Communication Review, 8, 4, October, 1978.

Guido, A.A. and Considine, J.: Laboratory Automation via a VM/370 Teleprocessing Virtual Machine. NCC, 1977.

Goldberg, R.P. (ed.): ACM Workshop on Virtual Computer Systems. Cambridge, (Mass.), March, 1973.

Goldberg, R.P.: Survey of Virtual Machine Research. Computer, June, 1974.

Goldberg, R.P. and Schwenk, H.S.: Virtual Machines for the Honeywell 6000 Family. COMPCON 76. Washington, D.C., September, 1976.

Goldberg, R.P., Perry, J.G., Schwenk, H.S. and Sockut, G.H.: Motivation for a Configuration and Integration Management Tool. COMPCON, Fall, 1978.

Hartmann, T. and Hendricks, E.: VNET (VM/370 Networking) User Experience. SHARE 48, Houston, March, 1977.

Hartung, R.L.: Virtualization of Tactical Computer Communication Interfaces. K-74 Project Status Report, NSWC Dahlgren Laboratory, (VA.), December, 1978.

Holley, L.H., Parmelee, R.P., Salisbury, C.A. and Saul, D.N.: VM/370 Asymmetric Multiprocessing. IBM Systems Journal, 18, 1, 1979.

IBM: Virtual Machine Facility/370: Introduction. IBM Corporation, GC20-1800.

IBM: Network Job Interface General Information Manual. IBM Corporation, GH20-1941.

IBM: VM/370 Networking (Programming RPQ PO9007). Program Reference and Operations Manual. IBM Corporation, SH20-1977.

Lam, C-Y. and Madnick, S.E.: Strategies for Interfacing Virtual Machines - A Case Study. MIT Sloan School, Center for Information Research. March, 1978.

MacKinnon, R.A.: The Changing Virtual Machine Environment. Presentation at SHARE 51, Boston, August, 1978.

MacKinnon, R.A.: The Changing Virtual Machine Environment: Interfaces to real hardware, virtual hardware and other virtual machines. IBM Systems Journal, 18, 1, 1979.

Marshall, B.: RASP-VM/370 Networking. SHARE 50, Denver, March, 1978.

NCSS: VP/CSS Programmer's Guide. National CSS, Inc., Norwalk, (Conn.), February, 1978.

Ohmori, K., Koike, N., Yamazaki, T., Ohmiya, T. and Nezu, K.: System Management of MICS-II - A Virtual Machine Complex. COMPCON, Spring, 1979.

Ohmori, K. et.al.: MICS-II - A Virtual Machine Complex Controlled by Dedicated Micro-Processors. Digest of Papers, COMPCON, Spring, 1978, p. 256-260.

Perry, J.G. and Hein, R.R.: Virtual Machines for a Tactical
    Environment. COMPCON, Fall, 1976.

Seawright, L.H. and MacKinnon, R.A.: VM/370 - A Study of Multiplicity
    and Usefulness. IBM Systems Journal,18, 1, 1979.

Simpson, R.O. and Phillips, G.H.: Network Job Entry Facility for JES2.
    IBM Systems Journal, 17, 3, 1978.

Schwartz, S.: Computer Communication Network Design and Analysis.
    Englewood Cliffs, (N.J.): Prentice Hall, 1977.

Thurber, K.J.: Computer Communication Techniques. ACM Computer
    Architecture News,7, 3, October, 1978.

Wecker, S.: DECNET: Issues related to local networking. U.S. Dept. of
    Commerce, Nat. Bureau of Standards. NBS Spec. Pub. 500-31.
    Report of a Workshop Held, August, 1977.

Weegenaar, H.J.: Virtuality and Other Things Like That. COMPCON,
    September, 1978.

Winett, J.M.: Virtual Machines for Developing Systems Software. Proc.
    IEEE Computer Society Conf., Boston, (Mass), 1971.

Anschriften der Autoren

G. Dedié
Siemens AG, DV WS SE SP112/DV WS SA
8000 München 70

J. Dorn
Siemens AG, DV WS SP
8000 München 70

H. Eberle
IBM Deutschland GmbH
Scientific Center Heidelberg
6900 Heidelberg

K.F. Finkemeyer
IBM Deutschland GmbH
Scientific Center Heidelberg
6900 Heidelberg

R.P. Goldberg
BGS Systems, Inc.
Lincoln, Mass. 01773, USA

H. Gümbel
Siemens AG, DV VM PP 31
8000 München 70

V. Haller
Messerschmitt-Bölkow-Blohm GmbH
Unternehmensbereich Flugzeuge, EDV
8900 Augsburg 1

G. Kost
Siemens AG, DV WS SP
8000 München 70

A. Levy
BGS Systems, Inc.
Lincoln, Mass. 01773, USA

R.A. Liuzzi
US Air Force
Rome Air Development Center (RADC/ISIE)
Griffiss Air Force Base, N.Y. 13441, USA

P.S. Mager jr.
BGS Systems, Inc.
Lincoln, Mass. 01773, USA

G. Mußtopf

Universität Hamburg
Fachbereich Informatik
2000 Hamburg 13

J.G. Perry jr.

Naval Surface Weapons Center
Dahlgren, Virginia, USA

A. Schaten

IBM Deutschland GmbH, EF Rechenzentrum
Entwicklung und Forschung
7030 Böblingen

H. Schmutz

IBM Deutschland GmbH
Scientific Center Heidelberg
6900 Heidelberg

H. Schwenk

BGS Systems, Inc.
Lincoln, Mass. 01773, USA

L.H. Seawright

IBM Scientific Center
545 Technology Square
Cambridge, Mass. 02139, USA

H. Seidlitz

Technische Universität Berlin
Fachbereich Informatik-Rechnerbetrieb
1000 Berlin 10

S.C. Vestal

Honeywell Inc.
Bloomington, Minn. 55420

G. Wessling

IBM Deutschland GmbH
8000 München 22

D. Zabel

Siemens AG, DV WS SE SP112/DV WS SA
8000 München 70

Anschriften der Programmausschußmitglieder

A. Endres

IBM Laboratorien
7032 Sindelfingen

E. Jessen

Universität Hamburg
Fachbereich Informatik
2000 Hamburg 13

F. Kopitsch

Siemens AG, D AP S3
8000 München 83

H.J. Siegert

Technische Universität München
Institut für Informatik
8000 München 2

H.R. Wiehle

Hochschule der Bundeswehr
Fachbereich Informatik
8014 Neubiberg

P. Wüsten

Siemens AG
8000 München 83